Scot[...]
Dept. [...]
U. [...]
Berkel[...]

"From
Fish
To
Gish"

By

Marvin L. Lubenow

**The exciting drama of a decade of
creation-evolution debates.**

CLP PUBLISHERS
San Diego, California

"From Fish To Gish"

Copyright © 1983 by Marvin L. Lubenow

Published by: CLP Publishers
 P. O. Box 15908
 San Diego, California 92115

ISBN 0-89051-094-6
Library of Congress Catalog Card No. 83-71222

Cataloging in Publication Data

Lubenow, Marvin L.

 "From fish to Gish."

 1. Creation. 2. Evolution. I. Morris, Henry Madison,
1918- . II. Gish, Duane Tolbert, 1921- . III. Title.

213

ISBN-0-89051-094-6   83-71222

ALL RIGHTS RESERVED

 No part of this publication may be reproduced, stored in a
retrieval system, or transmitted in any form or by any
means—electronic, mechanical, photocopy, recording, or otherwise—without the prior permission of CLP Publishers, with the
exception of brief excerpts in magazine articles and/or reviews.

Cover by Colleen Dossey

Printed in the United States of America

About The Author

Marvin L. Lubenow is the Senior Pastor of the 1,200-member First Baptist Church of Fort Collins, Colorado. He holds the Bachelor of Arts degree from Bob Jones University, the Master of Science degree from Eastern Michigan University, and the Master of Theology degree from Dallas Theological Seminary.

Pastor Lubenow has held the office of President of both the Conservative Baptist Association of Maine and of Massachusetts and has served for six years as a member of the Board of Directors of the Conservative Baptist Home Mission Society. Currently he is a member of the Board of Directors of the Conservative Baptist Foreign Mission Society. He is Chairman of the Academic Affairs Committee and a member of the Board of Trustees of the Denver Conservative Baptist Theological Seminary and on the Board of Trustees of the Southwestern Conservative Baptist Bible College, Phoenix. For years he has held membership in the Evangelical Theological Society and has presented a number of papers before that organization.

Pastor Lubenow's interest in the relationship of the Bible to science is reflected in his membership in the Creation Research Society, the American Scientific Affiliation (before which he has presented three papers), and the American Association for the Advancement of Science. He is a member of the Board of Directors of the Bible-Science Association and has been a speaker at four National Creation Conventions. He has also had three papers published in the *Creation Research Society Quarterly*.

He has given leadership in efforts to have the scientific evidences for Special Creation presented along with evolution in the public schools and is often used by the public schools as a resource person for creationism. His monograph, *Bones of Contention: The Bible and the Human Fossils,* demonstrates how the human fossil evidence supports Special Creation. He has been involved in several creation/evolution debates on university campuses.

Pastor Lubenow is included in *Who's Who in Religion* and in the 13th edition of *The Dictionary of International Biography*.

To Betty and Marilyn

My secretary and my daughter-in-law

Typing is not normally considered a spiritual gift,
but these two do it with a very special grace and love.

Contents

Introduction

I felt like a secret agent. As I sat in a geology lecture hall at the University of Michigan that fall day in 1975, I was aware that I was a "foreigner." All about me were graduate students and faculty members from the University of Michigan. I was a graduate student at a far less prestigious institution nearby—Eastern Michigan University.

However, there was a deeper reason for my "Daniel in the Lion's den" mentality. I was a creationist among 150 evolutionists. I had come, like the others, to hear William J. Schopf, Professor of Geology at UCLA, who is considered the world's leading authority on microscopic fossils known as Precambrian microfossils. Evolutionists believe them to be more than 600 million years old. I came to listen and to learn. I was not particularly interested in "blowing my cover" as a creationist.

During the discussion period after the lecture, I asked Schopf a question. Had he heard about an article written by a colleague of his at UCLA, Daniel Axelrod, and published in *Evolution* in 1959, telling of the discovery of over fifty different genera of land plants in the Cambrian? The question dealt with a tremendously controversial matter. It was like setting off a baby atomic bomb. Yet, I needed to know how Schopf would respond to it. Since the question was bound to attract attention, I tried to ask it in a casual, innocent way.

When the session was over, a young man who was also seated on the front row came over and stood directly in front of me.

"You're a Christian!" he declared.

I pleaded guilty as charged, but was astounded that he would know.

"When you asked that question," he continued,"my spirit said within me, 'He's a Christian, too!' "

This young man, then a graduate student at Michigan, had done his undergraduate work in geology at the University of Tennessee. While there, he had been one of the organizers of a creation-evolution debate held on that campus the previous January. It featured Henry Morris and Duane Gish against two University of Tennessee professors in one of the best-known university debates.

After talking together a bit, we both went over to where Schopf was in conversation with other students. At a break in the conversation, my new-found friend said to Schopf: "With the information that you presented to us today, you ought to debate the creationists."

"No thanks," replied Schopf. "A friend of mine debated them recently. He thought it would be a piece of cake and he didn't do his homework. He really got clobbered!"

Chapter 1

Moby Gym
Colorado State University

"Hey, Marv, you look scared to death!"

"I am!"

"What's the problem?"

"This debate is costing $3,300. I'm responsible for it—every bit of it. At one dollar a head, we need 3,300 people here tonight. If we don't have that many, I'm sunk."

"Oh!"

In a mild state of terror, I stood on the podium watching the people file in. It was 7:55 p.m. At 8:00, the creation-evolution debate at Colorado State University here in Fort Collins was to begin. Although we preachers are notorious for over-estimating the size of a crowd, I could not come up with more than 2,000. I believe in miracles, and I desperately needed one in the next five minutes.

Just as a drowning man's life flashes before him in an instant, the events that led to this potential disaster raced through my mind.

A year before, I had assumed the position of Senior Pastor of The First Baptist Church of Fort Collins. Dr. Duane Gish, Associate Director of the Institute for Creation Research, and Prof. Harold Slusher, a member of the geophysics faculty at the University of Texas, El Paso, had already been scheduled for a creation seminar in our church. I was delighted. I knew them as good friends for many years.

I had done a great deal of research on the creation-evolution debates in which Gish, Slusher, and Dr. Henry Morris, the Director of the Institute for Creation Research, had been involved. I had also attended one at Northwestern

University the year before. Why not, I thought, try to arrange a debate here at Colorado State? It seemed like such a natural thing to do. For the first time in my ministerial career I was in a university town. A creation-evolution debate would be a unique type of testimony both to the campus and to the community. Organizing one here would also give me more of a "feel" for the debates and help me to convey their real drama to the readers of the book I was hoping to write about them.

The first problem—as with almost everything in life—was money. I had none. Since I was so new at my church, and since none of my people had any first-hand knowledge of these debates and their potential, I did not feel free to ask the church to bankroll the project.

It was my desire to keep a very low profile in this matter. There are times when it is a disadvantage to be a clergyman. I felt that this needed to be a campus project with campus sponsorship. I went out calling.

My first stop was at the local Campus Crusade for Christ organization. Not only does Crusade have a high profile here at Colorado State, but each summer they hold their Institute for Biblical Studies for the entire Crusade organization on our campus. Further, Crusade has been involved in the sponsorship of more than fourteen of the creation-evolution debates held across the country.

Yes, the local Crusade leadership was very interested in the prospects of such a debate. No, they were not familiar with these debates nor did they know that many of them had been sponsored by their own organization on other campuses. There was just one problem. They had no money.

My next stop was the Navigators. Although they have a larger local staff than does Crusade, they are more low-key in their approach because of their emphasis on one-on-one discipleship. They, too, were excited about the possibilities of such a debate and gladly lent their full support. There was just one problem. They had no money.

Corbett Hall Fellowship is a large and active local organization on campus. They also thought that the idea of such a debate was excellent, and that it would answer many of the students' questions regarding the matter of origins. The debate format especially appealed to them. They assured me of their active participation. There was just one problem. They had no money.

Having carloads of moral support, I thought that I might as well touch all the bases. Inter-Varsity Christian Fellowship is large nationwide but rather small on campus. Their leader, Bob, was a bit hesitant to get involved since Inter-Varsity has not taken any particular stand against evolution—at least the theistic variety. Bob wasn't sure that he wanted to identify Inter-Varsity with one particular "brand" of origins. However, I assured him that the intellectual approach of the debate would fit in well with Inter-Varsity's own type of ministry. He finally came on board. There was just one problem. You guessed it. He had no money.

The intellectual impact of such a debate is remarkable. Some time after the debate, a philosophy professor with whom I was working on another project described the CSU debate enthusiastically as the greatest intellectual event that had been held on campus in the last ten years.

The debates have been financed in various ways. Some have been financed by the universities where they have been held as a part of a contemporary issues program. The Colorado State University Honors Program did contribute $200 to it and became one of the sponsoring organizations. That left only $3,100 to go. Other debates have been sponsored by local creationist organizations or by local churches. All of these methods allowed for free admission. However, it became apparent that it would be necessary to charge admission as the only remaining option. There is an old saying that people appreciate something more if they pay for it. Yet, I was afraid that by charging admission we would exclude some. There was simply no other way.

A debate at the University of Minnesota had been held the previous April. Their attendance of 5,000 was the largest attendance of any debate to date. My goal was to "beat Minnesota!" The fact that Fort Collins has a population base of 70,000 compared to a population base of well over one million for the Twin Cities area did not seem to be a major factor at the time. The Minnesota debate still remains one of the best-attended—equaled recently by the debate at Liberty Baptist College.

Having decided how the finances would be raised, I next

approached the problem of facilities. The auditorium-gymnasium at Colorado State University is an impressive structure. It seats approximately 10,000 and is where the university plays its home basketball games. Yet, for all its beauty, it looks strikingly like a huge sperm whale. It is therefore referred to locally as "Moby Gym."

I reserved the night of Friday, October 7, 1977, for the debate and calmly signed a contract for the rental of the building and a set-up for 6,300 people. The estimated cost of that alone came to $1,900. Other expenses involved matters such as honorariums for the debaters, newspaper advertising, printing of programs, purchasing of rolls of tickets, and the hiring of police and security personnel.

The membership of my own church provided three excellent support personnel for the debate. Dr. Fred Norwood, Professor of Business Administration and head of that department, graciously consented to handle all of the money and give an accounting of it. Chemistry professor emeritus Wendell King, who also serves as assistant score-keeper for all Colorado State University home basketball games, gladly consented to be timekeeper for the debate. Gene Kirby, a detective on the Colorado State University police force, willingly accepted the responsibility for matters involving security.

A very able moderator was found in Professor Michael McCulloch, Assistant Professor of Philosophy at Colorado State University and head of the University Honors Program. Mike is a devout Roman Catholic and has since become a good friend. His Irish charm lent warmth and humor to the debate. His fairness is demonstrated by a story he told at the opening of the debate:

> A Cardinal excitedly entered the presence of the Holy Father in Rome. He said: "Holy Father, I have good news and bad news."
>
> The Holy Father replied, "Give me the good news first."
>
> "We have just heard from Jesus! He is coming again! The Second Coming is at hand!"
>
> "Wonderful! Wonderful! But what could the bad news possibly be?" questioned the Holy Father.
>
> "Well," replied the Cardinal, "He called from Salt Lake City, and He sounded mad!"

Mike's application of the story was that no matter what position one espoused when he came to the debate, it wouldn't hurt to listen to the other guys. They just might be right!

The search for evolutionist debaters to oppose Gish and Slusher proved to be very frustrating, even though we had offered an honorarium of $200 to each one. I was teaching the University Bible Class in our church at the time. I asked the members of my class to approach professors they had in the sciences about being participants. They were consistently met with refusals. Finding evolutionists willing to participate has been the most difficult task in most of the debates. Many proposed debates have been cancelled because evolutionists could not be found who were willing to debate the issue.

I do not mean to imply that evolutionists who refused were necessarily afraid of the creationists. Some may have been, but in most cases the evolutionists were over-confident. Many who did participate have expressed the fact that they were not expecting and were not prepared for the type of rigorous scientific evidence that the creationists presented.

Some evolutionists refused because they felt that creationism was a dead issue that had been decided years ago. To them it would make as much sense to debate the flat-earth theory as it would to debate creationism. Others refused because they did not want to give the creationist movement status by participating in such an event.

I strongly suspect, however, that there is another reason why so many evolutionists have refused to debate the issue. Most scientists believe in evolution and many teach it. Yet it is not their major interest, and most have never examined with rigor the evidence for it. Many biologists teach it as part of biology, but have not studied it closely. The same could be said of botanists, zoologists, geologists, and other scientists. Hence, the challenge to defend evolution publicly in open debate is something that they are not prepared to do.

In our search for evolutionist debaters, we finally hit pay dirt—to use the expression in a strictly metaphorical way. I was calling on one of our church members, Ken Wollard, regarding another matter. Ken was a Colorado State University graduate student in anthropology. I happened to mention the proposed debate. He thought that possibly one of his professors would be interested. Dr. Michael Charney, Emeritus Professor of Anthropology, and one of the world's leading authorities in forensic anthropology and body identification, was indeed interested in such a debate. Charney had become quite well-known in the area because of his work on body identification in the famous Thompson Canyon Flood, just a few miles south of Fort Collins, in the summer of 1976. In terms of the 136 lives which were lost, it was the worst natural disaster in the history of our nation. Six Campus Crusade staff members also lost their lives in it.

Charney not only took up the challenge to debate, but even suggested one of his friends, zoologist Charles Wilber, to debate with him. Dr. Wilber was interested but felt very strongly that a geologist should be involved in the debate along with Charney. Students again consulted with every geologist on the Colorado State University faculty. None were interested. Wilber then consented to join Charney against Gish and Slusher, and the staffing for the debate was finally complete.

The weeks preceding the debate were feverish with excitement and activity. The Christian organizations on campus promoted the debate well. They also furnished ticket sellers and ushers. The printed program I designed had a response page so that questions could be asked, comments could be written, or one could indicate his desire for further information on creation or evolution. Among their duties, the ushers were to pick up the response slips between the main position statements of the debate and the rebuttals so that a question table, composed of both evolutionists and creationists, could organize the questions and direct them to the proper debater for the question period following the rebuttals.

As the coordinator, and the only one who had even seen a debate before, what seemed like a thousand details fell on me. These involved purchasing the rolls of tickets, lining up the security guards, determining the seating and the platform set-up, making sure that the public address system was adequate, setting up book tables, and planning the newspaper and other advertising.

Radio advertising was used, but newspaper advertising seemed to work best. Full page ads were placed in our local

newspaper, the Fort Collins *Coloradoan,* and the campus
newspaper, *The Journal.* Letters were sent to all churches in
northern Colorado and southern Wyoming asking them to
promote the debate and to attend it.

As I stood on that platform at 7:55, the agonizing questions
were: "Had we done enough? Was there a more appropriate
date than this Friday evening? Were there better ways of
promoting it?" My heart pounded as I awaited the outcome.
The attendance was approximately 2,000 (1,800 paid attenders
and 200 staffers). Others were ecstatic. They thought the
turnout was fantastic. They didn't have to pay the bills.

The $1,800 dollars from the paid attendance and the $200
from the Colorado State Honors Program made $2,000.
When we received the itemized bill for the set-up and rental of
"Moby Gym," it was $400 less than we anticipated. I don't
know why. I was afraid to ask. That meant that we were still
$900 short.

The next Sunday in my church I announced the financial
needs and asked people to pray. Two families made
contributions—one of $100 and the other of $600. A Sunday
School offering came to $200. I was very thankful to God
that He had supplied the needs. I was also thankful that I
would not have to go to jail.

Chapter 2

The Little One Before The Big One

As soon as the public announcement of an upcoming creation-evolution confrontation was made, a "little debate" erupted before the big one. This "little debate" took place in the campus and community newspapers.

It began with an evolutionist writing to express his displeasure regarding such a worthless and meaningless event as a creation-evolution debate. One or more creationists responded and the mini-debate was on. The amount of exchange that took place obviously depended on how much lead time was involved between the first public announcement and the debate itself.

Many of the debates precipitated a robust post-debate correspondence as well. In the case of the Tennessee and Texas Tech debates, this post-debate correspondence was lengthy and quite vitriolic.

Some people cringe at any adverse publicity for their cause. Actually, it depends on how popular the cause is as to how harmful adverse publicity is. In the case of evolution, it is so universally accepted that any adverse publicity is probably harmful. But since creationism as a public issue has been dormant for so many years, a case could be made that there is no such thing as bad publicity for it. Any publicity—good or bad—about creationism would serve to bring it to public attention and cause people to think about it. This result could only be good—no matter how adverse the publicity might be.

There is no doubt that these pre- and post-debate news-paper exchanges have heightened interest in the creation-evolution issue—even in the minds of those who were not able to attend the debate itself. Everyone loves a good "fight." And while the vast majority of these debates were of a very high order, there is no doubt that they were "fights" in the deepest sense of the word. Some of the most basic intellectual and spiritual issues were at stake.

In the Colorado State University debate, the first bombshell was a letter in the campus newspaper, *The Journal,* by Dr. Stephen M. Stack, Associate Professor of Botany and Plant Pathology at the university. Stack's salvo was such a "cheap shot" that Professor Michael Charney, as he began his defense of evolution in the debate itself, felt the need to issue a lengthy apology for it.

Stack first stated that he had been invited to be a debater, but had declined. He felt that creationism had been "intel-lectually decimated 100 years ago," and that the present creationist movement was just an attempt by Fundamentalists to bootleg their religion under the guise of science. Since the dictionary defined a debate as a regulated discussion between two matched sides, Stack contended that the proposed event was not really a debate because (1) evolution is science whereas creation is religion, and (2) evolution is a paleontological-biological subject and neither Slusher nor Gish had the credentials to speak on the subject. "One [Slusher] is a physicist who appears to have an interest in geology and the other [Gish] is a chemist who has abandoned his work to become a thinly veiled evangelist."

By no stretch of the imagination, Stack contended, could creationism be considered a scientific hypothesis. It's origin was in the "word for word literal interpretation of the English translation of the Book of Genesis (in spite of its contradictions)."

Stack used rather unfriendly terms to describe scientific creationists, such as pseudoscientific, impenetrably ignorant, modern relics of the Dark Ages, dogmatic, superstitious, informationally feeble opponents, and people who cite "non-scientific publications or misinterpret and misconstrue real scientific articles to serve their purposes." One would almost get the impression, reading Stack's letter, that he didn't care for creationists.

He concluded by stating that although scientific creationists are stubbornly ignorant, they are not stupid. The proposed debate was really a very clever set-up by creationists to propagandize the gullible. He felt that the debate served no meaningful purpose because creationists could not possibly give five minutes of solid scientific evidence for their cause, whereas evolutionists could not give all of the evidence for evolution if they were to speak for a lifetime.

The letter was really quite remarkable. In rather short compass, Stack had managed to include almost every charge or criticism that has ever been leveled against creationists. Thus the mini-debate began. I fired off a reply to Stack's letter which was published a few days later and the little debate before the big one was in full swing.

There is no question that Stack's venomous letter damaged the evolutionist cause. However, Charney handled it as a true gentleman. As he began his defense of evolution in the debate, he stated that an esteemed colleague of his on the Colorado State University faculty had treated this debate in a very cavalier fashion. Yet, the presence of 2,000 people testified to the fact that there were genuine issues to be faced and questions to be answered. He said that it pained him to see one of his colleagues treat an honest question with derision. He concluded by saying that if the academic community treats honest questions in the way Stack did, it deserves such terms as intellectual snobs, eggheads, ivy-covered professors in ivy-covered halls—to mention the nicer things that are said about them. His remarks were greeted with thunderous applause.

Chapter 3

A Funny Thing Happened on The Way to the Debate

On Monday of the debate week, I paid a visit to Bob Laughler, the editor of our local newspaper, *The Coloradoan*. Bob was a member of a Protestant church in our city and was a fellow Rotarian. We had placed full-page ads of the debate in his paper. I had every reason to think that I would be well-received.

"Bob, we are going to have 5,000 at the debate in Moby Gym this Friday night," I said. "You really ought to send a reporter to cover it."

He looked at me as if he were rising to a personal challenge. "If you have 5,000 people at that thing Friday, I'll give you my dessert at the next Rotary meeting." That really wasn't what I had in mind. I'm struggling with a problem because of too many desserts already. "Seriously," I said, "You ought to have a reporter cover this affair. There's been a lot of interest generated in it."

"W-e-l-l," he drawled, "You just don't know how hard it is to get reporters out on a Friday night."

I started to ask him what reporters did on Friday nights, or was there an understanding between the newspapers and the Cosmic Forces to make sure that nothing newsworthy ever

happened on Friday nights, or did he mean that there was
need for a special newspaper to report just Friday night
happenings, or . . . . I knew when I was licked. If arguing
would have helped, I would have argued. It was his absolute
and total lack of interest in the project that told me not to
look for a reporter there that Friday night.

The day after talking with Bob, I had a long-distance
telephone call from New York. It was George W. Cornell, for
30 years a religious writer for the Associated Press. He was
working on his Christmas series and had decided on the
general theme, "The Enigma of Human Origins." He was
thinking of including the views of various scientists, the
Biblical insights, the evolutionary questions, and concluding
with perfect humanity as seen in "Nazareth Man," Jesus.

As a part of the series, he thought of dealing with the
public debates on creation vs. evolution. To get more
information on them, he had contacted Henry Morris. Morris,
knowing of the upcoming Colorado State University debate,
had referred him to me. I told him about the debate, and he
asked that I send him a cassette recording of it as soon as it
transpired. It transpired. I sent the tapes.

At a late November Rotary luncheon, Bob Laughler called
me over to his table. "Boy, talk about having to eat crow! I
didn't think that debate was worth covering, and I've just
received an article out of New York on it this long," he said,
extending his arms about five feet. *He also gave me his
dessert.*

I was ecstatic. (I don't mean about the dessert.) One part of
Cornell's five-section Christmas series was devoted to the
Colorado State debate. And it would get Associated Press
coverage nationwide. That Bob would not publish it locally
was so foreign to my thinking that it never occurred to me to
ask him about it.

It never appeared. These articles, published all across the
nation during December 1977, never appeared in Fort Collins.
I didn't understand it. I kept waiting. Finally, after the
holidays were over, I asked Bob why.

"Marv, I just didn't have room."

I have never been a newspaper editor. But I do know how
much trivia goes into a small city newspaper. After all, the
70,000 people of Fort Collins don't get nationwide recognition

from a New Yorker every day.

More than five years have passed since that incident. I still don't understand. But I do know why they call our local paper, "The Daily Disappointment."

Chapter 4

Cornell on Colorado State

This chapter is an excerpt from Associated Press religious writer George Cornell's 1977 Christmas series entitled, "The Enigma of Human Origins." It comes from installment four of that series and is entitled, "Life's Origins Debated on College Campuses." I wish to thank Mr. George Cornell and Mr. Dan Perkes, head of the Newsfeatures Department of the Associated Press, for permission to use this excerpt.

A curving modernistic building on the Colorado State University campus looks vaguely like a white whale. Reminiscent of the big one in the classic Herman Melville tale, *Moby Dick,* the place is called "Moby Gym." There, about 2,000 students and faculty listened recently to a three-hour debate about the theory of life's evolution on earth.

The affair, featuring scientists on both sides of the issue, was one of about 50 such public debates that have been held on that question on American college campuses in the last four years.

"It seems clear when all the data are examined dispassionately, the emergence of life is the inevitable outcome of associational and organizational forces inherent in the chemistry of macromolecules," argued Colorado State zoologist Charles G. Wilber.

But University of Texas geophysicist Harold Slusher maintained that this violates known laws of physics. "Complexity, order, and arrangement do not arise spontaneously," he said.

The debate was arranged by student organizations, as have

been most of the others, some of them drawing up to 5,000 people, as at the University of Minnesota.

"The facts demonstrate that evolution has not occurred," argued biochemist Duane Gish of San Diego's Institute for Creation Research. " The fossil record reveals a systematic absence of transitional forms. It reveals, on the other hand, the sudden appearances of highly diverse forms of life, without preceding intermediate types."

"We have plenty of intermediate forms," responded Colorado State anthropologist Michael Charney, citing remains of early men, including recent finds in Africa. Acknowledging gaps in the general fossil record, he said, "We have to go out and search . . . . This is a vast earth. Lots of areas have not been covered."

Presiding at the debate, Colorado State philosopher Michael McCulloch laid down the ground rules. "It is not a religious debate, not a debate between scientists and religionists, but a debate between scientists."

However, the pro-evolutionists—and not their opponents—both brought up Scriptural creation accounts, terming them not scientific but religious. The anti-evolutionists contended that the evolutionary theory, dealing with unobserved, untestable concepts of origins, itself went beyond empirical scientific limits, necessitating faith in it, with evidence selected one-sidedly to favor it.

"The evolutionist is not dealing with a real universe," said geophysicist Slusher. "He's dealing with a universe that he builds out of his imagination."

However, zoologist Wilber contended that when anti-evolutionists "begin by postulating creation, attempting to interpret geology by using Scripture, then I say it's putting together things that were never intended to fit together and cannot be smashed together without destroying both."

No win-or-lose decision was attempted in the debate, the object being in such affairs simply to air the evidence on both sides.

Anthropologist Charney, challenging the Scriptural assertion that humans are "wonderfully made," said that far back in time, "we are descended from some quadrupedal animal on all fours" and "we bear many scars of the evolution . . . . The body of man is a hodgepodge."

The "upending of man on his two legs," has caused many physiological problems, he said, adding that it focused the weight on spine and pelvis, leading to backaches and other ailments, burdened the heart with pumping blood upward against gravity, causing circulatory problems, and overloaded the feet, causing fallen arches and bunions.

Also, he said, the "reduction in snout didn't take [place] evenly" in humans, leaving the problem of "oversized teeth in undersized jaws," resulting in dental troubles.

Biochemist Gish replied that if walking upright and reduced jaws caused disadvantages, it was contradictory to imply evolution produced them, since the theory holds that natural selection preserves improvements, not handicaps.

"These are all reasons why they should be selected against," he said. "It would seem that man never evolved in the first place." However, he contended that the physical problems were not inherent, but derived from slack living habits.

The debaters had 30 minutes each for opening speeches and 10 minutes each for rebuttals, with additional time for questions from the audience. Other excerpts:

Wilber: "All this complex universe derives from organization of a single, particular type of matter. From its earliest beginning, matter of the universe showed a dynamic state one might call 'Genesis' or becoming.

"It is adequate to assume that complex organisms resulting in unique relationship of macromolecules one to another is sufficient to account for the characters of highly organized structure that we refer to as living."

Slusher: "It's contrary to the second law of thermodynamics to say that you can start with an exploding cosmic egg and get a complex, ordered universe out of it. That law says that all spontaneous processes involving energy and matter move toward molecular entropy and disorder . . . .

"The particles would spread out and eventually reach a state of maximum entropy . . . . My students would laugh me out of the room if I said I saw an exploding building produce a more complicated arrangement than there was to start with. . . . . Raw energy going into any system, without external constraints, does not give rise to order. As physicists say, you've got to have a motor."

Gish: "If evolution is true, our museums should be literally overflowing with transitional forms . . . . The fossil record does not provide them . . . . What the fossil record does show is the explosive appearance of different kinds, with a lack of transitional forms."

Wilber: "The evolutionary pattern is seen only when the whole is observed, and not when the crack in the painting is exaggerated. No one can claim that the geological record is complete. No responsible scientist makes such claims . . . .

"When we talk about certain gaps . . . what's that due to? Simply to the fact that some professor hasn't put enough graduate students looking hard enough to find them. That doesn't mean we should stop being scientists."

Chapter 5

Be Sure Your Sins Will Find You Out!

It was a rather strange letter. The date on it was 27 December 1977. Since George Cornell's articles had not appeared locally, I xeroxed copies from those Mr. Cornell sent me and mailed them to Charles Wilber and Michael Charney. Charney had replied with a most cordial letter addressed: "My dear Marvin."

After thanking me for mailing the articles to him, Charney got to what appeared to be one of the purposes of his letter. He stated that he had always allowed the various positions on human origins to be presented in his anthropology classes, but he never had had any of his invitations returned. He implied that perhaps they (creationists) were afraid to subject their flocks to the evolutionary evidence. His reasoning escaped me. Although the general public was not aware of it, he certainly knew that I, a creationist, was responsible for the Colorado State University debate in which *both* sides of the creation-evolution issue was presented with special invitations going out to all of the area churches.

He concluded his letter by stating that he and Wilber had neglected to mention that even if all of the biological sciences were wrong regarding evolution, the disproving of evolution would not in itself guarantee that creation was the correct theory of origins. I was amused because Gish had made that very statement in the debate—that to disprove evolution does not in itself prove creation.

However, the most puzzling part of Charney's letter was the paragraph in which he stated that he had lost respect for the scientific objectivity of Dr. Gish. My first reaction was that he was going to level a serious charge at Gish: plagerism? fraud? bogus academic degrees? falsifying research?

None of the above. It seems that in one of Gish's articles he had quoted the famous evolutionist, Thomas Huxley. However, Gish had not taken the quotation from the original work of Huxley but from a secondary source—someone who had himself quoted Huxley. That person had apparently put the wrong page number down in the reference. Charney attempted to look up the reference but could not find it because of the incorrect page number. Charney claimed: "There is no such quote in the Huxley book."

There is no doubt that to use secondary references is discouraged in scholarly works, probably for the very reason about which Charney was complaining. It increases the possibility of mistakes in citations. But it was Charney's extreme language that struck me as being so strange. He claimed that Gish had "strayed from the rigid intellectual code of the scholar" and that Gish had forfeited "any claim to objectivity, to scholarship"! "All over one lousy quotation?," I asked myself. I felt that Shakespeare had put it well when he said, "I fear thou protesteth too much."

Charney did admit that Gish had promised to send him the proper page number for the quotation, but that so far Gish had failed to do so. Feeling that it really wasn't my problem, I xeroxed the letter and sent a copy to Gish. I put the original in my files and promptly forgot about it.

About a month later, I purchased some new works on the human fossils and on cosmology—two of my special interests. I had difficulty finding room for them in my study. Since all the shelves were full, and there was simply no place to build new shelves, I thought that it might be well to cull some of the older science works and discard them—thus making room for my new books. In contrast to theological works, scientific works quickly become obsolete. Many creationists have harmed their cause by quoting from out-of-date scientific works in dealing with the creation-evolution issue.

I began to suffer mixed emotions. On the one hand, I

wanted to keep my science library current. On the other hand,
I am a child of the Great Depression. I hate to throw anything
away. And there are some books which, although old, are
worth keeping. One certainly wouldn't throw away Darwin's
Origin of Species just because it was published more than 100
years ago. Yet, I needed to make room for my new books.

My eyes fell on a thick paperback, *Scientific American
Reader,* from 1953. It contained articles which had appeared
in the journal, *Scientific American,* between 1948-1952. I was
in the process of discarding it when my childhood training in
frugality surfaced. Perhaps, I thought, I had better look
through it to see if there is anything in it worth keeping. The
book was in sections, with each section covering a different
area of the sciences.

As I scanned the table of contents, I came to the section on
anthropology. My eyes stopped at an article in that section
entitled: "The Scars of Human Evolution" by Wilton M.
Krogman. Krogman was Professor of Physical Anthropology
in the Graduate School of Medicine at the University of
Pennsylvania. As I read the title, it struck me that this was
the same title which Prof. Michael Charney had given to his
presentation at the Colorado State University debate.
Overcome with curiosity, I turned to the article. Based upon
my memory—admittedly defective—there were a number of
similarities between Krogman's article and Charney's
presentation.

The similarities were so striking that at my first opportunity
I went to my cassette library, took down the tape of the
Colorado State University debate, and played it. I was aghast!
Except for some humorous and rather sensual remarks that
Charney had injected into his presentation, the presentation
by Charney and the 1949 article by Krogman were identical.
Word for word! Charney, the man who had questioned Gish's
scholarship because of one measly secondary quotation, had
actually plagerized his entire presentation and had not given
Krogman credit. There was not the slightest hint in Charney's
entire presentation that it was not his own work. If Charney
feels that a man forfeits his claim to scholarship when he uses
a secondary quotation, I wonder what he would say about
someone who plagerizes an entire article?

Should I tell Charney that he has been found out?

Chapter 6

You've Come A Long Way, Baby!

If there is one person to be designated the father of the modern creationist movement, that person is Henry Morris. No other person has so constantly and consistently enunciated Biblical creationism and the impressive scientific evidences that illuminate it. Others also have pioneered—some earlier than Morris. Some denominations, such as the Lutheran Church (Missouri Synod) and the Seventh Day Adventists, have had eloquent spokesmen for creationism. Yet, it is the name of Henry Morris which is synonymous in the popular mind with the rise of modern creationism. This association is richly deserved.

For the sake of history, movements must be dated. The originating date of a movement is usually some landmark event. Modern creationism has such an event—the publishing of the book, *The Genesis Flood,* in 1961, coauthored by Henry Morris and John Whitcomb. Morris was, at the time, head of the Department of Civil Engineering at the Virginia Polytechnic Institute and State University. He was also Professor of Hydraulics there and had written a definitive textbook on that subject. Whitcomb was Professor of Old Testament at Grace Theological Seminary.

History has a way of separating the permanent from the transitory. *The Genesis Flood* will prove to be as significant an event for creationism as the publication of Darwin's *The Origin of Species* was for evolutionism 100 years before. However, there is a difference. Darwin's book has lasted. *The Genesis Flood* is already obsolete. In the world of the fast-

moving sciences, no book involving a great deal of scientific
data, such as *The Genesis Flood,* can hope to remain current
for long. The reason the *Origin* has lasted so long is because it
is largely philosophy, not science. Even Darwin's friends
admit that he had precious little rigorous evidence to back up
his basic concepts.

However, there is a more recent phenomenon that has
projected the name of Henry Morris and his associate at the
Institute for Creation Research, Duane Gish, into the lime-
light and has launched the creationist movement into the
mainstream of late Twentieth Century history. This
phenomenon is the series of creation-evolution debates on the
university campuses. Although the court battles dealing with
creationism have captured the attention of the general public,
it is these debates which have impressed the student world.

It must be one of the ironies of history that these debates,
which have done far more than any other one thing to make
the intellectual world aware of the creationist movement, were
entered into by accident. Although Henry Morris and Duane
Gish have been accused of being professional debaters going
up and down the country setting traps for unsuspecting
evolutionists, neither Morris nor Gish had ever been in
debates before, nor had they studied debating technique. This
simply had not been a part of their plan for the promotion of
creationism. All of their 136 debates have been organized
entirely on the local level. One cannot help but feel that a
Higher Plan was involved.

These debates, which are of remarkable intellectual depth,
have tremendous popular appeal. That the debate format
should be in large part responsible for the land-swell of
interest in scientific creationism is another of the ironies of
history, for one of the most famous debates in history—that
between Thomas Huxley and Bishop Wilberforce in 1860—did
much to popularize and promote evolution in the last century.

The first "debate," in this ten-year series was in the Spring
of 1972. It was not really a debate at all, but a lengthy
confrontation between Duane Gish and one of the world's
leading evolutionary geneticists, G. Ledyard Stebbins. It all
started when a biology professor at the University of
California, Davis, was given copies of some of Gish's articles
and tapes. Amazed at the impressive scientific evidence for

creationism, the professor decided to devote one of his special study courses to the subject of creation vs. evolution. Approximately 40 students were enrolled.

At the conclusion of the course, he asked Gish and Stebbins, who was also a member of the Davis faculty, to come and defend their respective positions. While there, Gish was also scheduled for an evening lecture on campus. One of the reporters on the student newspaper was a Christian. She published a full-page article in the paper outlining Gish's arguments and challenged the faculty and students of the Davis campus to attend the evening lecture.

That evening over 800 students and faculty crowded the lecture hall beyond capacity. It was after Gish's lecture that the first creation-evolution "debate" took place. Stebbins and his fellow evolutionists on the faculty challenged Gish in a debate-like atmosphere for two and one-half hours. The confrontation created great excitement and interest on campus. The student newspaper gave excellent coverage to both sides with subsequent rebuttals. Later, Stebbins and Gish debated in a formal setting on the campus of Sacramento State University.

These debates have involved some of the foremost names in evolutionary thinking such as geneticist Stebbins, anthropologist C. Loring Brace of the University of Michigan, biogeologist Preston Cloud of the University of California (Santa Barbara), anthropologist Ashley Montagu of Princeton University, paleoanthropologist John T. Robinson of the University of Wisconsin, biologist John Maynard Smith of Sussex University (England), thermodynamicist Harold Morowitz of Yale, anthropologist Vincent Sarich of the University of California (Berkeley), biochemist Russell Doolittle of the University of California (San Diego), and physicist Max Herzberger, an associate of Albert Einstein, from the University of New Orleans. Many of the other debaters are well known by those in their fields because of their extensive research and publications.

Other famous names have also figured in the debates. Paleontologist Steven Stanley of Johns Hopkins University was a guest lecturer at the University of Wyoming and figured in the discussion period following the creation-evolution panel there. Stanley Miller, famous for his origin of life experiments, took part in the discussion period following a debate at San Diego State University. He declined an invitation by Gish to participate in an entire debate devoted to the origin of life. Famed geologist E. C. Olson served as moderator for the debate held on the campus of the University of California at Los Angeles (UCLA), and the moderator for the debate on the campus of Evergreen State College in Olympia was the Chief Justice of the Supreme Court of the State of Washington. In dealing with famous people, we certainly should not omit Gish's debate with Madalyn Murray O'Hair on Houston radio.

The climax of this decade of debate came in the 1981-82 academic year. In the October 1981 issue of *Science Digest*, Gish engaged in a creation-evolution debate with the famous evolutionist and popularizer of science, Isaac Asimov. The circulation of this magazine far exceeds the total number who had attended the debates up to that time.

Also, in October 1981, Gish debated biochemist Russell Doolittle, who had previously debated Morris and/or Gish four times. This debate took place at Liberty Baptist College, Lynchburg, Virginia, and was sponsored by the Old Time Gospel Hour. Jerry Falwell served as moderator. The attendance of 5,000 equaled the attendance record set at the University of Minnesota in 1977. However, this debate was designed for nationwide television coverage in 1982. Although the debates are continuing, this nationwide television exposure serves as a fitting tenth anniversary celebration for this remarkable phenomenon.

These debates constitute a frontal attack by creationists on the evolutionary establishment. It is one thing for creationists to confront school boards and P.T.A.'s, but for creationists to invade the hallowed halls of the university campus and confront evolutionists in their own private sanctuary has had profound effects on the student world. This creationist frontal attack is not just noted for its boldness. It also has the strategic element of surprise. Just when evolutionists thought that creationism was dead, the creationist shows up on campus very much alive to deal with the issue in terms of *science*. The result is that creationists are on the offensive and have a tremendous psychological advantage.

There is another sense in which creationism has an

advantage. Although we creationists would wish that men
would accept creationism because it is in accord with known
scientific principles, as well as being Biblical, modern man
asks: "What is new? What is contemporary? What is 'in'?"
Creationism benefits from this addiction to fads on the part
of modern man. Creationism—although very old—is just
being rediscovered. Evolution has been around a long time.
It's "old stuff." Further, evolution has not made good on its
promises. It has fed neither the mind nor the soul.
Creationism is riding the crest of man's desire for something
new. However, because creationism satisfies both the mind
and the soul, it is here to stay. It is the wave of the future.
These debates are like a breath of fresh air on the intellectual
horizon.

Never in these debates is an attempt made to establish a
"winner," either by popular vote or by a panel of judges.
These debates are instead a teaching mechanism to convey
information through a very exciting format. Still, there is a
sense in which creationists could not lose in such a
confrontation. Creationism is considered such an underdog
that just the appearance of a creationist on the same platform
with an evolutionist constitutes a moral victory for
creationism. The fact that the creationist is able to hold his
own is even more impressive.

However, the December 4, 1981, issue of the journal
Science, the official organ of the American Association for
the Advancement of Science, makes the following remark in
commenting on these creation-evolution debates: " . . . most
of which, incidentally, creationists have 'won' . . . . " Sometimes the accolades are not as direct. In the March-April 1978
issue of *American Scientist,* a reviewer is commenting on the
absence of paleontological evidence in so many evolution
texts. The result, he said, was a generation of evolutionary
biologists who are ignorant of the fossil record and therefore
"can be reduced to babbling by any creationist debater in
possession of more than two facts." Grudging admissions that
creationists have done very well in these debates can be found
quite often in evolutionist literature. There is a reason for this
concensus that creationists have "won." It is that
evolutionists have yet to satisfactorily answer the basic arguments of creationists—the problem of the fossil record and

the problem of the second law of thermodynamics mitigating against the increase in complexity over time which evolution demands.

Many creationists across the country have recently been involved in creation-evolution debates, including some of the newer staff members of the Institute for Creation Research. However, this work will limit itself to the debates of the two men who have pioneered and popularized the method—Henry Morris and Duane Gish.

Chapter 7

In the Beginning

University of Missouri, Kansas City

The University of Missouri at Kansas City is not without its academic accomplishments. Yet, no one would ever mistake it for the ivy covered halls of Harvard, Yale, or Princeton. None the less, it was here, on October 11, 1972, that the first of a remarkable decade-long series of formal debates on the creation-evolution issue took place.

Sponsored by the local chapter of Campus Crusade for Christ, this first debate was held in a university lecture hall with about 350 students and faculty in attendance. It was a very cordial affair—as most of them have been. The evening concluded with a reception and "rap-session" in a private home near the campus.

Henry Morris could afford to be relaxed. Since, in all probability, few expected him to win, he therefore had nothing to lose. Dr. Richard Gentile, Professor of Geology at the University of Missouri, Kansas City, could also afford to be relaxed. He had behind him the authority and prestige of the entire evolutionary establishment. It was, in one sense, a Twentieth Century replay of the conflict between David and Goliath. The student newspaper felt that in this case, too, the underdog clearly won.

When the early debates are compared with the later ones, considerable "evolution" is seen in the format of the debates themselves. The early ones were one to two hours in length, whereas the later ones were often three to four hours in length. In the early debates involving two speakers for each side, the two creationists often spoke first before the two evolutionists made their presentation. The later debates followed a regular debate format in alternating the two sides. The later debates reveal a sophistication on the part of the creationist and evolutionist debaters not seen in the earlier ones.

On the other hand, the creationist strategy has been quite consistent throughout all of the debates involving Morris and Gish. Their emphasis has centered on the laws of thermodynamics and the fossil record. According to the laws of thermodynamics, these creationists maintain that evolution *could not* take place. According to the fossil record, they affirm that evolution *has not* taken place. This clear approach has been partly responsible for the success in communicating their message.

Because so many evolutionists participated in these debates, a similar consistent strategy on their part could hardly be expected. What one would expect, and what did materialize, was a variety of arguments for evolution. An analysis of these arguments reveals the many ways evolution is being taught on the campuses today. It also reveals which arguments evolutionists themselves feel are most conclusive.

Obviously, it is impossible to reproduce all of the evidences brought by evolutionists in these debates. Nor is it the purpose of this book to detail the arguments used by creationists in establishing their position. Many fine publications are available documenting the creationist evidence. However, most of the debates had a distinct "personality." By emphasizing these individual personalities, we feel that an excellent overview of the whole can be obtained.

In the debate at the University of Missouri, Kansas City, Richard Gentile devoted most of his time to a philosophic principle which has been basic to historical geology and evolution. This principle of uniformitarianism Gentile described as a basic law: "The present is the key to the past." By this he meant that the physical and biological features of our planet were produced by the same processes that are at work today.

The phrase, "the present is the key to the past," seems innocent enough. Indeed, there is much truth to it. But there is a "hooker" in it also. Let me illustrate. Suppose someone told you that you were to explain your life and your existence referring only to processes going on in your life today. In some ways, that is not too difficult. Each day we eat. Each day we go to bed, sleep, and get up again. Each day our heart pumps blood through our veins, each day we breathe, and each day we move around.

However, in other areas "the present is the key to the past" just doesn't work. Perhaps ten years ago you had your gall bladder removed. That was a one-time event that cannot be repeated or understood in terms of events happening in your own life today. Four years ago your mother passed away. Obviously, that event also cannot be repeated today—or any other day. And, the most important event of your life, your own birth, likewise is a singularity, a once-only event, that cannot be repeated. Nor can it be explained by referring only to events going on in your life today. Notice that if you were limited in explaining your existence to only those events that are happening to you today, there is much in your life that could not be explained—including your own origin. Yet, that principle is the one that Gentile and other evolutionists would restrict us to in explaining the origin and history of the earth, life, and man.

However, there is an even deeper problem in applying the principle of "the present is the key to the past." How does the evolutionist know *with certainty* that nothing took place in the past history of the earth that is not going on more or less to the same degree today? Let us go back to the illustration of your own life. Before one could legitimately apply a principle such as "the present is the key to the past" to your life, they first would have to obtain a complete knowledge of every aspect of your life to know that the principle does indeed apply. As they studied your life and learned about your birth, your gall bladder surgery, and your mother's death, it would be obvious that the principle did not apply. If they sought to apply the principle anyway against the historical evidence, it is obvious that it would give a very false view of your life. If they sought to apply it to your life without complete knowledge, it would then be a philosophical belief regarding how a life should be interpreted rather than a scientific or historical fact. The point is that one must have a complete knowledge of your life to know if the principle can be legitimately applied.

The same thing is true in using that principle to interpret

the past history of the earth. The only way one can know that the principle legitimately applies is to have a total and complete knowledge of the past history of our planet. Yet, no human being has such knowledge. It actually demands that a person be omniscient—at least as far as the history of the earth is concerned. Obviously, only God has such knowledge.

Not only does the application of the uniformitarian principle demand a knowledge which no one has, but it also involves a prejudice against the supernatural. Gentile put it very directly when he said: "The doctrine of uniformitarianism is another way of saying that supernatural causes need not be involved to explain the real world of today." David Kitts (University of Oklahoma debate) said: "The uniformitarian principle, as I have formulated it, does not preclude catastrophes, it only precludes miracles."

Now, the real question is: "Is there any evidence that the supernatural or the miraculous has been involved in the past history of the earth?" There is both scientific and historical evidence that it has. Scientifically, the first and second laws of thermodynamics—to be discussed later—clearly imply that the universe could not have ordered itself, that the origin of our universe was brought about by an outside supernatural agency. The historical record of the Bible clearly states that there were at least two one-time events or singularities involving conditions that are not in operation today—the creation and the flood.

Scientists are quick to state that science deals with the natural, not with the supernatural. We agree. When one says that science deals with the natural, that at least allows for the possibility of the supernatural. There is no reason why science could not deal with the natural and also recognize the reality of the supernatural in the affairs of the world and of men— even though the scientist would consider that area outside his domain. However, the concept of uniformitarianism goes beyond that. It not only does not allow scientists to recognize the possibility of the supernatural, it denies the supernatural. It states that scientists are not to consider any event or any process in the history of the earth that is not going on to some degree today. It thus places the concept of creation and the flood "off limits" to the scientist.

It is not that those believing in uniformitarianism are

atheists. Many of them are Christians. Gentile himself stated that he considered the Bible a good book by which everyone should live. What uniformitarianism does is to separate nature and the Bible. The Bible is not to be used in interpreting nature because the Biblical statements about nature have no scientific value. Their value would be strictly religious. One thinks it strange that the God who created the universe would have so little to say about it that would be of scientific value. Even a superficial reading of the Bible makes it obvious that this divorce between nature and the Bible is not taught there. In fact, the Bible claims to have a great deal of authoritative information about nature.

Henry Morris' position statement in the debate was that the basic laws of nature—the first and second laws of thermo-dynamics—make evolutionary theory impossible. Gentile did not even address this issue. In his rebuttal, Morris pointed out that some leading evolutionists are themselves questioning the validity of the uniformitarian concept. Uniformitarianism, he explained, really involves two separate ideas. One is very true and the other very false. The concept of the uniformity of the laws of nature is very true. It goes beyond geology for it is basic to all of science. In fact, one could not do science without it. Creationists subscribe to this idea as enthusiastical-ly as do evolutionists. (Morris didn't mention it, but it is also taught in the Bible: Gen. 8:22.)

However, the second idea imbedded in uniformitarianism—that the rates of geologic processes have always been the same in the past as they are today—is false. It is unprovable. This is the aspect of uniformitarianism which would deny Special Creation and any intervention by God in the Flood. It is this concept which drives science to an atheistic position. It is not necessary that scientists hold this view. However, many do. They believe that they must do so in order to be good scientists.

It is obvious that the model of origins and earth history which Henry Morris and Duane Gish develop in these debates is similar to the Biblical model found in Genesis. Yet, it is their contention that this same model of origins and earth history can be developed independent of the Bible—*and strictly on the basis of scientific laws and evidences.* The following chapters record their efforts.

Chapter 8

The Gaps Are Real, and They Are A Problem
University of Oklahoma

An aerospace engineering professor at the University of Oklahoma, Edward Blick, was responsible for arranging the first debate in which both Henry Morris and Duane Gish took part. On January 15, 1973, over 1,000 students attempted to crowd into the 500-seat student union auditorium. Opposing Morris and Gish were two evolutionists of stature from the University of Oklahoma faculty. David B. Kitts, Professor of Geology, is a noted paleontologist and philosopher of science. Hubert Frings, Professor of Zoology, is the author of a standard biology textbook.

Henry Morris invariably begins by defining terms. In all of his debates he first defines the creation model, then the evolution model. However, instead of giving his own definition of evolution, he gives the definition formulated by the famous evolutionist, Sir Julian Huxley. It goes as follows:

> Evolution in the extended sense can be defined as a directional and essentially irreversible process occurring in time, which in its course gives rise to an increase of variety and an increasingly high level of organization in its products. Our present knowledge indeed forces us to

the view that the whole of reality is evolution—a single
process of self-transformation.[1]

Morris points out that the two models, evolution and
creation, are diametrically opposed. They both could not be
correct. Whereas the creation model calls for a decrease in
order and complexity in nature over time, based upon the
universal second law of thermodynamics, Huxley's definition
of evolution calls for an increase in order and complexity in
nature as time goes on.

Frings, however, took sharp issue with Huxley's definition
of evolution and substituted his own. "Evolution is
'modification over time,' and that's all it is," he insisted.
Many other evolutionists use similar definitions of evolution
such as "change through time." Now, a precise definition of
evolution is very important—as we will try to show. The
question is: "Who is right, Huxley or Frings?"

Perhaps the best way to answer the question is to look at an
evolutionary chart. Although these charts vary in size, shape,
and color, they are remarkably consistent in one thing. They
all show single-celled life at the bottom. Above them would be
multi-celled organisms, and then more complex ocean life.
About one-fourth of the way up are the first animals with
backbones—the fish. Working our way further up the chart
would be the amphibians, the reptiles, the mammals, and the
primates, with man at the very top of the chart. No one can
deny that man, with his remarkable brain, is the most
complex form of physical life in the universe—as well as the
most recent.

Notice that as we move up the chart we do see change. But
notice also that the word *change* is not specific enough to
accurately describe what is happening. It is not just general or
random change. As we go from a single cell up to man, it is a
very specific type of change. It is *a directional change
involving increasing complexity*. Any other type of change
would not satisfy the evolutionary chart. Huxley is right. A
proper definition of evolution must state that it is a

---

1. "Evolution and Genetics," Chapter 8 in *What is Science?* (Ed., R.
    Newman, New York; Simon and Schuster, 1955), p. 278.

directional change involving increasing complexity over time.

Does it matter? Yes, it does! The definition of evolution determines the type of evidence that one must produce to support it. Since evolution is a very specific type of change involving increasing complexity through time, the evolutionist must demonstrate that unaided nature is able to produce such changes. He must also produce objective evidence that such changes have indeed taken place. The evolutionist simply cannot produce such evidence.

This is why Henry Morris has emphasized the laws of thermodynamics so forcibly. When properly understood, the second law of thermodynamics is the single most powerful argument against evolution. It states that the normal, spontaneous direction of natural processes is toward decreasing complexity—not increasing complexity. "As time goes on, order goes down," Morris says.

For this reason, the evolutionist likes to bootleg into the argument a deficient definition of evolution. By defining evolution as "change or modification over time," evolutionists then feel free to introduce any change in nature as evidence for evolution. By this definition *all of us* are evolutionists, for all of us readily admit that there is change in nature.

The question to be asked is: "Could a downward change or a lateral change produce what we see on an evolutionary chart—that amoeba-to-man scenario?" The answer is obviously "No!" However, if you thumb through the pages of any high school or college biology text, you will discover that all of the alleged evidences for evolution presented in such texts involve changes which are lateral rather than upward. The famous "peppered moth," used in virtually every evolutionary textbook as living proof of evolution, is really a lateral (rather than an upward) change.

Creationists should be vigilant to point out these deficient definitions of evolution and the resulting defective evidences used to support it. One is really at a loss to explain the continual use of these faulty definitions. Is it possible that many evolutionists don't really understand the kind of evidence needed to support their theory? Or is it possible that they do!

A second feature to come out of the Oklahoma debate deals

with the scientific method. Since the time we were in junior high school, we have been told that the scientific method begins with experiments and observations. These observations are used to formulate an hypothesis. Further successful testing results in the development of a theory, and ultimately, if there is continued confirmation, the formulation of a scientific law. Not only is that order universally taught in the classroom but half of the evolutionist speakers in these debates reported that this was indeed how the scientist worked. This emphasis on experiment and observation at the first stages of the scientific method gives it a solid, objective reputation as being trustworthy.

However, a funny thing happens on the way to the philosophy of science department. Kitts tells us that this is not at all the way science really operates. Dealing with how one goes about reconstructing the past history of the earth, he said: "I hold, along with every other academic philosopher of science in this country, that theories cannot be generated out of observations." Kitts is reflecting the pioneering work of Sir Karl Popper, the famed philosopher of science from the University of London. What Kitts is saying is that science does not work according to the well-known scientific method, even though virtually everyone—scientist and layperson alike —thinks that it does. Theories are not generated out of cold, hard facts. Theories are generated out of the fertile brains of men. Then, facts or observations are examined to see if they fit into the theories. Kitts is right when he states that every philosopher of science in the country believes that. What it means is that there is more philosophy in scientific theories than most scientists themselves realize. We are quite mistaken if we think that theories start with factual observations.

Another statement by Kitts will reveal the importance of this distinction. Kitts said, " . . . the fossil record is perfectly consistent with the creationist point of view, and the problem is not what the fossil record tells us, but what evolutionary theory tells us." This is because "the geologist does not test theories against events. He tests events against theories." In other words, evolutionary theory determines how the fossils are to be interpreted. The importance of theory and philosophy in the interpretation of facts cannot be overemphasized when we consider the implications of the theory of evolution. Evolution is not a theory based upon facts. It is instead a theory into which the facts are placed and made to fit.

A fascinating portion of Kitts' presentation dealt with the gaps in the fossil record which Gish had emphasized as evidence against evolution. For instance, the evolutionist claims that reptiles evolved from fish. If this had actually taken place, the modern synthetic view of evolution demands that millions of years would have been involved in the process. During this time, as Gish pointed out repeatedly, the fins of the fish involved in this transition would have slowly and gradually changed into the feet and legs of the amphibian.

Since fish fossils are found in great abundance, and since amphibian fossils are quite abundant also, it would be the normal and expected thing to find transitional forms between the fish and the amphibians, that is, forms where the fins have partially become feet and legs. That absolutely none of the expected fossils have been found is a great embarrassment to the evolutionist. Since fish fossils are found and amphibian fossils are found, the area between them—where the transitional fossils should be, *but aren't*—is called a *gap*.

Not only are the transitional fossils between fish and amphibians missing, but all of the expected transitional fossils that the evolutionist hoped to find between the major categories are missing. Thus the fossil record is full of gaps and completely lacking in transitional forms or bridges. Kitts himself had written about this problem at about the very time of this debate. His statement was so straightforward and honest that Gish has quoted Kitts in almost every debate since then.

Kitts wrote: "Despite the bright promise that paleontology provides a means of 'seeing' evolution, it has presented some nasty difficulties for evolutionists, the most notorious of which is the presence of 'gaps' in the fossil record. Evolution requires intermediate forms between species, and paleontology does not provide them" (*Evolution,* Sept. 1974, p. 476). After the Oklahoma debate, Kitts walked over to Gish and Morris and reportedly said: "Well, the gaps are real, and they are a problem."

All of this makes Kitts' performance during the debate

rather humorous. In the light of what Kitts himself has written, one can't help but wonder if he were serious. First, he tried to pretend that Gish was less than scientific when he spoke of "regular and systematic gaps" in the fossil record. Kitts responded: "Now, what are regular and systematic gaps? I think I know what a gap is, but what is a regular and systematic gap? How does one distinguish a regular gap from an irregular gap?"

Then Kitts tried to argue that the gaps were actually the result of the classification system of Kitts' teacher, George Gaylord Simpson, who has the most widely accepted classification scheme for the 32 orders of mammals. Kitts argued that Simpson distinguished orders of mammals on the basis of whether they were delineated by systematic gaps. So there is a perfect circular argument. The gaps are systematic because they delineate orders, and the orders are orders because they are delineated by gaps.

Let me try to illustrate what Kitts is saying. Suppose in a large valley there were many different animals grazing together—cattle, horses, camels, elephants, rhinos, elk, sheep, goats, and deer. Let these grazing animals represent the fossil record. Now, suppose that you gather the different types of animals into their own groups. As the horses, cattle, and other animals are gathered into their own individual herds, the differences between cattle and horses and between cattle and rhinos become more obvious than when they were all mixed together.

Let this process represent the organizing of the fossils into their similar groups. Now, the question is: "Were these gaps or distinctions between cattle and horses and between cattle and the other animals created by you when you organized them, or were you able to organize them because the differences or gaps were there already?" I think we would all agree that the gaps or differences were there already. We did not create them. Organization was possible because they were there. The same is true of the fossil record. It is not that organization creates the gaps. We are able to organize the fossils because the gaps are there. Kitts' comment after the debate is more to the point than his hedging during the debate: "The gaps are real, and they are a problem."

Chapter 9

Never Again!
Sacramento State University

Was the debate at Sacramento State University (a) funny,
(b) disgusting, (c) scholarly, (d) sacrilegious, (e) emotional, (f)
exciting, (g) provocative, or (h) insulting? The answer is: "All
of the above." World famous geneticist G. Ledyard Stebbins,
from the University of California, Davis, gave one of the best
defenses of evolution of the entire debate series. In striking
contrast, the presentation by evolutionist Richard M.
Lemmon, biochemist of the University of California,
Berkeley, was without question an all-time low in the ten
years of debates—with the possible exception of the
evolutionist debaters at Bridgewater State College in
Massachusetts. Lemmon was as insulting as Stebbins was
scholarly.

The debate was held on March 1, 1973. Fifteen-hundred
people tried to crowd into the Music Auditorium designed to
seat 450. Attempts earlier in the week to obtain larger
facilities were refused. The debate was one of only two in the
series in which a Minister of the Gospel was one of the
creationist debaters. (The other occasion was when I teamed
with Dr. Gish in a debate at Wheaton College on the age of
the earth.) The Rev. James C. Boswell, a local pastor, and
Duane Gish were the creationist speakers.

A statement by the moderator, Prof. Angus Wright, set the
"tone" of the debate. "I like to feel that my credentials as
moderator go beyond just having a loud voice and knowing
where the bathrooms are. It is well known that I am not well
versed in the concepts of science, and that I am even less
attuned to the ways of the Lord. So, I feel that I was chosen

as moderator because there was no good reason to believe that I came about by either evolution or creation. This makes me a fully qualified, unbiased observer."

Lemmon's entire presentation was a breaking of one of the cardinal rules of debate and logic. The issue to be debated was, "Which model offers the better explanation for origins: special creation or organic evolution?" Instead of speaking to the issue, Lemmon attacked the credibility and rationality of creationist scientists, including Gish, and ridiculed Gish and Boswell for their literal belief in the Bible. This technique, attacking the man rather than the issue, is known as an argument *ad hominem* (against the man). It is poor debating technique, faulty logic, and is considered in all circles to be anything but "kosher."

Specifically, Lemmon said that creationists, including Gish, were not qualified to be called scientists because they believe in things that are illogical. These things include the statement of faith of the Creation Research Society, the idea that Christianity is right and every other religion is wrong, the idea that the earth was created before the sun in creation week, the fact that Joshua caused the sun to stand still, the matter of Jonah's three days and three nights in the belly of the whale, Levitical laws regarding ceremonial cleansing of women after childbirth, and the Biblical command that witches are to be put to death.

He stated that he and Stebbins were there because they felt that someone should speak up against creationist attempts to have creationism taught in the California schools. (This was an issue before the California Board of Education at the time.) He said that if these bills were passed, California teachers would be forced to teach "things that they know are not science."

Lemmon then listed the various scientific and religious organizations that were opposed to this California legislation. It is rather amusing that Lemmon would make such an appeal based on authority, because scientists have long prided themselves in the fact that they do not appeal to authority. That is, what people say or believe or think about scientific matters is not supposed to matter to the scientist. It is only what the cold, hard facts of scientific experimentation say that really matters. After stating that nineteen California Nobel

Laureates were opposed to the legislation, he asked: "Can one Nobel Laureate be found to support the creationism our opponents are advocating?" Although Gish did not respond to this particular challenge, the truth is that one could be found who had been honored by the Nobel committee.

Stebbins, in his presentation, emphasized the fossil record. He claimed that correspondence he had with famous paleontologists, such as Alfred Romer and George Gaylord Simpson, revealed that many transitional forms have been found in the fossil record. His main emphasis was on a fossil bird known as *Archaeopteryx*, claimed by many evolutionists to be a transitional form between reptiles and birds. He also argued for the legitimacy of circumstantial evidence in support of evolution.

A remarkable incident took place during the question period at the end of the debate. In order to understand its significance, a bit of background is necessary. According to evolutionists, the first time life appeared in abundance was at the base of the Cambrian geologic period, about 600 million years before the present. The life in existence then, evolutionists say, was entirely ocean life. In fact, evolutionists believe that land life could not have existed at that time because there was no oxygen in the atmosphere. It took almost 200 million years for the ocean plants to put sufficient oxygen into the atmosphere to sustain land animal and land plant life. Thus, on any evolutionary chart or in any natural history museum diorama, land plants will not appear until the Silurian Period, and land animals are not thought to have appeared until the Devonian Period of geologic history.

Yet, in the June 1959 edition of the journal, *Evolution,* Daniel I. Axelrod published a review article documenting the discovery of approximately 60 genera of woody (land) plants in Cambrian strata. That land plants would appear in the fossil record at the time when abundant life first appears is exactly what creationists would expect. However, it is devastating to evolutionary theory. For some reason, these discoveries are virtually unknown among evolutionists.

Gish, during the question period, made reference to these amazing discoveries of land plants in the Cambrian. Stebbins, who is a world-renowned authority in genetics and paleobotany, was shocked and dumbfounded by these statements and demanded to see the references. Gish produced them. Axelrod was at U.C.L.A. when he wrote the article in question. However, at the time of the debate he was an associate of Stebbins at the University of California, Davis. Stebbins was completely unaware of the discoveries set forth in the article by Axelrod. The incident unnerved him. He vowed that he was going to talk to Axelrod about it as soon as he returned to Davis. This scene had a profound effect on the audience as the debate concluded. Reports, allegedly coming from Stebbins, were that he would never again debate anyone from the Institute for Creation Research. And so far, he hasn't.

Chapter 10

Nothing But the Facts!

Van Nuys, California

Imagine that you are a biologist doing field work in Tibet. While studying the Tibetan flea, you make a remarkable discovery about its sex life. You have discovered a "fact." You verify it with repeated observations and experiments. Now, having discovered a "fact," what does your discovery mean? What is the significance of the "fact" that you have unlocked from nature?

As you reflect upon it you realize that this "fact" stands unrelated to anything else unless you incorporate it into some comprehensive philosophy of nature. It is disconcerting to realize that such a solid, established "fact" has so little meaning and significance all by itself.

However, place your discovery into a creation context. Suddenly, your discovery reveals a new aspect of the innovative nature and originality of the all-wise and all-powerful Creator. Or, if you place the fact you have discovered into an evolutionary framework, it could be an extraordinary illustration of the alleged "creative" powers of mutation and natural selection. Notice that facts do not necessarily give meaning to any particular theory of nature, but a theory of nature can give meaning to the facts that are placed in it. A group of isolated facts without a theory or philolsophy to connect them has little meaning. This is what David Kitts was emphasizing in the Oklahoma debate.

Thus we see how important a theory or philosophy of

nature is. Yet, this philosophy of nature is often beyond experimental or observational proof. It is usually said that the theory of nature which is able to receive and explain well the greater number of individual facts is the preferred theory. However, since it is up to the individual to decide which concept best explains the data, it is obvious that personal preferences can enter in and that a high degree of subjectivity is involved.

Morris and Gish insist that the creation model explains more facts or data and explains them better than does the evolution model. In the Van Nuys debate, Morris gave, as he usually does, a description of the creation "model," as he and Gish prefer to call it. According to Morris, the creation model involves four elements. Although they build this model on scientific evidence alone, I show in parentheses the Biblical analogies.

1. A period in the past of special creation of the universe and the various categories of nature, by means and processes which no longer operate. (Creation Week)
2. A condition in which the universe and nature are now being conserved or maintained. (The concept of God's Providence in operation since Creation Week)
3. A principle of decay superimposed upon the universe and nature. Conservation in quantity, and decay in quality. (The Fall)
4. At least one period in history of worldwide catastrophe. (The Flood of Noah)

One could legitimately ask, "If the creation model is better able to handle the facts of nature, why doesn't the scientific world accept it?" The answer actually lies in the realm of theology. The scientific world is a part of the larger "world" of which Jesus Christ spoke in the Gospel of John, chapters 14 through 17. This world prefers to be independent of God and not acknowledge Him. Perhaps we could answer the question by asking a deeper question. Why would a scientist having no relationship with God want to accept a supernatural model of origins—especially if he has the option of choosing a naturalistic model? Is it not more in keeping with his nature that he choose the naturalistic, secular model and reject or ignore the supernatural model?

Perhaps this best explains the statement by William T.

O'Day, a postdoctoral fellow at the University of Southern California, in the Van Nuys debate. He said: "Organic evolution is a theory so well supported that in my own mind and in the mind of the great majority of living scientists it has assumed the status of fact."

This debate was the first one to be held in a church, the First Baptist Church of Van Nuys. Fifteen-hundred people were present on that occasion in September, 1973. Both O'Day and his fellow evolutionist debater, David Morafka, Assistant Professor of Biology at California State College, Dominguez Hills, were emphatic that evolutionary data made faith in a literal interpretation of Genesis absurd. Although Morafka stated that he was not a Christian, both men went to great lengths to assure the audience that evolution posed no threat whatsoever to Christian morals and ethics—in spite of its incompatability with a literal interpretation of Genesis.

O'Day is not the only evolutionist who believes that evolution is a fact—and says so. In the Sacramento State University debate, Richard Lemmon quoted the famed scientist, Harold Urey, as saying: "The evidence in regard to evolution as a fact impresses me as strongly as evidence for universal gravitation." Because this type of statement is so common, it is well to examine it critically.

Notice the anaolgy Urey tries to make. He compares the evidence for evolution with the evidence for gravitation. *There is no analogy.* Gravitation is the force that binds us to the earth. While there is much that is not understood about it, it is a force with which we deal every second of our lives. Further, any school child can do experiments with it, and all of us observe gravity in action in everything we see and touch. Yet, Urey has the audacity to compare the evidence for evolution with the evidence for gravitation.

There is no experiment we can perform to demonstrate evolution. If evolution is happening at all, it is happening so slowly that it cannot be seen even in the entire lifetime of an observer. To compare the evidence for evolution with the evidence for gravitation is nothing short of raw propaganda and a great disservice to science and to the scientific method.

There is a disturbing lack of logic in the thinking of many evolutionists which we will attempt to bring out. The statement by Urey is just one example. This lack of logic is often undetected because of the high regard we have for scientists as being educated people. Scientists themselves tend to believe that because they are scientists, everything they say is scientific. The public should realize that this is not necessarily so.

While scientists are highly trained, their training—though extensive—is very specialized. Very few scientists have had courses in logic or in the philosophy of science. Yet, these areas are basic in dealing with the creation-evolution issue. Scientists often make philosophical statements but do not recognize that they have left science and entered the realm of philosophy. The ability to weigh and sort out evidence and to give each item of evidence its proper value is also an area in which most scientists are not well trained. Only this fact can explain the statement made by Urey comparing the evidence for evolution with the evidence for gravitation.

In the Van Nuys debate, Morafka brought up an argument against creationism which had been seldom used. Gish had emphasized the tremendous explosion and diversity of life appearing suddenly in the Cambrian Period. He contrasted that with the remarkable absence of life in the Precambrian Period. Even if one grants the legitimacy of the Precambrian microfossils, the gap between the microscopic fossils of the Precambrian and the highly organized and diversified life of the Cambrian is immense. The evolutionary ancestors of the Cambrian animals simply are not to be found. This fact is continually emphasized by Gish. Although Gish has not actually said it, the implication of his remarks is that the Cambrian Period represents the time when creation took place —disregarding, of course, the evolutionary time scale which Gish would not accept.

Although all of the animal phyla were found in the Cambrian except the vertebrates, Morafka jumped upon that fact emphasizing that since no vertebrates—fish, amphibians, reptiles, birds, mammals, or men—are found in the Cambrian, the Cambrian could not be used as evidence for Special Creation. It simply did not fit the creation model. Neither Gish nor Morris responded to Morafka's argument because when the Van Nuys debate took place in 1973, there was no answer for it.

This all changed in 1978. John E. Repetski of the United

States Geological Survey reported finding fish fossils in the Upper and Middle Cambrian. Although it has not caught the imagination of the general public like the finding of Lucy in Ethiopia by Carl Johanson, the finding of fish fossils—vertebrates—in the Cambrian is without question the most significant fossil discovery in the last twenty years. It lends additional credibility to the creationist position and presents additional problems for the evolutionist. Morafka can't use that argument anymore.

Chapter 11

Archaeopteryx *Is For the Birds*

Pennsylvania State University

We usually assume that it is quite easy to determine whether something is or isn't. Sometimes that doesn't seem to be the case. So it was on the campus of Pennsylvania State University on October 10, 1973. The debate centered largely on the presence or absence of transitional forms in the fossil record. Duane Gish said there were none. Gish's opponent, Roger Cuffey, said there were many. He showed slides of a number which he claimed qualified as transitional forms.

Roger Cuffey is a Christian. He is the first one of a number of debaters in this series who is a member of the American Scientific Affiliation. The ASA, as it is affectionately known by its members, is an organization of Christians having advanced degrees in the physical and social sciences. It was founded over 40 years ago. Morris and Gish, together with many other recent creationists, were members of it. Over the years, the complexion of the organization has changed. Now its membership is composed largely of theistic evolutionists. Morris and Gish both withdrew their membership because of prejudice against recent creationism. I am probably one of the few recent creationists currently holding membership in the ASA. As such, while not an extinct species, I certainly represent an endangered species as far as that organization is concerned.

When one person says there are no transitional forms in the fossil record, and the other says there is an abundance of them, it is obvious that they are not talking about the same thing. Cuffey talked about sequences of fossils intergrading from one form to another in successive rock layers. He claimed that these changes were evolutionary changes, and that there were many examples of them in the paleontological literature. Cuffey felt that the case for organic evolution had been adequately demonstrated by the late 1800's. In a letter in the ASA *Journal,* March 1971, he wrote: "It is time for evangelical scientists to stop wasting time fooling themselves that evolution did not happen." In a later issue, March 1972, he asks if it is any wonder that paleontologists have concluded that organic evolution was the method of creation "and that those ignoring such overwhelming scientific evidence must have nothing worthwhile to say concerning religious matters as well?"

Gish pointed out that the sequential changes Cuffey called transitional forms were really very small changes that did not represent evolution at all. They were merely examples of genetic variation. It has been demonstrated, Gish declared, that environmental matters such as changes in salinity, temperature, pressure, acidity, and the presence of polutants can all bring about the types of changes Cuffey called evolutionary changes. Evolution would have nothing to do with these changes because they are brought about independent of genetic mutations. Evolutionary change must involve mutations.

Cuffey stated that there was no evidence more crucial in the creation-evolution issue than the fossil evidence. Yet, the total number of professional paleontologists was really quite small, and not many students have studied enough paleontology to be qualified to speak on the subject. He stated that the creationists who were speaking about the fossil record were not really qualified to speak on the subject—an obvious reference to Gish. It was not the only time that Gish's authority to speak on the fossil record would be challenged. In a panel held at the University of Wyoming just a few months later, paleontologist Donald Boyd said: "Almost all paleontologists are evolutionists, whereas the best creationist interpreter of the fossil record is a biochemist!"

Gish acknowledged that he was not a paleontologist. However, as an educated scientist he was able to read the literature, weigh the evidence, and draw his own conclusions. Further, he declared, the type of fossil evidence that the theory of evolution demanded was such that even a ten-year-old kid could recognize it. He was referring, of course, to the alleged transition of fish to amphibians and reptiles to birds. A fossil involving half-fins and half-feet (fish to amphibian) or having half-feet and half-wing (reptile to bird) could easily be recognized as a transitional form by a child.

In all of his debates, Gish places special emphasis on the lack of transitions between fish and amphibians and between reptiles and birds. There is a definite reason. When we deal with fossils, we deal almost entirely with skeletons. Fossilization is a rare phenomenon. Usually only the bones are found as fossils. Yet, although amphibians are supposed to have given rise to reptiles, and reptiles given rise to mammals, the skeletons of these three forms are very similar. Great controversy exists in interpreting some of these fossils. The major differences between amphibians, reptiles, and mammals are found in the nonskeletal parts which normally do not fossilize. These include such things as skin, scales or hair, warm-bloodedness or cold-bloodedness, and differences in the number of chambers of the heart.

In the alleged evolution of the vertebrates, there are two areas where evolution would have involved easily recognizable skeletal changes. One area is the fish to amphibian transition where the fins of the fish would have changed gradually over millions of years into the feet and legs of the amphibian. The other area is the reptile to bird transition where the front feet and legs of the reptile would have changed gradually over millions of years into the wings of the bird.

Because of the abundance of fossils discovered, and because of the vast periods of time involved in these alleged transitions, Gish stresses that the evolution from fish to amphibian and from reptile to bird—both involving significant skeletal changes—should be easily demonstrated from the fossil record. Even one or two of these fossils, if discovered, would be enough to demolish creation and thoroughly establish evolution. Yet, not a single such transitional fossil has been found.

To emphasize this fact, Gish shows a series of color slides which I took at the Field Museum of Natural History in

Chicago. The photographs were taken of a display entitled:
"Amphibians pioneered the conquest of the land." The first
picture shows a crossopterygian fish—a legitimate fish found
in the fossil record. It is considered by evolutionists to be the
type of fish from which the amphibians evolved. The second
picture shows a labyrinthodont, a legitimate amphibian found
also in the fossil record. The third picture shows the type of
animal we would expect to find in the fossil record if
evolution were true. It is a form with half-fins and half-feet—
a true transition between a fish and an amphibian. However,
the wording beneath it reads: "Inferred Intermediate." In
classic lines from almost all of his debates, Gish replies:
"Inferred, indeed! It is purely imaginary! This museum, with
one of the largest and most complete fossil collections in the
world, could not supply a single fossil of a transition between
fish and amphibians. And so they had to call upon the *artist*
to furnish what the paleontologist could not supply!" This
remark is followed by much laughter from the audience.

In the alleged reptile to bird transition, there is a fossil
which almost every evolutionist milks for everything it is
worth. It is a fossil known as *Archaeopteryx*. This fossil was
mentioned in three-fourths of these debates, and a picture of
it is found in almost every biology textbook mentioning the
word, "evolution." About five of these fossils are known to
exist, several of them found in the Upper Jurassic of Bavaria.
Evolutionists call it the perfect transitional form. The fact
that creationists have not accepted it as a legitimate transition
between reptiles and birds is proof to evolutionists that
creationists are simply blind to the evidence.

We must admit that in *Archaeopteryx* the evolutionist did
seem to have a point. It has some features—such as its
elongated boney tail, functional finger on its forelimb, and
conical teeth—that are reptile-like. Other features—such as
wings and feathers—are bird-like. Still other features—such as
its breast-bone, somewhat expended braincase, and
incompletely fused forelimb bones—seem to be intermediate.
Evolutionists claim that if it weren't for the clear imprint of
feathers, *Archaeopteryx* would certainly have been classified
as a reptile. In fact, some evolutionists now claim that it was
just a reptile with feathers.

It is at this point that logic and the ability to weigh the

various evidences reveals its importance. Of the unique qualities of *Archaeopteryx,* which ones are important enough to be diagnostic, and which are just incidental? Many evolutionists debating Gish have claimed that one must consider the whole package of traits, and the package of traits demands that *Archaeopteryx* be classed as a transitional form. Stebbins (Sacramento State University debate) devoted much of his time to the merits of *Archaeopteryx* as a transitional form. Morafka (Van Nuys debate) likewise gave it top billing as a transition. Cuffey highlighted *Archaeopteryx.*

Creationists, along with some notable evolutionist authorities on birds, have consistently maintained that *Archaeopteryx* was a bird. Their logic is solid. The zoological definition of a bird is "a vertebrate with feathers." Any animal with a backbone and feathers is a bird. It is the *feathers* that are diagnostic of birds. There is tremendous variation among birds. About the only thing they have in common is feathers. The other features, no matter how similar they are to other classes of animals, are not significant. To illustrate his point, Gish mentions the duckbill platypus. Here is an animal with a duckbill and webbed feet that lays eggs. Should it not be classed as a bird? Because it is living today, we can study it. We know that its diagnostic features demand that it be classed as a mammal. Yet, Gish maintains, if it were extinct and found only as a fossil, its webbed feet and duckbill would cause quite a controversy as to how it should be classified.

Gish deals with the so-called "reptilian features" of *Archaeopteryx.* Commenting on the fact that *Archaeopteryx* had teeth but that modern birds do not, he states: "Some other ancient birds had teeth, but some did not. Some amphibians have teeth, but some do not. Some reptiles have teeth but some do not. Most mammals have teeth, but some do not." Then, amid tremendous laughter, he says: "And I'll wager that some of you have teeth, and some do not!" His point, of course, is that the presence or absence of teeth is not diagnostic. Gish invariably quotes evolutionists to prove his point. His favorite quotation in this area is from W. E. Swinton, evolutionist and authority on birds, who writes: "The origin of birds is largely a matter of deduction. There is no fossil of the stages through which the remarkable change from reptile to bird was achieved" (Marshall, A. J., editor. 1960. *Biology and Comparative Physiology of Birds.* New York: Academic Press, p. 1).

Gish has demonstrated great boldness in taking on authorities in paleontology regarding the bankruptcy of the evidence in the fossil record for evolution. In the early years of these debates, when *Archaeopteryx* was flying at him from virtually every evolutionist who faced him, Gish couldn't know of a remarkable discovery being made at that very time that would strengthen the creationist cause.

Working in Dry Mesa Quarry in Western Colorado, paleontologist James A. Jensen of Brigham Young University discovered fossil bones of birds as old as *Archaeopteryx* (by evolutionary dating methods) but much more modern in form. This discovery was first reported in *Science News,* September 24, 1977, and has yet to appear in the technical literature. Later, when Jensen was giving a public lecture at the Denver Natural History Museum, I asked him during the question period if his new bird fossils were essentially like modern birds. He replied: "They are similar—they are much more like modern bird bones than they are like *Archaeopteryx.*"

The discovery of a relatively modern type of bird contemporary with *Archaeopteryx* seems to indicate a greater antiquity for birds and casts a serious question on their evolving from reptiles. Also, if modern birds were living alongside *Archaeopteryx,* that fact effectively removes *Archaeopteryx* as a transitional form between reptiles and birds. For *Archaeopteryx* could not have played a part in the evolution of birds if modern type birds were already well established at the time. The creationists are right! Yet, *Archaeopteryx* continues to fly across the debate podium time and time again.

The Pennsylvania State University debate centered largely on the presence or absence of transitional fossils. Cuffey declared there were many. Gish declared there were none. The real issue goes deeper. It goes back to our discussion in the University of Oklahoma debate on how one defines evolution. The reason Cuffey claimed that there were so many transitional forms is because of how he views evolution. His definition of evolution was essentially "change through time." Thus, any change at all becomes evidence for evolution, and any fossil in the rock strata a bit different from the one below it becomes a transitional form.

None of Cuffey's illustrations showed evidence of one kind of organism changing into another kind of organism. They were all illustrations of genetic variation. Genesis 1 states that all life shall reproduce after its kind. This does not mean that all animals are exact carbon copies of their parents. We know that much variation is possible. There are four billion people on planet earth at this moment. Each one is different. Yet, each is readily identifiable as a human being, and each reproduces after his kind.

However, there is a limit to this variability. Laboratory experiments have demonstrated that there are definite genetic limits to each organism's potential for variability. Whether it's a matter of developing a sugar beet that has more sugar, or radiating a fruit fly to see what type of mutation can be produced, there is a limit to variability. In fact, creation could be defined as "variation within limits" whereas evolution could be defined as "variation without limits." A study of evolutionary evidences will reveal that all of the changes, as Gish pointed out, are nothing more than variation within limits. When this fact is realized, it is obvious that the transitional forms are still missing and that *Archaeopteryx* is for the birds.

Chapter 12

You Really Have To Depend On Us!

University of Wyoming

There is a saying that Laramie, Wyoming, is not the end of the world, but you can see it from there. Actually, the University of Wyoming has a beautiful campus and is well known for its Department of Geology. After all, why shouldn't it be. The state of Wyoming has more geology than people.

Henry Morris and Duane Gish held a creation-evolution panel on that campus on February 8, 1974. Opposite them were three members of the University of Wyoming faculty. This exchange was "historic" in that it marked the first time in these debates that a reference was made to an entirely new concept of evolution—an approach which seeks to explain the absence of transitional forms in the fossil record. This new concept has now fully flowered and is called the "punctuated equilibrium" model of evolution. Although traditional neo-Darwinists are still in the majority, a very sizable minority of evolutionists have embraced the newer model.

Darwin, himself, conceived of evolution as proceeding at a steady, gradual, continuous pace. He was very much aware that the fossil record in his day did not support that view. He considered this lack of fossil support the most obvious objection that anyone could have regarding his theory. Time, he felt, would eventually justify his thinking. As more fossils were discovered, the missing transitions would turn up. The later synthetic view, known as neo-Darwinism, held substantially the same attitude. Thus, for over 100 years evolutionists have been looking for and hoping for transitional forms to confirm their theory. They truly have been walking by faith.

Creationists have been pounding unrelentingly at this crack in the evolutionary wall. While some evolutionists were desparately trying to create transitional forms out of the fossils they did have, others were admitting the reality of the gaps and trying to explain them. It was only a matter of time before something had to give. Something has given—evolutionary theory. Instead of having a theory that required transitional forms, they now have a theory that does not need them.

Having followed the evolution of evolutionary thinking for many years, there is no doubt in my mind that the incessant pressure of creationists is largely responsible for this new direction in evolution. The reader should be aware, however, that every evolutionist worth his salt will violently deny that creationists had anything to do with it. They firmly believe that the change would have come even if there hadn't been a creationist closer than six light years away. They ascribe the change to the self-correcting nature of science. One cannot help but wonder how effective that self-correcting principle would have been if Henry Morris, Duane Gish, and others like them hadn't been lurking in the background. Unfortunately, we will never know.

The story began years ago and is connected in a rather humorous way to the debates chronicled in this book. Gish often quoted from the writings of Richard Goldschmidt. Goldschmidt, an avid evolutionist, was a Jewish refugee from Hitler's decimation of German science. He was a geneticist on the faculty of the University of California, Berkeley, and died in 1958. His extensive genetic research had convinced him that although mutations might be responsible for minor evolutionary changes, the leaps between species and between the higher taxa had to be explained by an entirely different mechanism. His knowledge of the fossil record, with its systematic gaps, confirmed his own genetic research.

In his work, *The Material Basis of Evolution,* published in 1940, Goldschmidt proposed a concept he called the "hopeful monster" mechanism. He felt that new species arose abruptly by a huge mutation known as a macromutation—the type of mutation that would produce a two-headed calf. He recognized that the vast majority of macromutations would be lethal. But occasionally, by sheer good fortune, he felt that they might create organisms adaptable to a new mode of life. His thinking was based, in part, on the idea that relatively small changes in the very early development of the organism could result in vast changes in the adult animal.

Gish tells the Goldschmidt story with rare form. When the neo-Darwinists treated Goldschmidt's theory with disdain because there was not a shred of evidence for it, Goldschmidt would reply that it was cheap criticism, because there wasn't a shred of evidence for slow and gradual evolution either. Gish would then laughingly say that he agreed with both schools of thought—there was not a shred of evidence for either one.

Gish would describe the "hopeful monster" mechanism as: "Something laid an egg and something else got hatched." He went on to say: "Let me first explain what a terrible shock that must have been to mama reptile! In all good faith you lay a good reptilian egg and some strange critter comes out. But it must have been an even greater shock to papa reptile! He could well have sued her for divorce, claiming infidelity." Referring to the abuse heaped upon Goldschmidt by the neo-Darwinists, Gish would then say: "They preferred to think that Goldschmidt was the one who laid the egg."

Gish had been rather severely criticized for his references to Goldschmidt. I frankly wondered about the wisdom of them myself. While they were genuinely funny and provided a degree of levity in what could otherwise be a heavy presentation, I felt that they referred to a situation in the 1940's and 1950's that had little relevance today. Creationist John N. Moore, who, until his recent retirement, was Professor of Natural Science at Michigan State University, had privately urged Gish to cease referring to Goldschmidt in the debates. G. Ledyard Stebbins (Sacramento State University debate) stated that he had known Goldschmidt personally and that Goldschmidt was led astray by wrong information from the German paleontologist, Otto Schindewolf. This was to imply·

that Gish was using questionable material. David Kitts (University of Oklahoma debate) claimed that Gish had used Goldschmidt very badly.

Either Gish had a special "feel" for what was going on, or he knew something that the rest of us did not know. For quietly, behind the scenes, as a result of the absence of the transitional forms that Morris, Gish, and others had been harping on, some of Goldschmidt's concepts were being revived. In the June-July 1977 issue of *Natural History,* Stephen Jay Gould wrote an article entitled, "The Return of Hopeful Monsters," in which he predicted that in the 1980's Goldschmidt will be largely vindicated in the world of evolutionary biology. (Actually Gould and Niles Eldredge first presented a paper on "punctualism" to the scientific community back in 1972.)

In 1981, Steven M. Stanley, another pioneer in this new evolutionary concept, wrote what may become the classic statement of it, *The New Evolutionary Timetable.* This is a popularization of his more technical work, *Macro-evolution,* published in 1979. These ideas quickly spread throughout the geologic community and appeared often in the debates. Geerat Vermeij (University of Maryland debate in 1976) disavowed Goldschmidt, but then claimed that what Goldschmidt had proposed was possible. In 1977, Arthur Boucot (University of Oregon debate) also used the new model to explain the systematic absence of transitional forms.

In his reference to this newer concept in the Wyoming panel, invertebrate paleontologist Donald Boyd claimed that creationists want to hold evolutionists to a model in which change is slow and steady. Evolutionists, he said, won't stand still for that. They have reason to believe that rapid genetic modification can take place in small populations isolated from the main group with its well-adapted gene pool. Thus, very few transitional forms would have existed and the chance of their becoming fossilized would be remote. These concepts lie at the heart of the new model.

Referring to Norman Macbeth (a lawyer and critic of evolution), Gish called this model "the game of small numbers." He pointed out that according to natural selection, the successful populations are those that survive, evolve, and reproduce in larger numbers. Hence, they should leave a good fossil record. The new model, obviously designed to explain the absence of transitional forms, plays down the historic role of natural selection in evolution. In this sense, it is truly revolutionary.

Steven Stanley, Professor of Paleobiology at Johns Hopkins University, was a visiting lecturer on the Wyoming campus at the time of this panel. He not only attended, but made the first comment from the audience in the discussion period. He attacked Morris' use of the second law of thermodynamics as evidence against evolution since no law, he said, could be regarded as absolutely proven in science. However, since the laws of thermodynamics have been observed and studied for several hundred years, and no exceptions to the laws have ever been found, certainly these deserve the status of laws—if anything does. If the trend in science seems to be away from calling anything a law, the concepts of thermodynamics should still be given the very highest regard in interpreting scientific phenomena.

The panel discussion at the University of Wyoming would not be called an intellectual "heavy-weight"—as some of the debates have been. However, it has no peer for its genuine and original humor. Paleontologist Boyd claimed that if *Archaeopteryx* was 100% bird, then he was a monkey's uncle. Since, as a thoroughgoing evolutionist, his belief would make him a monkey's uncle, that would make *Archaeopteryx* 100% bird. But I don't think that's what he had in mind.

Professor of Biology Robert George stated that if he had a choice, he would prefer to be created by God. He told of his shock when he learned there was a high probability that he was related to a chimpanzee. Although it doesn't contribute to any aspect of human pride in him, he felt that he was forced to recognize that "the darn monkey looks like me in the first place." He claimed that if he could, he would sell out evolution theory quickly. If he could disprove it, he would probably win the Nobel Prize and $100,000. But as a scientist, he had to face the facts.

In speaking of thermodynamics, George became confused. He said: "If I wanted to demonstrate a low entropy system, I would take a gun and shoot somebody in the audience. Then we could all sit around and watch him decay." He was associating low entropy with low organization, whereas low organization is associated with high entropy—entropy being a measure of disorder.

He told about the problems the early creationist, Couvier, had with extinctions. Couvier felt that nothing God created could become extinct. Then they began finding mammoths and eight-foot giant sloths as fossils. Couvier was quite disturbed because he said, in George's words: "We can't find these animals in the woods!" Finally, he came up with the idea of successive judgments by God, which George described as God's "banging the earth very hard!"

When Morris observed that he and Gish had stuck to science, but that the evolutionists kept bringing God into the discussion, George said: "Who brought God into this thing? They did! They are very clever. They don't mention God, but they talk about creation. What does creation mean? It means God." He said that he noticed that during the whole hour Morris and Gish talked they didn't mention God once. "Very, very clever!"

George kept referring to creation and the supernatural as "magic," which had no place in science. He wanted to know why God couldn't have used evolution to bring man about, rather than magic. Morris gave a remarkable refutation of these comments in which he declared that it is the evolutionists who actually believe in magic. They resort to magic when they postulate that the tremendous increase of order from primeval random particles to the marvelous complexity of man's brain was brought about by mutation and natural selection in opposition to the second law of thermodynamics. "If evolution is true, one must postulate miracles at every stage of the evolutionary process to elevate something from a simple to a complex system when the natural processes go in the opposite direction," declared Morris.

Professor of Anthropology, George Gill, stated that there was a tremendous gradient of transitional fossil forms from apes to man. When Gish cited some fossil discoveries of Richard Leakey which would call this "tremendous gradient" into serious question, Gill replied: "First, I think we should send Richard Leakey back to school for a few years, since he never got even a B.A. degree." This

is an amazing statement considering the fact that Richard
Leakey has discovered more fossils of significance in the study
of the origin of man than any other person in history. Nor
does it seem that growing up under his parents, Louis and
Mary Leakey, would in itself be a trivial education in
anthropology.

When Gill mentioned vestigial organs such as gill slits on
human embryos and tail bones on humans, Gish replied: "I
can certainly understand why Dr. Gill would be prejudiced
toward gill slits!" However, he went on to explain that this
series of bars and grooves never opens up into the throat, and
so they are not slits. Further, they do not have anything to do
with the respiratory system, but actually form something else.
Therefore, they are not gills. "If they are not gills, and if they
are not slits, I don't know why evolutionists persist in calling
them 'gill slits.' " When Gish explained that the "tail bone"
with which people are occasionally born is just a fatty tumor
that is easily removed surgically, Gill replied jokingly: "If I
were his coccyxical vertebra, I would object to being called a
tumor on his back-side."

The attitude of the panel can be described in the words of
Dr. George who admitted that as individuals, scientists can be
biased, biggoted, stupid, and everything else one can think of.
But "as a group it's amazing how objective they can be." His
statement to the audience was: "You really have to depend on
us!"

Chapter 13

Don't Put Words In My Mouth!

University of Lethbridge

We have all seen the sign in retail businesses which reads: "This is a non-profit organization. We didn't plan it that way, but it is." Things do not always turn out as planned. Although the proposition statement of the debates always stated that the scientific evidences in the creation-evolution issue were to be addressed, many of them did not turn out that way. The Biblical or the religious element was often brought up by the evolutionists—and sometimes at great length. Morris and Gish would then remind the audiences which side was talking about science (the creationists) and which side was bringing up religion (the evolutionists).

The debate which Gish had at the University of Lethbridge, Lethbridge, Alberta, Canada, on February 21, 1974, was typical of those debates in which not a shred of scientific evidence was presented for evolution. Gish's opponent in the Lethbridge debate was Job Kuijt, Professor of Botany at the University of Lethbridge. Before the debate, Kuijt declared that if any Christian testimony was given as a part of the debate, he would walk out. He was given assurances that the debate was to be entirely on the scientific evidences for creation and evolution. Kuijt, however, made no reference to scientific evidences in his own presentation. After first claiming that creationists document their case by quoting evolutionists out of context, he devoted the rest of his time to an attack upon the authority of the Bible and its literal

interpretation as practiced by Evangelicals and
Fundamentalists. In his rebuttal, Gish reminded Kuijt that he
wasn't playing by the rules. After demanding that no
Christian testimony be given, Kuijt then used his time to give
his own humanistic testimony.

Morris and Gish have often been accused of quoting
evolutionists out of context. Kuijt's charge was far from the
first or the last. Some Christians who disagree with Morris
and Gish on creation have also accused them of misquoting
authorities. The charge is so serious and is repeated so often
that it is well to consider it.

Morris and Gish use many quotations from evolutionist
sources in their presentations. In fact, they never quote
anyone but evolutionists. They always inform their audiences
that the person being quoted is an evolutionist. They always
give the source or reference for the quotation so that a person
may check it out for himself. They go to great lengths to state
that the person would not agree with the creationist position.

Their reason for quoting only evolutionists is twofold. First,
there is a very mistaken but pervasive idea in the scientific
community that one cannot be a good scientist if he believes
in creation. Thus, to quote a creationist—no matter how
scientific and accurate he may be—does not carry any clout.
It is sad but true that people will accept the words of an
evolutionist on almost any subject, but will question the
authority of a creationist even in the area of his specialty.
This is prejudice with a vengeance! Thus, Morris and Gish
quote evolutionist authorities regarding the facts of science—
be it thermodynamics or the fossil record—because they know
that these people will be accepted as authorities.

A second reason is a bit more subtle. In a court of law, if a
witness for the prosecution testifies of some fact which aids
the defendant, that person's testimony is especially important
—and may even be decisive. The fact that the witness is not in
sympathy with the defendant would remove any possibility of
prejudice or partiality toward him. It would also remove the
possibility of perjury and establish instead a high probability
of truthfulness as to the facts of the case. Thus, lawyers try
very hard to get an opposition witness to testify to something
that will aid their case. This type of testimony is considered to
be of the very highest quality.

This is the thinking of Morris and Gish in quoting evolutionist authorities. It is a very astute and clever strategy and it has been amazingly effective. The creation-evolution controversy is not just a scientific one. It is a philosophical one as well. It is truly a battle for the mind. In this struggle both sides utilize "psychological warfare." Being able to quote evolutionist sources to support the facts of the creationist position is a part of this "psychological warfare."

The charge is made that they misquote these authorities or quote them out of context. What does that mean? The charge of misquoting is quite easy to explain. Suppose in a telephone conversation you tell me that you are thinking of going downtown tomorrow. There are several ways I could misquote you. I could say that you were definitely going downtown tomorrow, whereas you stated that you were just thinking about it. I could say that you were thinking of going downtown today, whereas you had mentioned tomorrow. I could say that you were thinking of going downtown and then to the museum—thus adding something you had not said. There is a saying: "Don't put words in my mouth because it isn't sanitary!" Anytime we put words in someone's mouth to make them say something they didn't say, we are misquoting them. If done intentionally, it is called "lying!" If done unintentionally, it is more excusable, but it does not change the fact that the person has been misquoted.

The matter of quoting out of context is more subtle. It also amounts to making a person say something he didn't mean to say, but it is an easier trap into which to fall. Suppose in telling me about your thinking of going downtown tomorrow you said that you would consider going only if your check arrived in the mail. I could quote you exactly in telling someone that you were thinking of going downtown tomorrow. But if I did not mention the matter of your check arriving, I would be quoting you out of context. Even if I quoted your words precisely, there was a condition involved which formed the context of your words that I had not mentioned.

There are other ways in which I could quote someone out of context—that is, not taking into consideration the flow of their thinking when I quote a particular passage. I could take something written about one subject and quote it perfectly, but apply it to a different subject or situation. I could take something written about a specific area or subject and generalize it—giving it a much broader meaning than the person intended. Or I could quote so few of the author's words that the true meaning of the author is unclear, or distorted, or actually changed. An over-zealous person may grasp a statement thinking that it supports his view without really comprehending the nature of the statement. Whether it is done intentionally or unintentionally, the effect is the same. It puts words in a person's mouth which he did not really say.

Having researched virtually every quotation Morris and Gish have used in their debates and panels by checking the primary sources carefully, I am convinced that Morris and Gish are not guilty of either misquoting or quoting out of context. The real problem is deeper than that. I believe, as a result of my own research, that the charge has a psychological element to it.

Kuijt zeroed in on a quotation Morris and Gish have often used in their debates. It is a quotation from a chapter written by E. J. H. Corner, an evolutionist at the Cambridge University School of Botany. The quotation is found in the book, *Contemporary Botanical Thought,* edited by Macleod and Cobley, on page 97:

> Much evidence can be adduced in favour of the theory
> of evolution—from biology, bio-geography, and
> palaeontology, but I still think that, to the unprejudiced,
> the fossil record of plants is in favour of special creation.

Kuijt stated that he wrote to Professor Corner and asked him two things: (1) Is the statement cited correctly, and (2) Is it or is it not taken out of context? Corner allegedly replied that the citation was correct, but that it was taken completely out of context. Personally, I think that there is nothing more foolish than writing to an author and asking him if he has been quoted out of context. Assuming that the author writes with a degree of clarity, all an intelligent person has to do is to turn to the page from which the citation came and check it out. To make sure, read the entire page—or the entire chapter.

There is far more here than meets the eye. Corner's quotation has been used so extensively by creationists in their writings that I am sure he is very sorry now that he ever wrote it. It is to be expected that he would claim that the quotation was taken out of context. In the rebuttal, Gish took the time to read the entire page from which the Corner quote was taken. It was very obvious to all that Gish had not taken the quotation out of context. The entire page is full of statements regarding the weakness of evolutionary theory in explaining the origin of the flowering plants. There was no doubt in anyone's mind that Corner was saying exactly what Gish claimed he said.

I mentioned that there was a deeper reason for the unfounded charge that Morris and Gish quote out of context. My research has convinced me that evolutionists are embarrassed and psychologically dismayed that creationists use their own words against their position. Even though their words are used properly, evolutionists consider it immoral for creationists to do such a thing. Even though this type of thing is normal in scholarly research and writing, evolutionists consider it immoral that creationists should use the facts of nature to support creation if those facts appear in a work written by an evolutionist. The thinking and the attitude of evolutionists in this regard is weird beyond belief. Kuijt writes:

> Creationists who cite statements from Simpson and Dobzhansky blithely ignore the fact that these people, after a lifetime of working at the forefront of biology, are more convinced than ever of the evidence in favor of evolution.

In other words, Kuijt is saying that because Simpson and Dobzhansky are evolutionists, no creationist has the right to refer to their writings in any way that would support creationism. When Corner writes " . . . that to the unprejudiced, the fossil record of plants is in favour of special creation," no creationist has the right to use that statement to further the cause of Special Creation. The fact that it is an accurate quotation doesn't matter either. Since Corner is an evolutionist, his words are "off limits" to creationists.

If this attitude were applied universally, it would be the end of all scientific research. The truth is the evolutionist can't handle the fact that there is evidence which supports creation. He doesn't know how to respond except to make the absurd claim that Morris and Gish quote out of context. Gish put it very well when he said: "Evolutionists don't own the facts of science."

Chapter 14

Didn't God Know Any Zoology?

University of Cincinnati

Alex Fraser is a feisty Englishman. Alex Fraser is also Professor of Genetics at the University of Cincinnati. When the bell sounded on the evening of October 24, 1974, he and Duane Gish came charging out of their respective corners. The ensuing intellectual bout was a "no-holds-barred" affair.

Fraser first declared that he was an agnostic. He stated that he preferred the fun of waiting until he died to find out what was going on. "If you know, it takes all the fun out of the game."

There are four possible systems regarding God and the universe, he declared. The first possibility is that there is no God—just the universe and no worries. The second possibility is that the universe is operating by law with God outside the universe minding His own business. A third possibility is that God is interfering in the universe, but only at the point of human self-identity or self-consciousness.

With any of these first three positions, Fraser claimed, scientists have no problem. The fourth possibility was the cosmology of Genesis. Here, Fraser declares war. This cosmology by "the god of the middle-eastern tribes is completely and irrevocably incompatible with science." (By "science" he means the evolutionary scenario.) "I'm a great compromiser," he said, "but on this one—no compromise."

The burr under Fraser's saddle turned out to be the time problem. Citing geologic sedimentation rates and the radioactive decay rates, he declared that Bishop Ussher's time scale —even if expanded to 15,000 or 20,000 years—was out of the question. The earth had to be hundreds of millions of years old.

Fraser's argument went something like this. Either the earth is hundreds of millions of years old or someone has been deliberately fooling around with the sedimentation rates so that we don't come up with the 6,000 year figure. The same thing must have happened to the radioactive decay rates. If the earth is only 6,000 years old, then when God formed the universe, He put the radioactive decay products "in there in exactly the right amounts to make damn sure we got the wrong answers." If that was God's idea of a joke, Fraser found it rather hard to accept. All of the measurements of science and the constants of nature, he said, would have to be revised to account for the recent age of the earth because "God dibbled the evidence." He felt that if all of our measurements are wrong, we are in a very dicy situation. We can't be sure of anything because God is playing games with us.

Fraser called the vast array of living organisms a jig-saw puzzle. When you put the pieces together to try to bring order out of the system, the pattern that naturally falls into place is an evolutionary one. He stated that if everything we know might be "a grand and gloriously complicated and really remarkably sophomoric cosmic joke, then really, I want out. I'm just not interested." The Biblical time scale, "one little book," was the problem.

There is no question but that the central issue in the creation-evolution controversy is the time question. There is also no doubt that the most offensive element in the time issue is the literal interpretation of Genesis with its strong implication for a recent creation. Morris and Gish continually stick to the issue of creation vs. evolution. Although they both believe in a recent creation, they emphasize that no matter how old the earth is, evolution is impossible. Yet, the time issue continually comes up. Evidence for vast ages for the earth is considered evidence against creation and for evolution. Evolutionists are painfully aware that any evidence for a recent creation strikes at the jugular vein of evolution.

Behind Fraser's comments are three totally unwarranted assumptions. The first is that the earth is obviously old. The second is that the earth and life obviously evolved. The third follows from the first two. If the earth is really young and life was really created, when to the human mind it is so obvious that the earth is old and that life evolved, then God is a practical joker who created a lie.

To say that the earth is obviously old is nothing more than a value judgment. We have no way of knowing what an "old" earth would look like compared to a "young" earth. To say that life obviously evolved because we can arrange the various categories of life in an order going from simple to complex—from amoeba to man—does not in the slightest prove that this is the way life appeared on earth.

Once, in a college course in paleontology, the professor gave each of us a packet of over 100 metal objects including nails, tacks, paper clips, and other items. He was trying to teach us systematics or taxonomy—the study of the classification of living forms. Our task was to arrange all of these metal items into relationships and sequences. Although each student had a different arrangement, there was a general similarity. Yet, the fact that we were able to arrange these items in a sequence from simple to complex didn't prove that they evolved. Big nails didn't evolve from little nails, even though we were able to arrange them that way. The fact is that almost anything can be arranged in an "evolutionary" sequence—simple to complex or generalized to specialized. Once, for the fun of it, I arranged my wife's shoes in an evolutionary sequence. But that did not prove that they evolved.

Why is it so important to man that the earth be old and that life have evolved? There are definite reasons for both. While man strenuously objects to a creation just a few thousand years old, he doesn't object to the idea that God created the original matter which exploded twenty billion years ago in what is called the Big Bang. The reason is that a God who is twenty billion years away is no threat to man. Such a God is very distant and quite benign. Such a God will let man do as he pleases. In fact, a God twenty billion years away is like no God at all. Men like it that way. A God who created the world just a few thousand years ago is much too close for comfort.

In the same way, if man evolved from the lower animals over a vast period of time, then man has no direct relationship to God. And, if man has no direct relationship to God, he then has no responsibility or accountability to Him. Man prefers it that way, too. But if God created man directly as man, it is obvious that man owes a debt of worship and obedience to the One who is so directly involved with him. Not only does this again put God too close for comfort, but it means that man is not free to "do his own thing." There is every reason why man prefers an old earth and the evolution of life, and the reason is not at all scientific, but spiritual. It flows from the fallen nature of man and his basic desire to be free from God and His authority.

What about this matter of God's being a practical joker who created a lie? It would be hard to imagine how God could have spoken more clearly than He did in Genesis that He created plants as plants, animals as animals, and man as man. The creation account of Eve certainly does not admit to any evolutionary scenario. Obviously, if the earth evolved by naturalistic means out of a cloud of gas and dust, it would take an immense amount of time to get to its present condition. But God clearly tells us He didn't do it that way. If words and language have any meaning at all, Genesis One does not teach evolution. The evolutionist first rejects the clear teaching of Genesis. He next postulates an evolutionary history for the earth and life. He then accuses God of lying. The problem is in the mind—and soul—of the evolutionist. Morris comments: "Give an evolutionist six days and he'll take a billion years!"

Alex Fraser had a second line of argument against the concept of creation. He didn't feel that the animals and plants of today reflect the perfection that one would expect if they were created by God. Fraser started with the whale—which is a "whale" of a problem for the evolutionist. Because whales are mammals, an evolutionist would predict that they have descended from land mammals, says Fraser. So, you dig inside and find that they have some relics of pelvic bones. By disuse, these pelvic bones have been reduced bit by bit until now they are just tiny bones used to anchor a few muscles.

"If we say that God did it that way," Fraser stated, "my reaction would be: 'Didn't God know any zoology? Such a silly way to build an animal!' " He feels that the animals in nature are not the beautiful, precise mechanisms that we would expect if God had done the job. Instead, they are "God-awful compromises, they are messes." A good biology major in his fourth year, Fraser felt, could do a better job in designing them.

Evolution, Fraser continued, would predict such a situation. Whereas we expect perfection from God, evolution is an expedient, opportunistic, minimal solution system. Whatever is the least that will do is enough—until the selection pressure forces the organism to develop a little bit more. Evolution will settle for the very least that will do the job.

The compromises that Fraser sees in nature, together with some mixed up chemistry here and there, force him to conclude that the creative God was an amateur. The only way you could have God at the level of awesome majesty that Fraser would require was to suggest that God had a tremendous sense of humor. He created the animals but made them look as if they had evolved.

The early amphibians and reptiles were such crude animals that they looked like "they had been constructed by a high school kid." However, the evolutionary process refined them, so that the later amphibians and reptiles were "pretty slick pieces of machinery," Fraser declared.

Fraser's statements are really quite absurd. Morris and Gish point out that the second law of thermodynamics would explain the imperfections in nature very adequately. There is a Biblical counterpart to the second law—the curse upon all nature—which gives the spiritual dimension of these imperfections. However, Morris and Gish seldom mention this aspect because of their desire to establish the creation model on strictly scientific grounds. We need not take Fraser's comments too seriously until high school kids *do* construct reptiles and fourth year biology students redesign whales.

Fraser's third area of discussion was genetics—his specialty. The genetic system is a marvel of design and accuracy. Its origin is one of the major unsolved problems of evolution. Creationists do not have that problem. Although the genetic system is far more accurate than any machine man has ever made, about once in every 100,000 cell divisions a mistake in this copying process occurs. These mistakes are called "mutations." It is hard to understand how mistakes in a highly ordered structure could be the means of improvement. This, however, is the heart of evolutionary theory. Mutations, which are totally random events, are the raw material for new evolutionary species.

Evolutionists have yet to demonstrate a single mutation that is, without question, beneficial. Everyone is agreed that more than 99% of them are harmful, and many even lethal. Theory has it that occasionally there is a small one that is beneficial in bestowing upon its possessor a very slight advantage over others of the same species in the struggle for existence. This slight advantage makes its possessor more successful, and this advantage is passed on to future generations. When a large number of these very small beneficial mutations have occurred, there will be, it is thought, a significant enough change in the organism over its distant ancestors that it could legitimately be called a new species.

Some evolutionists believe that as more beneficial mutations occur, the differences become even greater than those on the species level and that the higher categories are formed in this way. The newer breed of evolutionists who subscribe to the "punctuated equilibrium" model believe that mutations are responsible for only the smaller changes and that species level changes and beyond have another mechanism as yet unknown.

Fraser took issue with the idea that mutations are intrinsically bad. He stated that he has taken a gene that was lethal, selected and modified the background until it was a perfectly good recessive gene with all of the lethality gone. A bad gene, a mutation, is bad only against a certain background. If that gene has a different background or context, it can be beneficial. That a geneticist like Fraser can do this I have no doubt. How this would work in nature or in evolutionary history without the aid of a highly trained geneticist to direct the process he did not explain.

In this entire debate series, the most difficult task for the evolutionist—other than to explain how evolution occurred in the presence of the second law of thermodynamics—was to come up with a beneficial mutation. Some of the claims were astounding. Other were hilarious. Frank Awbrey (Palomar

College debate) cited a mutation in fruit fly experiments in which the flies had four wings. The only problem was that they couldn't fly. It is not clear how this could be considered a beneficial mutation and thus be evidence for evolution.

One of the most astounding statements made in these debates was made by cell biologist and geneticist Martin Samoiloff (University of Manitoba debate). Morris and Gish often point out that in experiments with fruit flies, over 1,500 generations of these insects have been observed in mutation-producing experiments. Although some very strange fruit flies have been produced, the end result has been an insect that is still 100% fruit fly. It has not begun to change into anything else. Yet, mutations are supposed to be the raw material which allows an organism to change into something else. Much of this fruit fly work was done by Hermann J. Muller of the University of Indiana.

Samoiloff had studied under Muller. He told of an occasion when Muller came into the laboratory furious. He had read a pamphlet stating that although Muller had worked with 1,500 generations of mutant fruit flies, he had yet to produce a bumblebee. Muller, according to Samoiloff, said publically for all to hear: "If I were selecting for a bumblebee, by now I would have had it!"

Samoiloff claimed that the goal of the experiments was the selection of single gene characteristics, such as flies without eyes, flies without wings, and flies that were sterile. Samoiloff concluded: "If the goal of the experiment was in fact to generate butterflies, Muller would have done it!" We might well ask, "Why wasn't the goal of the experiment to produce bumblebees or butterflies from fruit flies?" Could anything have demonstrated the possibility of transmutation better than that? The simple truth is that it was not done by Muller and it has not been done by anyone else because it can't be done. I am amazed that Muller would have made such an audacious statement. I am even more amazed that Samoiloff believed him. We still await the production of bumblebees and butterflies from fruit flies.

Perhaps the most humorous illustration of a mutation claimed to be beneficial was made by Aharon Gibhor (University of California, Santa Barbara, debate). He stated that a featherless chicken had been produced by mutation. He made two claims for this event. First, he claimed that it was a beneficial mutation for chickens in very hot climates! Now, chickens are known all over the world. They are also common in hot climates. They do very well there with feathers. It is difficult to understand how Gibhor knew that they would do even better without feathers. However, Gibhor made a second claim that was even more unbelievable. Feathers are diagnostic of birds. The zoological definition of a bird is: "a vertebrate with feathers." Gibhor claimed that since this chicken no longer had feathers, it was no longer a bird. Hence, it qualified as a transitional form between a bird and something else. Perhaps if we took the scales off of an alligator, it would no longer be a reptile.

In all of this, evolutionists have missed—accidentally or intentionally—the main point that Morris and Gish are trying to make. Evolutionists explain that mutations are the mechanism furnishing the raw materials for evolution. Yet, a mutation is a defect or mistake in a highly ordered genetic system. Before one can have mutations, one must have a genetic system. You can't have mistakes in a system before you have the system itself. The question Morris and Gish continually ask is: "How did this complicated genetic system arise in the first place?" They get no answer.

Chapter 15

Chitty, Chitty, Bang, Bang!

University of Tennessee

Science can really be a fun thing. George Schweitzer proved it in the debate at the University of Tennessee on January 14, 1975. Schweitzer has an impressive academic career. He is Distinguished Professor of Chemistry at Tennessee and also has a doctorate in the philosophy of religion. A theistic evolutionist, he authored a chapter in the volume, *Evolution and Christian Thought Today,* produced by the American Scientific Affiliation. Schweitzer did not address himself to the subject of the debate with Morris and Gish. His presentation, totally devoid of any scientific evidence for evolution, dealt instead with the philosophy of science and with the formulation of scientific models.

However, his presentation was without question the most entertaining of the entire series. In a later debate at Columbus College, Columbus, Georgia, evolutionist William Frazier accused Harold Slusher of trying to be a stand-up comedian. The charge was unwarranted, but neither Slusher nor anyone else could compare with the professor from Tennessee. In all of this, I do not mean to disparage Schweitzer. He is an excellent communicator and a master teacher. His presentation on the various models of origins was superb. No one who heard it will ever forget it. It was just that the lack of scientific evidence from Schweitzer, as well as from his colleague, Tennessee biologist Arthur T. Jones, was glaringly obvious to all.

Schweitzer stated that the scientist tries to do with nature just what every human being tries to do with his own life—get it all together. Yet, no organizing scheme in science is completely satisfying. They all have shortcomings. Lest their particular scheme prove to be wrong and they cry a lot, he encouraged students not to commit themselves irrevocably to any of them. He suggested that some sophomore out there making a "D" in geology might, in a few years, come up with a whole new organizing scheme that will be better than any we now have. "You know," he said, "I want to be free to go along with that poor sucker, don't you?"

His description of the contemporary organizing schemes of origins was as arresting as any "show and tell" presentation could ever be. The first model he described was probably the Genesis model of recent creationists. He called it the "Zapper" model. Zappers, he said, believe that the major categories of life appeared suddenly out of nowhere—zap! Some of the zappers, he continued, believe that it happened in a period of four days [?] about ten thousand years ago. Since then, "nothing really great has happened."

The second model he called the "Oozers." This was obviously the neo-Darwinian concept with life coming from nonlife about three billion years ago and then slowly oozing onward and upward to the present life forms. He said that he knew fast oozers and slow oozers, but most oozers he knew were slow oozers.

The third "gang" he described as the "Jumpers." Although he didn't say so, this group is probably the "progressive creationists." He said that they believe that things happened over a long period of time, but that these folks didn't like the oozing. They believe that life occurred in rapid jumps or bangs at certain points over geologic time.

Another group, described as "sort of a fun group," are the "Five-second-agoers." He lamented the fact that there weren't many of them around anymore. They believe that the whole works appeared just five seconds ago with a built-in history. He told the audience that if they remembered coming into the auditorium that night, that didn't prove anything because they were created just five seconds ago with their memory built-in. "How do you disprove that? I don't know."

He stated that there were variations on these themes. There

are fast oozers and slow zappers. Then there are the combined oozers and jumpers. They like some oozing and they like some jumps. This, which was his own personal view, he called "Oozer-jumper," and referred to it as the "chitty, chitty, bang, bang" theory. It was a reference to the newest evolutionary model, "punctuated equilibrium." He went on to explain that he did not know what the ultimate truth was and urged people to "hang loose." In the meantime, they should trust the experts.

It was obvious that Schweitzer did not consider Genesis as having a great deal of historical information for the study of origins. In a later debate with another scientist from the Institute for Creation Research staff, Schweitzer described Genesis One as a great hymn to creation. The six days are the six stanzas of the song or poem. As impressive and as spiritual as that sounds, the idea is that since Genesis is poetry, we do not expect it to be literally true or historically accurate. We all know that in poetry there is a freedom or "poetic license" that is not normally found in other forms of literature.

However, this concept—very popular with those who want to give lip service to Genesis without having to take it literally —sounds believable only because so many people are ignorant of Hebrew poetic style. Whereas the nature of English poetry is to be nonliteral, Hebrew poetry is just the opposite. The nature of Hebrew poetry is to be very literal. Hence, to say that Genesis is poetry does not give one authority to ignore its literal meaning.

Schweitzer then attempted to separate science and religion so that "our science and our religion wouldn't get disastrously mixed up." He did this by making a distinction between "mechanism" and "meaning." Since evolution is so logically connected to a naturalistic, atheistic interpretation of the universe, and creation is so obviously connected with the work of God, Schweitzer tried to demonstrate that these associations do not necessarily have to be the case. Scientists are chiefly interested, he maintained, in mechanisms. He had proposed a number of these mechanisms, such as "oozing." On the other hand, the meaning of it all was a religious question. The two are not related.

To illustrate, he suggested that even if one should be

convinced that the zapping mechanism was the correct
one—that is, everything appeared suddenly, instantaneously,
in four days—that doesn't give us the meaning of it. Does it
automatically mean that God did it? No! One possibility, he
felt, was that about 10,000 years ago a fleet of rocket ships
might have landed on earth, dumped out all the animals,
planted all the trees and bushes, and then left. "And heaven
forbid," he uttered, "it might have been a gang of atheists!"
In this way he stated that the mechanism and the meaning are
different and are not necessarily related.

Other possibilities, he continued, would be for the great god
and goddess of ancient Egypt to have cooked them up and
dumped them out. Or, a great herd of divine three-toed
celestial elves could have done it. It could even have been by
chance. Perhaps the nature of this universe is that every
billion years on some planet—zap! "There is," you say,
"another possibility—God did it." "You're right," he
asserted, "but that is true of all the mechanisms."

As entertaining as Schweitzer was, he was something less
than convincing. If anyone is so mentally constituted as to
feel that his other suggestions for zapping—space ships,
Egyptian gods, three-toed celestial elves, or accidents—have
any merit, nothing I am able to say would change their minds.
It is rather interesting that to suggest other meanings for
zapping or sudden appearance, he had to resort to paganism
and fairy tales. The fact is that there is only *one* real
explanation for the sudden appearance of the universe and life
—the creative power of the almighty God revealed in the Holy
Scriptures.

There is a *direct* relationship between mechanism and
meaning—in contrast to what Schweitzer stated. The whole
message of Romans One is that God has ordained a relationship between mechanism and meaning. Because there is a
relationship between the two, men stand guilty before God if
they reject His testimony in nature. It is a deep and serious
concern to creationists that theistic evolutionists show as little
regard for Romans One as they do for Genesis One. The
attempt to reconcile science and Scripture by the concept of
theistic evolution results in an illegitimate offspring which is
not the true progeny of either science or Scripture.

The entertainment of the evening turned to high drama in

the question period. In the course of answering a question
about the alleged simple to complex arrangement of the
fossils, Gish cited the article by Daniel Axelrod from the
journal, *Evolution,* regarding the discovery of over fifty
genera of land plants in the Cambrian. This was the same
evidence that shook up Stebbins in the Sacramento State
debate two years earlier. When Gish spoke of these land
plants in the Cambrian, a voice shouted from the audience:
"That's a lie!" The voice was that of Robert E. McLaughlin,
Professor of Paleontology at the University of Tennessee.
After the debate, he came rushing to the platform demanding
that Gish document his statement regarding land plants in the
Cambrian. When Gish produced two articles from the
journal, *Evolution,* some witnesses say that McLaughlin
claimed they were forgeries. Gish recalled that he did charge
that one article had mistranslations of Russian to French to
English.

McLaughlin then wrote a letter to the Knoxville News-
Sentinel in which he accused Gish of just about everything
except murder and adultery. He claimed that the whole debate
was staged, that the audience was carefully selected to respond
at proper times, that Morris and Gish have left a wake of
discord and bitterness from coast to coast, that Gish used
deceptive and faulty evidence, that he misquoted authorities,
that he knows nothing about paleontology, and that questions
from the audience were screened before they got to Morris or
Gish. He especially charged that a slide Gish showed depicting
Cambrian animal life was actually of the Silurian Period 120
million years later. These and other mistakes, he asserted,
were all missed by the audience because of the clever
deception of the creationists.

The moderator of the debate, Robert W. Glenn, Professor
of Speech and Theatre at the University of Tennessee,
responded with a letter in the same paper a few days later. He
stated that he didn't think that McLaughlin knew what he was
witnessing. In a debate, if one side uses incorrect data, it is
the duty of the opposing side—not the audience—to point
that out. That's what a debate is all about. He also answered
the other charges made in McLaughlin's letter.

Gish also wrote a letter to the newspaper. He documented
the slide he used as being from the American Museum of

Natural History in New York and labeled "Cambrian Diorama." He remarked that it is regrettable that a professor charged with teaching paleontology at the University of Tennessee did not have a better understanding of the difference between the Cambrian and the Silurian Periods of geologic history.

Chapter 16

Cheating When The Heat's On

University of New Orleans

If you were assembling a jig-saw puzzle, how would you proceed? Would you place it outside in the sun so that the energy from the sun could do the work of organizing the puzzle? Or would you utilize the conceptual and organizational powers of your mind, together with the energy of your body, to do the task? The question seems absurd. The answer is obvious. In both cases, energy is involved. The real question is: "How is energy best utilized to organize the puzzle?"

It may be difficult to believe that such a seemingly obvious solution to a seemingly absurd question lies at the heart of the creation-evolution controversy. The question, "How is energy applied to develop increased complexity?" occupied a substantial part of most of the creation-evolution debates.

The problem involves two of the basic laws of science. They are called the first and second laws of thermodynamics. "Thermo" is the Greek word for "heat." "Dunamis" is the Greek word for "power." Although the word, "thermodynamics," can be a rather intimidating word, it really means "heat power." Its details can become quite involved in physics and mathematics. Its basic concepts are really quite easy to grasp. Henry Morris has done much to popularize these concepts and was one of the first to apply them to the creation-evolution issue. The fact that the basic concepts of thermodynamics are virtually unknown to so many people is a reflection on the quality of science education in our nation today.

One continually hears the remark that creation-science is bad science. Actually, just the opposite is true. Creationists are demanding that we return to basics. We have become very enamored with the gadgets of our technology, but few people understand the basic laws that are at work in the world. A young person might be able to fire a rocket, but has no idea what makes that rocket work.

Some years ago, the science writer, Isaac Asimov (who later had a debate with Gish in the pages of *Science Digest*), wrote several articles for the *Smithsonian* magazine. He was lamenting the fact that science students know so little about the two laws which are basic to all of science and universal in all of nature—the first and second laws of thermodynamics or "heat power." Asimov quoted C. P. Snow as saying that the laws of thermodynamics are as basic to science as the writings of Shakespeare are to literature. Since we teach Shakespeare in junior high school, Asimov asks why we do not teach the laws of heat power there also? These laws are absolutely universal because every process in nature involves the taking up or the giving off of heat in some way. Among other things, they explain why a chemistry equation must always balance, why a bouncing ball does not continue to bounce indefinitely, and why we cannot make a perpetual motion machine.

The fact is, to Asimov's dismay, these laws are not taught in high school and are barely taught in college. Although I took a science major in high school and later took a master's degree in physical science at a state university, I would never have heard of these two basic laws of science had it not been for the writings of Henry Morris and other creationists. Although creationists recognize these two laws as foundational arguments against evolution and in favor of creation, they are somewhat difficult to use because there is such widespread ignorance of them. One gets the idea that people think that creationists made them up. (Actually, it probably was creationist scientists who first formulated them in the early 1800's.) There can be no doubt that if these basic laws had been consistently taught, the absurdities of evolutionary theory would have been recognized long before now. Only

today—largely through the work of creationists like Henry
Morris—are evolutionists coming to grips with these two basic
laws and the problems they pose for evolution.

Whether it is Morris and Gish debating together, Morris
alone, Gish alone, or one of them with someone else, the laws
of thermodynamics or heat power form a basic part of
the creationist presentation. The outline that is always used is:
(1) The laws of thermodynamics show that evolution could
not take place, and (2) the fossil record shows that evolution
has not taken place. Thus far, evolutionists have failed to give
a satisfactory answer to the thermodynamic argument. Some
have not even tried. Some of the answers given are incredibly
naive, showing that many evolutionists do not understand
what creationists are saying and do not understand how
nature works.

The first of several debates devoted to the matter of
thermodynamics was held on February 4, 1975, at the
University of New Orleans. Henry Morris' opponent was Max
Hertzberger, one of the world's leading optical physicists, and
a protege and colleague of Albert Einstein. (The night before,
Morris had debated William Craig, geologist on the University
of New Orleans faculty, on the question of the fossil record.)
A native of Germany, Hertzberger spoke with such a heavy
accent that I question if many were able to understand him.

Hertzberger stated that the universe as a whole is not a
proper object of scientific study since we can only observe a
small portion of it. He also emphasized that the beginning
and the end of the universe are beyond the observational
horizon of science. Further, we cannot observe the infinitely
large and the infinitely small, where he felt the laws of nature
probably change. In all of this, of course, he is correct. It is
refreshing to hear someone of his stature acknowledge it.

Regarding the second law of thermodynamics, Hertzberger
stated that most physicists, including Boltzman, have
misinterpreted the second law. If interpreted according to the
mathematical definition of "minimum action," the second
law would allow for both increases and decreases in entropy—
entropy being the term for the measure of disorder. Hence,
the second law, he felt, cannot be used either for or against
evolution. There seemed to be the tacit admission that as it is
normally defined, the second law does present problems for

evolutionary theory.

In illustrating his point, Hertzberger used an optical lens. Although he was difficult to understand because of his accent, he seemed to be saying that as light passes through the lens there is an increase of entropy or disorder on one side of the lens and a decrease in entropy on the other side. Since the format of the debate did not allow Morris to offer a rebuttal, he was not able to respond to this obvious case of "cheating" with regard to the second law.

Creationists recognize that there is design in the universe. In spite of this design, according to the second law, the universe is running down. As time goes on, the universe loses order, organization, and information. What Hertzberger did was to introduce into the system additional design—man-made design in this case—in the form of a lens. When additional design or information is introduced into a natural system, one can get a reduction in entropy. During the question period, someone pointed out to Hertzberger that his illustration of the lens involves an intelligence who designed the lens. It was not a random situation at all, whereas evolution is said to be a random situation.

Hertzberger responded to this questioner by "cheating" again. Referring to the questioner, he said that entropy increases when you are young and decreases when you are old. (I think he meant to say just the opposite.) "You go through all the stages of evolution," he declared. What Hertzberger failed to comprehend was the difference between the development of a human being and alleged evolutionary development. A human being has an incredibly complex genetic program teeming with information directing the growth of the organism. In contrast, Morris declared, there is no plan or program in evolution to direct an increase in order or complexity.

Henry Morris has been a pioneer in acquainting people with the laws of thermodynamics, or heat power, and their application to the study of origins. These laws continue to be powerful arguments for creationism. They seem unanswerable. The first law is called the conservation law. It states that the sum total of matter-energy in the universe is a constant. A creationist could phrase it that the amount of matter-energy created by God at the beginning has not changed. It is called the conservation law because matter-energy cannot now be created or destroyed. We can change matter into energy. We do that when we burn a log in the fireplace. In nuclear reactors we can change energy into matter. In other words, while there are many ways in which matter and energy can be interchanged, the sum total of matter-energy in the universe always remains the same. It is a constant. In a sense, the first law of thermodynamics is like a bookkeeping system. Since matter-energy cannot be created or destroyed, the books must balance in every scientific experiment or in every heat transfer in nature. All of the matter-energy must be accounted for.

It is tragic that this first law is so neglected in science education for this law is basic to an understanding of nature. It is because of this law that we can predict what will happen in science. In fact, it is this law that gives rationality and sense to the universe. Let me illustrate. Suppose in a natural process or in a scientific experiment matter or energy could just pop into existence out of nowhere. Or suppose that matter or energy could just disappear for no reason whatsoever. Science would be impossible. Nature could not be comprehended. We would have no way of knowing what would happen in the world from one moment to the next. Every second would be full of surprises and uncertainty. Since our emotional and mental health demands a degree of stability, life would literally be hell without this first law of thermodynamics.

Nothing in science is more important than the concept of repeatability. Yet, all of this is based upon the first law. The fact that an experiment done in the sixteenth century can be repeated in the seventeenth, the eighteenth, the nineteenth, and the twentieth centuries with the very same results is because of this conservation law of thermodynamics. Without it, one simply could not do science.

This first law of thermodynamics has profound implications regarding the origin of the universe. If matter-energy cannot be created or destroyed, then the universe could not have created or ordered itself. It must have, as Morris emphasizes, been created by an agency or power outside of, and independent of, the natural universe. The conservation processes that we see at work in the universe can only conserve what was originally created. They cannot create anything new. Since creative processes are not going on now, it also means that the question of the origin of the universe is outside the area of scientific investigation—just as Hertzberger stated.

The second law of thermodynamics involves two concepts. The first is the matter of the direction in which natural processes go. This one-directional element of natural processes is called "time's arrow." For instance, heat always flows from a hot body to a colder body—never the reverse. Gases always flow from a high pressure to a lower pressure—never the reverse. Liquids and gases will mix naturally, but will not separate naturally. By our adding design or intelligence to the system, we can make things go the other way, but in nature these processes go in only one direction.

There is another concept associated with the second law. It is the concept of decay, disorder, or loss of complexity. In other words, the "arrow of time" not only points in one direction, but it points downward in that direction. The directional nature of the second law could well have been in effect from the beginning of creation—that is in Creation Week—because it is so necessary to a rational universe. However, the degenerative aspect of the second law—referred to as the law of increased entropy—was probably superimposed upon nature at the Fall. The effect of the second law is that as time goes on, order in the universe goes down. Another way of saying it is that while the quantity of matter-energy in the universe remains the same, with the passing of time the quality decreases or degenerates.

The term, "entropy," is not a common term, but the concept behind it is not difficult. Let us refer to an earlier illustration—the burning of a log in the fireplace. In the burning of a log, some of the matter is transformed into energy. However, once used, that energy is degraded in the sense that it is no longer available for future work. Although that energy has not been destroyed, it is impossible to reclaim it and use it again. It is unavailable.

Every energy-transforming situation in the universe involves a portion of the energy passing from the available to the unavailable category. In the working of a steam or gasoline engine or an electric motor some of the energy is lost in the form of heat. The loss of this heat energy is unavoidable. It is the price that we pay to do work. The measure of this loss of energy or order is called "entropy." Increasing entropy means increasing disorder. Decreasing entropy means decreasing disorder or increasing order.

Like the first law, the second law also has profound implications regarding the history of the universe. When extended or extrapolated into the future, it means that all of the useful or available energy will eventually become unavailable. At that point the universe will experience a "heat death," for no more work can be done. Remember that energy, like water, must always flow downhill in order to do work.

However, the more remarkable implication is when we extrapolate into the past. As we go back in time, the matter-energy of the universe becomes more and more available or useful and the universe becomes more and more ordered or complex. Finally, we reach a point where all of the matter-energy of the universe becomes available, useful, ordered. At that point, the available matter-energy of the universe equals the total matter-energy of the universe. We cannot go further back in time because one can't have the available matter-energy of the universe greater than the total amount.

Thus, the second law of thermodynamics not only testifies to a point of creation for the universe, but it also testifies to a universe which was created in a highly organized, complex form. The two laws of thermodynamics together are amazing testimony to the concept of creation.

It cannot be too strongly emphasized, as Morris does in all of his debates, that these laws have been tested and experimentally verified for almost two hundred years. The laws of thermodynamics were first developed at the time of the invention of the steam engine. Because they deal with the transfer and exchange of heat, and because every process in the universe involves the transfer or exchange of heat, these laws of thermodynamics have been found to be universal laws. They apply to every process. No exceptions have ever been found. If anything deserves the status of laws of science, these do. Engineers are very familiar with the effect of these two laws. They refer to the first law in this way: "You can't get something for nothing." Of the second law, they say: "You can't even break even."

In the University of New Orleans debate, Morris contrasted the concept of evolution with the two basic laws of the universe—the first and second laws of thermodynamics. The concept of evolution alleges that as time goes on, the complexity and order of the universe increases. However, the second law of thermodynamics declares that the universe is running down and that disorder or entropy is increasing. The two concepts are diametrically opposed. Evolutionists assume that there is some force or process inherent in matter that allows it to order itself. In the Colorado State University debate, Wilber said that the nature of matter was one of "genesis or becoming." (This was taken from the French theologian-paleontologist, Teilhard deChardin.) Slusher, in his rebuttal, stated that according to the second law, the inherent nature of matter was not one of "becoming," but one of "going." Thermodynamics indicates clearly that evolution is not science, but an atheistic, naturalistic, mechanistic philosophy.

The laws of thermodynamics can be expressed in ways other than that of classical thermodynamics. The great physicist, Boltzman, who died in 1906, discovered that entropy was equivalent to the logarithm of the probability. Thus, probability theory can be used to express the chances of life evolving from nonlife and the chances of living forms evolving with increasing complexity over time. Henry Morris often uses such illustrations in these debates to show the improbability—yes, the impossibility—of evolution taking place.

A third way of expressing the laws of thermodynamics is in the form of information theory. This is especially helpful in showing how thermodynamics relates to living organisms with their marvelous genetic code. When the second law is applied to information theory, it demands that any chance event, such as a mutation, will decrease the information content of a message, a code, or a genetic system, thus increasing the entropy.

At the University of New Orleans, as elsewhere, Morris states that increased complexity can be accomplished when four conditions are satisfied: (1) an open system so that matter and energy can flow into the system, (2) available energy, (3) energy conversion systems or motors to take the raw energy and convert it into usable energy to do work, and (4) a code, blueprint, pattern, template, information system, ór intelligence to direct the growth.

One of the great mysteries of these debates is the way in which evolutionists claim that one can get order and increased complexity using only an open system and energy from the sun. Try putting that puzzle together that way. The truth is that evolutionists don't really get order that way either. They always "cheat" (as Hertzberger did) and try to bootleg order into the system without admitting what they are doing. I am convinced personally that many of them have not thought through the problem and do not realize what they are doing. They either start with a degree of order or they slip order into the system somewhere along the line. All of this is really "cheating," since evolution is a random process. Morris points out that mutations and natural selection, the alleged mechanisms for evolution, do not satisfy the criteria for getting increased order or complexity. Neither mutations nor natural selection is a code or an energy transforming mechanism. Yet, both a code and an energy transforming mechanism are necessary to get growth or increased complexity. Morris gets rather poetic when he states of mutations and natural selection: "Neither is either, and so both can't be both. But you have to have both [a code and an energy transforming mechanism] to get growth!"

Hertzberger declared that: "The men who wrote the . . . Christian Scriptures are men of their times, and if they spoke about physical or other problems, they have the prejudices of their times, too." In contrast, Henry Morris concluded his presentation by stating that in the light of the first and second laws of thermodynamics, the most scientific statement one could make about the origin of the universe is: "In the beginning, God created the heavens and the earth."

Chapter 17

From Blob to Bob

Texas Tech

You are standing on the display lot of an automobile dealership. The salesman shows you a car with a fender bent and folded. The hood is torn so that you can see the bare metal edges. You detect 14 partial paint jobs. The last paint job was to repair the door. The paint is on bare metal because the earlier paint had been sanded off. The odometer reads 6,000 miles. You conclude that it really means 106,000 miles or even 206,000 miles, and it has turned over or perhaps been turned back.

The salesman says: "Look at those tires; hardly any wear!" He claims that all that paint was put on at the factory to protect the metal, and that the car was actually damaged in a rain and wind storm last night. "It's a cream puff," he declares.

As Rae Harris, Professor of Geoscience at Texas Tech University, Lubbock, gave that illustration, he turned to the debate audience and said, "How many of you would buy that story? How many of you would buy that car?" Harris believes that the earth is very old. In fact, he believes that an old earth proves evolution and disproves creation. The car in his story represents the earth. The paint layers represent the sedimentary rock layers of earth, some of which have been bent and folded like the hood and fender of the car. The odometer reading of 6,000 miles represents the age of the earth according to some creationists. However, just common sense tells one that this car has far more than 6,000 miles on it. So, one has merely to look at the earth with a bit of reason to see that it is far, far older than 6,000 years. He feels that the earth's surface has so much paint on it—sedimentary rock layers—that no single short term catastrophic event, like The Flood, can be acceptable as an explanation.

The attendance (2,700) set a new record for the debates to that time—February 9, 1975. Both Henry Morris and Duane Gish reminded those assembled on the campus of Texas Tech that the age of the earth was not the subject of the debate. Although both men believe that the earth is young (not necessarily 6,000 years old) they declared that evolution is impossible no matter how old the earth is. In fact, they mentioned that many creationists do believe that the earth is old, but still reject evolution. Thus, Harris' arguments were off target.

Much of Harris' presentation dealt with geological phenomena which he felt proved that the earth was very old. One of these was a famous cliff in Yellowstone National Park called Specimen Ridge. It is mentioned or pictured in almost every general geology textbook as one indication of the antiquity of the earth. Harris stated that the following sequence was repeated on that ridge or cliff 17 times. First there was a deposit of volcanic ash. Then a soil layer developed by the weathering of the ash. A forest then grew in the soil—with some trees measuring three feet in diameter. Then the forest was buried by a subsequent volcanic ash fall and eventually some of the trees became petrified. It is obvious that if this sequence was repeated 17 times, and if each sequence involved just one thousand years (a modest estimate), this one geologic formation is older than some creationists ascribe to the entire earth.

I mention the Yellowstone National Park illustration given by Harris for two reasons: First, because it is found so extensively in geology texts as evidence for an ancient earth; second, because I have been there. I visited it in the summer of 1971 with a team of creationists—including professional geologists—to determine if the evolutionary interpretation of the site was the correct one.

We confirmed that the ridge or cliff was indeed made up of layers of rock. On the side of the cliff were 17 benches,

or steps, or ledges with petrified trees on many of them.
Although it is true that the ridge is made up of layers
of rock, evolutionists have always assumed that those layers
of rock inside the ridge had petrified trees in them, too. Yet,
no one has ever dug into the ridge to find out for sure if this
is the case.

We discovered that there is another interpretation of the
geologic history of this ridge—an interpretation that is not
only possible, but far more likely. It is that these 17 ledges
were on the cliff or ridge before the forest grew there. The
forest then grew on the entire ridge with trees on all of these
different levels. A single volcanic eruption covered the entire
ridge and buried all of the trees at the same time. They
subsequently became petrified and constitute one of the most
famous petrified forests in the world today.

Evolutionary literature is full of illustrations of geologic
formations that are alleged to have taken vast amounts of
time for their formation. It should be realized that no one
witnessed the formation of these geologic structures, so any
explanation of their formation is obviously a personal
interpretation. The key question to ask is: "Is that the *only*
possible explanation?" Specimen Ridge in Yellowstone
National Park, usually explained in geology texts as being 17
layered sequences involving many thousands of years, can
better be explained as a single event requiring just a fraction
of that time.

Gish states that a creationist is free to accept either a long
or a short time span for the age of the earth, depending on
his assessment of the evidence. Evolution, however, demands
a vast time scale. Therefore, the evolutionist will
automatically interpret geologic processes with that in mind.
He doesn't even ask the question: "Is there another way of
interpreting the evidence?" Yet, if evolutionists seek to prove
that the earth is very old, based upon geological formations,
they must first demonstrate that these geologic features could
not have been formed in any other way than one involving
vast periods of time. This type of demonstration, of course, is
impossible. It is for this reason that the dogmatism
evolutionists display in their assertions regarding the age of
the earth is out of keeping with a proper scientific attitude.

Rae Harris was not the only debater to use this type of

evidence against Morris and Gish. A few months before the
Texas Tech debate, Morris had a debate with Frank Roberts
on the campus of Wheaton College. The theme of that debate
was the legitimacy of Flood Geology. Roberts is a Christian, a
member of the American Scientific Affiliation, and a graduate
of the same seminary from which I graduated. He then earned
a doctorate in geology. To prove that the earth could not be
young and that the Noachian Flood could not account for the
geologic evidence, Roberts also used geological formations
that he claimed demanded vast amounts of time in their
formation.

Two years later another Christian, David Krause, a member
of the American Scientific Affiliation, debated Duane Gish on
the Dearborn Campus of the University of Michigan. He also
used the same type of evidence that he thought was contrary
to a recent creation. Krause was especially offended by the
idea of "apparent age."

In the Texas Tech debate, as in many others, Morris
revealed that geologists, such as Derek Ager, Professor and
Head of the Department of Geology and Oceanography at the
University College of Swansea, and a past President of the
Geological Association of Great Britain, are now recognizing
that all of the sedimentary rock features could have been—and
probably were—laid down very rapidly. The closing words of
a recent book by Ager are: "The history of any one part of
the earth, like the life of a soldier, consists of long periods of
boredom and short periods of terror." If the rock layers were
laid down rapidly, the alleged vast periods of time must be
inserted between the layers. It should be obvious that it is
impossible to determine how much time—if any—elapsed
between layers of rock. The philosophic nature of the old
earth arguments is apparent.

It is clear that there is circular reasoning in the geologic
column. The rocks are dated by the fossils they contain, based
upon an evolutionary sequence, and the fossils, in turn, are
dated by the rocks in which they are found. Some
evolutionists have tried to get around this by claiming that the
geologic column was formulated before Darwin's time. It is
thought that Darwinian evolution and the geologic column are
two independent lines of evidence that tend to confirm each
other. This thinking is based upon gross error. The

assumption is that evolution was unknown until Darwin invented it. Nothing could be further from the truth.

Michael Kendall, Professor of Anatomy at the University of Nevada, Reno, in his debate with Morris on that campus, gave an excellent survey of evolutionary thought going all the way back to the ancient Greeks. Charles Darwin did not invent evolution. Darwin's grandfather was an ardent evolutionist. The idea of evolution with its simple to complex development was well-known in England when the early geologists were formulating the geologic column. There is no question but that evolutionary concepts lurked in the background as the geologic column was being pieced together.

Rae Harris tried to avoid this circular reasoning by claiming that the geologic column was constructed on the basis of stratigraphy—entirely apart from the fossils. He quoted several geologists to that effect. Morris had no difficulty in quoting many evolutionary geologists declaring that rocks are very definitely correlated by the fossils they contain. There is simply no other way. Just as a rose is a rose is a rose, so Cambrian limestone is the same as Silurian limestone is the same as Devonian limestone is the same as Triassic limestone is the same as Cretaceous limestone. The only way to correlate is by the fossils contained therein.

Harris asserted that the rocks are sequenced independently of the fossils, and thus constitute a marvelous confirmation of evolution. He went on to say: "I, or any other geologist, would have great fame, and maybe even a salary increase [much laughter], if we were to discover fossils of mammals under the coal beds, fossils of reptiles under the Silurian limestone, bones of elephants and dinosaurs together, or fruit trees [apples] in the Cambrian." Statements like this sound very impressive. They imply that evolutionists are tremendously open-minded and will follow wherever the facts lead. Actually, some remarkable discoveries like these Harris suggested have been made, but have been totally ignored.

The falsehood of Harris' statement was exposed by Gish when he produced evidence from the article by Daniel Axelrod in the journal, *Evolution,* that woody land plants had been found in the Cambrian. This was the very thing that Harris had said would bring great fame and possibly a salary increase to anyone who discovered it. In spite of many documented discoveries of this sort, the evidence has been totally ignored by evolutionists for almost 30 years, simply because it would destroy evolutionary theory.

In fact, Harris' words were put to the test twice. Not only did Gish drop one bombshell about woody land plant fossils discovered in the Cambrian, but he dropped a second bombshell regarding the recent discovery of cuttlefish fossils in the Lowest Cambrian rocks in California. This discovery was reported by Firby and Durham in the November 1974 issue of the *Journal of Paleontology*. The find of a large squid-like mollusk with cone-shaped teeth was of major significance for several reasons. First, it extended the range of the Class Cephalopoda from the Late to very Early Cambrian. Second, cuttlefish, which are very complex invertebrates, had not been reported previously from rocks earlier than the Jurassic—400 million years younger than the new find. Third, these fossils represented predators 100 million years older than any that had previously been found.

The predatory feature has special significance because evolutionists believe that rapid and far-reaching evolutionary changes took place in the Late Precambrian and the Early Cambrian. Since all of the major animal phyla are found in the Cambrian, it means that the bulk of evolutionary diversity had to take place before that time. The reason so much evolution could take place, evolutionists explain, was due to the absence of predators. During times of rapid evolutionary change it is assumed that animals would be more susceptible to predation. They would be in a transitional phase from one type of organism to another or from one ecological niche to another. The finding of very capable predators at the base of the Cambrian is thus a blow to evolutionary theory.

These two bombshells shook Harris more than he showed. In his rebuttal, he had to admit that he had not heard about them. In fact, he expressed amazement that these "wonderful fossil finds" had not been reported in the literature. The way he said it carried the implication that Gish had made it all up. When Gish produced the articles and the documentation, he had nothing more to say—at least in the debate.

Three days later, a letter to the editor written by Harris appeared in *The University Daily*, the campus newspaper. It revealed the full extent of his embarrassment when Gish

presented evidence of which he was not aware. He seemed
particularly stung by Gish's implication that if cuttlefish are
found in the Jurassic rocks and now have been found in the
Lower Cambrian, with a 400-million-year gap in between,
perhaps there is an error in the evolutionist's interpretation of
the fossil record and that there is not a 400-million-year
spread between the Jurassic and the Lower Cambrian after
all.

Harris claimed in his letter that when he read the article in
the *Journal of Paleontology,* he was extremely disappointed to
learn that Gish "would misquote by error or design" from the
article so "that an apparent 'win' might be achieved in a
scholarly debate." Harris claimed that the authors of the
article did not state that they had found a cuttlefish, which is
in the genus Sepia, but that they had actually assigned their
find to a new and different genus, Campitius. He concluded
by saying: "I cannot help but resent on a personal and moral
basis being made to publicly say that I have never heard of
such an important paleontological find, when in fact the find
had not occurred."

Although Harris did not send Gish a copy of his letter,
someone else did. Two weeks later Gish's reply appeared.
Gish called the letter by Harris a smokescreen to cover up the
fact that Harris and his associate had not defended evolution
theory against its fatal weaknesses. Gish stated that although
the technical article very cautiously refrained from calling the
find a fossil cuttlefish, Firby and Durham, when talking to
reporters for the Associated Press and United Press
International, repeatedly referred to it as a cuttlefish. The
technical article itself stressed its similarities to a cuttlefish.
Further, Gish pointed out, most paleontologists tend to assign
distinctive names to their finds. Gish felt that when the
discoverers of the fossil referred to it as a cuttlefish, he had
every right to do the same.

Harris' associate in the debate was Robert J. Baker,
Professor of Biology at Texas Tech. Baker said: "I believe
that evolution is a fact." Among other things, he felt that
house fly resistance to DDT enabled one to see evolution in
action. He expressed amazement that so many evolutionists
say that evolution is not observable when this type of
"evidence" is available.

In referring to the similarity of the wing of a bat to the flipper of a whale, Baker spoke of evolution having a plan. Like Hertzberger (University of New Orleans debate) and others, he was bootlegging design into the evolutionary process. Schweitzer (University of Tennessee debate) tried to do it by bringing God in at every step of the evolutionary process. Leading evolutionists all recognize that evolution has no plan or design. Random mutations, which are the alleged basis of all evolutionary innovations and improvements, are the exact opposite of any design or plan.

A humorous sidelight of the debate was that Gish referred to amoeba-to-man evolution as "from fish to Gish, and from horse to Morris." Rae Harris said that he preferred to think of it as "the way to Rae." But Robert Baker took the prize when he called it "from blob to Bob." He then went on to say, amid much laughter, that some of his students might not think that was much of an evolutionary step.

Chapter 18

The Dating Game

Calvary Chapel, Costa Mesa, California

Referring to the Biblical account of creation and the Fall, evolutionist Bayard Brattstrom said that he "wanted to put in a plug for the snake." Brattstrom, a herpetologist who studies snakes, took part in the first of two debates held at Calvary Chapel, Costa Mesa, California. The first debate was in the Fall of 1975 with 2,800 in attendance. The second was in the Fall of 1976 with over 3,000 in attendance. Chuck Smith, the pastor of this dynamic church, served as moderator on both occasions. Henry Morris and Duane Gish participated in the first debate. Gish and Harold Slusher were in the second.

Brattstrom started, as so many have done, with an inadequate definition of evolution: "change through time." If one includes in the definition the necessary concept of organisms developing from simple to complex, he faces two problems. First, there is no evidence for it. Second, it cannot be observed in our present day. By using an improper definition, lateral changes in present-day organisms (which are just cases of genetic variation) are introduced as evidence for evolution. Introduction of this illegitimate evidence also makes evolution observable—thus "qualifying" it as a scientific theory.

Brattstrom, however, outdid his fellow evolutionists. He introduced changes in architecture, men's and women's clothing, language, morals and ethics, and even changes in the packaging of Betty Crocker products to illustrate the fact that everything changes. Since everything changes, he had to accept the fact that organisms change also. He felt that change is the only absolute in the universe.

He went to great lengths to show that evolution is not in conflict with any of the world's great religions—specifically mentioning Hinduism and Roman Catholicism. In fact, he said, the only two groups that oppose evolution are fundamental Catholics and Bible Fundamentalists. His attempt to make creationists a very small minority and the "odd couple" among religious people was not new. What he didn't say was that those faiths which place the highest authority and accuracy on Genesis are opposed to evolution, while those religions that have a low view of Genesis, or no view at all, are compatible with evolution.

Although he was supposed to be dealing with the scientific evidences for evolution, he continued to talk about the Bible. He claimed that the Bible has been distorted by many trans-lations—a claim revealing his ignorance of how translating work is done. He then did his own Bible translating. Genesis 1:1 should read, "From primordial energies gods were created." This, he felt, would put Genesis in agreement with the Big Bang theory of cosmology, as well as with Hindu creation stories.

Brattstrom's rebuttal was also off target. He actually gave his personal testimony, saying that he was not an atheist nor an agnostic, but a scientist. (The analogy in that statement eludes me.) Through his practice of yoga and zen meditation, he felt that he had experienced what one might call the energy of the universe. His concluding statement was: "I, myself, have no personal need for God. I believe in myself."

Brattstrom's associate in the debate was zoologist William Presch. Both men are professors at California State University, Fullerton. Although Presch spent a great deal of time attacking the Genesis account of creation and the flood, he did devote some time to scientific matters. However, his evidence was entirely from situations that involve genetic variation. He called it the creation of new species.

The Biblical "kinds," Morris and Gish emphasize, are not to be equated with the scientific category called "species." "Species" is a word controlled and defined by the scientific community. In fact, there are problems with its definition.

When we identify the Biblical "kinds" with the scientific word, "species," we do the Bible a grave injustice. They are different. If we equate them, all an evolutionist need do is to claim that he has produced a new species and he can claim to have disproved the Bible.

Presch cited the creation of a virus by scientists as the creation of life. Although he did not spell it out directly, the implication was that if man is able to create life, God didn't. This type of thinking permeates the mind of the evolutionist. Yet, it is totally without logic.

Gish asks the question, "If man could create life, what would it take?" First, it would take thousands of the most highly trained and skilled scientists. Second, they would be working in beautifully designed multimillion-dollar laboratories with the most sophisticated equipment. Third, they would be utilizing discoveries which thousands of scientists before them had made over hundreds of years. What does all of this emphasize? It emphasizes that the creation of life demands intelligence and thought—just the opposite of the evolutionist idea that life arose by accident. The creation of life by man would simply demonstrate that life had to be created by an intelligence in the first place. It certainly would not prove that life arose by chance.

Gish further emphasized that a virus is far from a living thing. Defining life at the cellular level—a most reasonable definition—he described the difference between a virus and a living cell as the difference between relative complexity and incredible complexity. A virus is just nucleic acid with a protein coat. It is no more living than are genes. It does not have any of the properties commonly ascribed to life. Viruses produce no energy. They have no enzymes. They synthesize no building blocks. They have no metabolism. They do not grow. They do not respond to stimuli. They cannot replicate themselves.

When a virus gets inside the living cell, the living cell replicates the virus. Gish declared that a virus cannot bridge the gap between the nonliving and the living. He feels that possibly viruses are mutated genes that have become harmful and are no longer under the control of the cell. Gish also emphasized that man did not even create a virus. He started with a virus, took it apart, and put it together again. That is quite different from creating a virus out of nothing or out of its basic chemicals.

The second debate at Calvary Chapel a year later featured two scientists from the University of California, Irvine. They were Gary Lynch, neurobiologist, and George Miller, chemist. The second debate was excellent in every respect. In contrast to the first debate, the evolutionists in the second debate did not bring religion into the issue, but maintained a strict adherence to scientific matters.

As Lynch began, he had projector difficulties. He commented, "I see we have the absolutely standard slide problems." He was quite comforted to know that it happens in church as well as at the university. When the problems persisted, he said laughingly to his associate, "George, we've been sabotaged!" What is humorous is that almost every evolutionist who had projector problems in these debates made a joke regarding a creationist "conspiracy." It seems that evolutionists trust creationists about as much as creationists trust evolutionists.

Lynch gave a fascinating talk on what would normally be a very dull subject—the brain casts and teeth fossils of man's alleged primate ancestors. Lynch is not a paleontologist, but entered this area because of his study of the human brain. It occurred to him that if he knew how the human brain had originated and the stages through which it passed, it would help him in his understanding of the human brain today.

There is certainly truth in the fact that a knowledge of the origin of the human brain would help us understand it. However, Lynch did not prove evolutionary ancestry for man and his brain. He merely assumed it. Lynch was not dogmatic in his approach, and he was aware that he was dealing with circumstantial evidence. But if man does not have an evolutionary origin, then Lynch's conclusions are wrong because his data are wrong. It is a fact of life that our decisions and conclusions are only as valid as the quality of our information. It would be fascinating to see what under-standing of the brain Lynch would come to if he worked on the postulate that man was created in the image of God.

George Miller gave an excellent presentation on radiometric dating. However, he concerned himself almost entirely with carbon-14 dating. While it was most informative, carbon-14 does not give great ages for things, and it is not where the real issue of the time question lies.

It is beyond the scope of this work to go into the technical details of radiometric dating. Harold Slusher has written an excellent monograph on it. However, since the dating methods were a vital part of these debates, let me instead give an incident that I believe goes to the very heart of the fallacy in the radiometric dating methods.

In late March and early April 1977, I took part in the Creation Week program sponsored by the Midwest Center of the Institute for Creation Research. My assignment was to speak in a number of Chicago area churches and to give a presentation on the Genesis Flood in Edman Chapel at Wheaton College. I was also asked by Gish to write up the debate held at Racine, Wisconsin, for the ICR *Acts and Facts*. That article constitutes a chapter in this book.

I was picked up at O'Hare Airport, Chicago, by the car in which Henry Morris was riding. He had to be rushed into downtown Chicago to record a TV talk show on station WGN. One of the other participants in the talk show was Peter J. Wyllie, Professor of Geological Sciences at the University of Chicago. I mentioned to Morris that I had met Wyllie at the Annual Convention of the American Association for the Advancement of Science in Denver just a month before. Wyllie was one of the featured speakers. Since Morris had not met him, he asked me to introduce them when Wyllie arrived at the studio. I did.

In the course of conversation with Wyllie, I told him how much I appreciated a recent book of his, *The Dynamic Earth*. I then asked him a question about the radioactive dating methods that had been puzzling me. Wyllie responded by saying that the radiometric dating methods were not his area of expertise. "You may have noticed," he said, "that I did not go into them in my book."

When he and Morris got into their mini-debate on the TV talk show, Wyllie's entire argument against creation and for evolution was based on the radioactive dating methods. When the recording for the program was over, he and Morris continued in a lively but cordial discussion. At a break in the conversation, I remarked to Wyllie that I was a bit surprised that after telling me that the dating methods were not his area of specialty, he had based his whole argument against creation upon them. He smiled. I then asked him if he were aware of the basic assumptions upon which the dating methods depend.

"No," he replied, "I remember studying about that in graduate school, but I've forgotten what they are."

Since the basic assumptions behind the dating methods are the key to the whole problem, and since very few people are even aware of what these assumptions are, let me pose the problem I presented to Wyllie that afternoon.

There is about as much lead-206 in the rocks of earth as there is uranium-238. Lead-206 comes from the radioactive decay of uranium-238 in a 14-step process. The half-life of uranium-238 is 4.5 billion years. That means that it would take 4.5 billion years for one-half of a given amount of uranium-238 to decay to lead-206. In fact, it is because there are equal amounts of uranium-238 and lead-206 that it is believed by evolutionists that the earth is one half-life of uranium-238 old, or 4.5 billion years.

There are several assumptions latent in that estimate for the age of the earth that are philosophical in nature and totally beyond proof. The first assumption is that all of the lead-206 in the rocks of the earth today has come from the decay of uranium-238.

Although we know that all human beings come from their mothers through the birth process, yet we also know that the first two human beings did not come into existence that way. So, although lead-206 comes from uranium-238 *now,* there is absolutely no reason why God could not have included the element lead-206 as a part of His original creation. In other words, there is no reason why all of the lead-206 had to come from uranium-238.

The other assumption is that there was no lead-206 in the rocks of the earth at its formation. This assumption is contradicted by the theory of evolutionary cosmology itself. It is this problem which neither Wyllie nor anyone else has been able to answer for me.

By examining the light from the stars, we can determine the elements which make up the stars. Each element gives off a particular wave length of light. We know in this way that there is lead in the stars. However, there are actually four isotopes of lead. Three of them are products of radioactive decay—lead-208, lead-207, and lead-206. Lead-204 is not the product of radioactive decay. The difference in these isotopes is in the weight of the nucleus. But the light emitted by the elements in the stars comes from the electrons which surround the nucleus. Hence, one cannot tell as he studies the light from the stars which isotope of lead it is. All the isotopes of lead emit the same wave length of light.

However, according to evolutionary cosmology, the earth and the solar system are supposed to have formed from the gas and dust of an exploding star—or stars. If there is lead in the stars, and if the earth was formed from the remnants of exploded stars—as evolutionists believe—then there would have been lead in the material which made up the earth at its formation. Since there is no way of determining what isotope of lead is in the stars, there is no way of ruling out the possibility that there was lead-206 in the earth when it was formed. If there *was* lead-206 in the earth at its formation, the question is: "How much?" It is impossible to answer that question. Yet, one must know the answer to it before he can use the uranium-238 to lead-206 dating method to date the earth.

It seems that there is a built-in ambiguity in this system which would disqualify it as a dating method. The problem of the initial amounts of daughter products in the rocks when they formed is not unique to the uranium-238 to lead-206 sequence. It is a problem in all dating methods which has not been solved. Creationists challenge the fact that these radio-active materials are dating methods at all. We feel that it is all just a "dating game" or a numbers game that has no relation-ship to the actual age of things.

Chapter 19

The Duane and Madalyn Show

Wichita and Houston Radio

Radio talk shows provided the setting for two lively exchanges on the creation-evolution issue. In almost every way, the shows were as different as the two cities of Wichita and Houston. The Wichita show was at night. Houston was in the morning. In Wichita the evolutionists were relatively unknown. In Houston, the evolutionist was a world-famous figure. In Wichita the evolutionists were professors at church-related colleges. In Houston it was the famous atheist leader, Madalyn Murray O'Hair. There was only one thing that the talk shows had in common—the evolutionists all agreed that God has no business in science.

A third radio talk show "debate" took place on October 21, 1980. The scene was Jim Frey's popular "clear channel" program on WHO radio, Des Moines. Gish's opponent was the well-known science writer, Robert Schadewald. Unfortunately, no transcript or recording of this program is available for study. WHO is an extremely powerful clear-channel station which covers 40 states. Station estimates are that 1.5 million people heard the debate.

The Wichita program was on Kathy Warren's "Night Line" on Station KFH, April 14, 1977. The station estimated that there were 250,000 listeners to the program. Opposite Gish and Slusher were George Potts, Assistant Professor of Biology at Friends University, and Louis Bussjaeger, Assistant Professor of Biology at Kansas Newman College. Both are

Wichita institutions.

Kathy Warren began the Wichita program by asking a question: "Is the creation-evolution issue a matter of religion vs. science?" Gish and Slusher answered in the negative. They pointed out that in origins, both positions demand a basic faith commitment regarding our view of the universe—either theistic or atheistic. However, Potts and Bussjaeger felt that it was entirely an issue of religion vs. science. They emphasized that whereas religion deals with faith, science deals with observations and empirical evidence. All four of the participants, in fact, emphasized strongly that science deals only with testable empirical data. This, in a sense, became the theme of the evening.

Kathy then asked the evolutionists about what she called the "first beginning."

Bussjaeger: "Initially there was spontaneous generation—life from nonlife."

Gish to Bussjaeger: "Since you insist that creation is religious, presumably because it involves a creator, I presume that your evolutionary process and mechanism is totally mechanistic—God is not involved, God is not necessary, in this process."

Gish obviously went for the jugular vein. Since Potts and Bussjaeger were both professors in church-related colleges, this was a delicate question for them to field. Their caution in responding was obvious. Yet, the question was not out of bounds. It is a question basic to the whole issue and with far-reaching implications.

Bussjaeger: "I'll answer as Darwin answered. Modern biology has rendered unnecessary the use of a vitalistic or a God-centered version of design. But it doesn't rule out divine providence. It just renders it unnecessary."

Gish: "Let me ask you the question again. The theory of evolution, as you are teaching it and believing it, does it or does it not require God?"

Bussjaeger: "It's a natural historical process that does not require God, it does not negate God, it does not address God."

Gish: "It doesn't in any way involve God in the actual process?"

Bussjaeger: "Like I say, God is separate from

science . . . ."

Gish interrupts: "I'm not talking about science. I'm talking about evolution."

Bussjaeger: "Evolution is science."

Gish: "Do you require God in any way in your evolutionary process, or is He involved, yes or no?"

Bussjaeger: "He does not need to be involved."

Gish: "Now you said that this [evolution] is not a question of religion. Yet, the thing that you are teaching is completely atheistic, totally mechanistic. You said that creation must be excluded [from science and from the public schools] because it is religion. If you have an atheistic theory, it is as religious as creation. You are taking a particular religious view, a totally atheistic, materialistic, mechanistic view of origins. That is a religious position. It's as religious as creation. As a matter of fact, when you go to origins you can't avoid this ultimate question of theism or atheism."

Potts and Bussjaeger both violently deny that evolution is intrinsically atheistic.

Potts: "Theistic causality is not a parameter of science. Science cannot and will not deal with that. Science is not atheistic. It is nontheistic by the set of rules that it runs on. In science we don't talk about original origins. If I take off my laboratory smock as a scientist and put on my collar as a theologian and talk about creation, then I feel that I am in the right area to be talking about this. Science cannot talk about origins that are nonmaterialistic."

Potts is here setting forth quite clearly the contemporary scientific philosophy—which is atheistic. When Potts says that science can't talk about theistic origins, it isn't that there is some cosmic rule or law against it. It is that science has *chosen* not to talk about theistic origins. Since there are only two options, when science chooses to exclude theistic origins, the only other alternative is atheistic origins. Unfortunately, many Christians have accepted without discrimination this atheistic philosophy of science. Pott's statement that science is not atheistic, but nontheistic, is merely playing with words. The meaning is the same.

Kathy: "Dr. Gish, do you feel that a person who believes in evolution must be an atheist?"

Gish: "His theory is atheistic. Dr. Potts said that it

[evolution] has to be totally mechanistic. It cannot involve God in any way. In the laboratory today, a scientist can work without invoking God. However, in origins you can't do that. You absolutely have to place yourself in some faith commitment. You can't study origins from a scientific point of view because you can't recapitulate the origin of the universe, the origin of life, or the origin of a single living thing."

Slusher commented on Bussjaeger's claim that life came from nonlife. Spontaneous generation is a violation of the work of Louis Pasteur that life comes only from life. When one believes that life evolved from nonlife, Slusher declared, you have left empirical science and gone on faith that something happened.

Kathy: "Is Darwin's theory of evolution in direct conflict with Pasteur?"

Bussjaegaer: "Pasteur disproved spontaneous generation in the present situation. Life from nonlife occurred in the beginning . . . "

Slusher interrupts: "Is that faith, Dr. Bussjaeger, what you are remarking there? You said it happened in the beginning, but you do not know that experimentally! Would you say that that is an act of faith on your part?"

Bussjaeger: "No, it's not a matter of faith. In science you have theories. A theory is only a tool—something to use." He then mentions Stanley Miller's origin of life experiment which Gish later shows has no relevance to the issue because it did not actually simulate the alleged primeval earth conditions, but had human intervention in the form of a trap.

Slusher continues to bear down on the inconsistencies of the evolutionist position: "You remarked earlier tonight that you believed in the principle of uniformity—that the laws and the things we observe today have acted in the past. Do you see life coming from nonlife today? You said a minute ago that Louis Pasteur disproved that. Why is it possible, when you say you speak scientifically, for you to say that you disbelieve in spontaneous generation today, but to say that it could have happened in the past? If you have not observed this happening experimentally, isn't it an act of faith on your part to say that it did happen?"

Potts: "Absolutely not."

Slusher and Gish both laugh as Slusher continues: "Then what would you say is the scientific basis for it, Dr. Potts?"

Potts: "The basis is the empirical data, and it's overwhelming!"

Slusher: "What is the empirical data that life arose by chance?"

Potts: "The universe is full of empirical data from which inferences are made upon origins!"

Slusher: "Tell me what that empirical data is. Give me one instance of it!"

Gish: " . . . that life arose spontaneously!"

Bussjaeger: "I'm not talking about life arising spontaneously!"

Potts: "You put those words in Dr. Bussjaeger's mouth! You are the ones that brought this up!"

Slusher: "You said the universe is full of empirical evidence that life arose from nonlife. Cite me one bit of empirical evidence that it happened that way! Take Mars for instance— no sign of life, the moon, no sign of life!"

Kathy interrupts as things were getting out of hand with everyone talking at once. She says to Bussjaeger: "Is it putting words in your mouth to say that life came from where there was no life?"

Bussjaeger, sounding a bit shaken and probably wishing that he were a million miles from Wichita, finally responds: "No."

Kathy: "Okay, and if that is not happening today, are you saying that conditions were such that that could have happened at the beginning?"

Bussjaeger: "Yes, that's the point!" He then goes into a discourse that creation is religion and evolution is science. They are separate and that science deals with empirical evidence.

Gish: "As creationists, we go by the empirical evidence. What has been suggested here tonight is totally outside the empirical evidence. They are suggesting that life came from the inanimate. The entire evolutionary scheme is *not* what we see going on today. It's a supposition, an hypothesis, a belief, but it does not deal with science. To insist that we all believe as atheists or act as atheists when we deal with origins is not right."

And so it went on into the night. The constant demands by Gish and Slusher for empirical evidence to back up the claims of evolutionists Potts and Bussjaeger produced nothing of substance.

At the end of the program, Kathy asked each of the four participants to give what they felt were the basic areas of disagreement between creation and evolution.

Gish began by stating that he and Slusher had been quoting precise empirical evidence for creation all evening. In response, they had been given nothing but empty statements on the part of the evolutionists.

Bussjaeger claimed that creationists modify the facts to fit the theory. They will not modify their theory to fit the facts. This whole debate, he felt, had been settled in the 19th century.

Before the summary, Slusher had spoken on the second law. Bussjaeger had claimed that Slusher had misquoted it. In his summary, Slusher documented his remarks on the second law and offered to give his time to Bussjaeger if he could show where he had misquoted the second law. Bussjaeger did not respond.

Potts concluded the program by stating—as he had all through the evening—that creation was a theological theory whereas evolution was a scientific theory. The two could not be mixed.

The confrontation between Gish and atheist leader Madalyn Murray O'Hair was on Ben Baldwin's "The Talk of Houston" show, on the 50,000-watt station, KTRH. The station estimated that there were 160,000 listeners to the program. Mrs. O'Hair is not known for her courtesy in allowing others to speak. She has a unique, intimidating style. For much of the one and one-half hour program she and Gish were talking at the same time. Hence, there was probably more "talk" on that talk show than on any other show of similar duration.

Gish and O'Hair made initial position statements. Gish presented evidence for creationism as well as problems intrinsic to evolution. O'Hair then stated that scientists should work on the unsolved problems humanity faces rather than merely giving the simplistic answer of "God" to the areas of reality we do not understand.

One could only be amazed at the ease and boldness with which Mrs. O'Hair spoke on subjects about which she knew nothing. She likened the world to a computer. Since it is easy to use a computer, it is easy to see how the world could have evolved. Since a computer is highly designed by intelligent beings, and the evolution of the world allegedly took place by naturalistic, chance processes, the analogy is not immediately apparent.

Since every answer on a computer is a "yea or a nay," so each step of the evolutionary process, including the building up of complex organic compounds, had a 50-50 chance of taking place, according to her. Mrs. O'Hair then proceeded to tell Gish, who had spent 20 years in biochemical research synthesizing these complex molecules, how easy it was for these complex molecules, like DNA, to be built up from their constituent parts. Her logic was that when they disintegrated, they disintegrated into their basic building blocks, so it should be just as easy to put them together!

Although Mrs. O'Hair was not knowledgeable of the details of the evolutionary scenario, she was quite satisfied with the theory. "It doesn't worry me at all that the ape-like ancestors of man turn out to be apes," she said. "What did we expect them to be?" She plead for increased effort to unravel the past history and origin of the world rather than to assume a miraculous origin. She objected to such an origin because "that miraculous origin always leads us back to church and the acceptance of Jesus Christ as our personal Savior, and this is the thing that bothers me the most."

Because there was so much confusion on the program with both Gish and O'Hair talking at the same time, moderator Ben Baldwin tried to give some direction by asking Gish a question.

Baldwin: "How does your belief relate to the version described in Genesis in the Bible?"

Gish: "This is the basis of creation, of course. To be a creationist, one must be a theist. You have to assume that there is a God, a creator."

O'Hair: "But you said that we were going to talk only about that which is provable." (Gish had not made such a statement.)

Gish: "Oh no. Origins is outside of the provable."

O'Hair: "Isn't that convenient for you!"

Gish: "Well, it's convenient for the evolutionist, too!"

O'Hair interrupts: "Where is man in the Cambrian fossils?"

Baldwin to Mrs. O'Hair: "Let me get an answer to my question here first."

Baldwin to Gish: "Do you accept as literal fact that God created Eve from a rib of Adam?"

Gish: "I believe that is essentially what God did, yes! I believe God brought Adam and Eve directly into being, and that man has been essentially human since his creation."

O'Hair interrupts: "He zapped them down from outside of the universe?"

Gish ignores that absurd question and gives a survey of the fossil record demonstrating the discrete creation and appearance of the individual categories of animal life.

O'Hair interrupts: "And isn't it funny that there is no fossil of man, no fossil of your Adam and Eve!"

Gish: "Oh, there are fossils of man. You don't find them in the Cambrian, as you mentioned, because the Cambrian is a marine environment."

O'Hair: "But after all, Adam created the fish in that marine environment, so if the fish are in the Cambrian period, Adam would have to be there too."

Gish again explains that the Cambrian is a marine environment so that we would not expect to find man in those rocks.

O'Hair: "Answer one question. Did or did not Adam create the fish?"

Gish: "No, he did not."

O'Hair: "Oh, then you do not accept the Bible at the same time you're asking the Bible to be put in the schools?"

Gish: "The Bible says that God created those different kinds."

O'Hair: "That depends on which chapter of Genesis you read."

Gish: "Adam was the final creation."

O'Hair: "That's right, and God brought the fish to him and had him name each individual kind of fish!"

Gish: "No, the Bible says He brought the animals to him."

O'Hair: "Then Adam's skeleton should be with any of

them on any of the land area.''

Baldwin interrupts at this point to take a call from a listener. Later on, the subject returns to the Genesis account of creation. O'Hair tells about a certain spider indigenous to Texas, but claims that at the alleged time of creation Texas was a sea. She asked how God could have created this particular spider under those conditions.

Gish: ''God created certain basic kinds and in each kind there is a certain limited variability.''

O'Hair: ''That's clever!''

Gish: ''Well, it fits the facts.''

Gish, in response to remarks made by O'Hair about the flood: ''May I suggest, Mrs. O'Hair, that you read what the Bible has to say, and then you will know what it says.''

Mrs. O'Hair is probably the most famous and vocal ''enemy'' of the Bible and prayer in public life. Because of her intense opposition to the Bible, we naturally assume that she has some knowledge of its contents. Whatever her knowledge of the rest of the Bible, it must have come as a shock to the listeners of this talk show to realize that although she treated the Biblical account of creation and the flood with extreme ridicule, she had virtually no knowledge of what the Bible actually said in these areas.

O'Hair continued her statements that the world was quite different in former ages and that there is much we don't know about those conditions.

Gish countered with the fact that what we *don't* know is not the problem. It is what we *do* know—about thermodynamics, probability, and the fossil record—that makes evolution impossible. He then uses the illustration of a watch which has as its purpose to tell time and thus testifies of a watchmaker.

O'Hair interrupts shouting: ''The watch evolved! Did or did not the watch evolve?''

Gish: ''No, madam.''

O'Hair shouts: ''The watch evolved! The watch evolved from an hour-glass!''

Gish: ''No, it was created by an intelligent human being.''

O'Hair: ''The watch came idea by idea, piece by piece over a long period of time through a process!''

Gish: ''Was there an intelligent creator involved?''

O'Hair: "There was an observer involved!"

Gish: "You are translating random, chance, naturally occurring processes with no intelligence to a process that involved intelligence, planning, and direct creation. You are demonstrating the total weakness of your position when you do that."

Baldwin states that their time is running out and that each should make a closing statement. O'Hair again attacks the simplistic answers given by creationists.

Gish: "I think our listening audience can discern for themselves who has been simplistic here today and who has argued the case on known scientific principles and scientific evidence."

Regarding the public schools, Gish concluded by asking: "Why must we admit the science of atheists and exclude the science of Christians?"

Chapter 20

As Literal as Broiled Fish

University of California, Santa Barbara

When we look at the amazing variety in nature, our first impression is that every organism is unique. Yet, further study reveals that there are similarities and patterns that allow us to systematize things—to bring order out of complexity.

In the same way, these 136 debates (at the writing of this book) involving 172 different evolutionists can be grouped or arranged in definite categories—in spite of surface differences. For instance, one would not expect debates held in San Diego with humanists who spent their entire time attacking the Bible to have much in common with a debate held on the campus of the University of California, Santa Barbara, involving Preston Cloud, internationally famous biogeologist. Yet, for all practical purposes they were identical. Cloud is also a humanist and one of the signers of the Humanist Manifesto.

Although these debates were to be on the scientific evidence, they soon became something else. Humanism's creed is: "Man is the measure of all things." Since the humanist admits to no higher authority than man, himself, it is not surprising that the issue soon became the scientific and historical accuracy—and hence the authority—of the Bible. Out of this came another issue—the nature of evidence.

The repeatable, experimental, empirical evidence for evolution is not strong enough to convict a known thief of petty larceny. In stating evolution to be a fact, evolutionists seem unable to comprehend the nature of the evidence needed for evolution. Since evolution is alleged to be an historical, directional, nonrepeatable process, it means that—like history —only evidence dealing with the past has any validity. Gish put it this way: "Evolution is history, and history is not the stuff of science."

Historical evidence is just as valid a type of evidence as scientific evidence. However, the two are quite different in their nature. They have different criteria for establishing valid evidence. They use a different methodology.

With the exception of the fossils, all of the types of evidence used to support evolution are of present-day phenomena. As such, they are irrelevant. Let me illustrate. George Washington is supposed to have crossed the Delaware River on one of his campaigns. However, there is no way that I could verify that fact today by scientific experiments. No matter how often I cross the Delaware in a boat, that in no way proves that Washington crossed it that way. At best, it only demonstrates that he *might* have done it. It can never demonstrate that he *did* it. The evidence needed is not *scientific* evidence, but *historical* evidence, such as written testimony by Washington himself or by others who were eye-witnesses or had first-hand knowledge.

A few evolutionists who understand the nature of evidence are honest enough to admit that the only proper source of evidence for evolution is the fossil record. Here, however, evolution faces another problem. Paleontologist Arthur J. Boucot (University of Oregon debate) states that less than one per cent of all the fossils show any hint of gradation, and these are at species-level and almost entirely sea shells. In other words, even these "transitions" are just illustrations of genetic variation.

Boucot admitted—along with other evolutionists, including David Kitts and G. Ledyard Stebbins—that the evidence for evolution is entirely circumstantial. Circumstantial evidence is evidence that is not conclusive because it is capable of more than one interpretation. Boucot used an illuminating illustration. He likened the fossil record to a motion picture film. A motion picture film is made up of a number of individual pictures or frames. These he likened to the individual rock layers containing fossils. Just as each picture is actually complete in itself, so each of the rock layers is complete in itself. However, when you speed up the film in a projector, the human eye sees the people in the individual pictures as moving—that's why we call it moving pictures. Just as the movement in the pictures is an illusion, so when we "speed up" the various fossils in the rock layers, we get the sense of movement, change, or development. This is interpreted as evolution. Boucot was candid enough to admit that this, too, might be an illusion.

To strengthen their case, evolutionists try to liken the fossil record to written history. That's why they call it "natural history" or "historical geology." The fallacy, however, is that while in written history we have human observers telling us how two independent facts of history are tied together, in the geologic record we do not have anyone to tell us how two fossils might be related. In the Colorado State University debate, Charles Wilber said: "Now, the geological record is another form of history; that's all it is." He reasoned that if we can't depend on the geological record, we can't depend on written history either. Then he felt Luther, Lincoln, Washington, Thomas Aquinas, Jesus, Aristotle, and Moses would all be called into question. "All we know about them," he said, "comes from history and from historical records."

Harold Slusher, Gish's associate in the Colorado State University debate, gave—amid thunderous applause—one of the best responses to this weird association of the geological record with written history. "I have never heard of anyone observing the origin of life in a shallow sea," he replied. He stated that if history which is written down on the basis of observations and eyewitnesses is in the same category as the unwitnessed and unobserved geological record, "then speaking as a physicist, I have a very improper method as to what constitutes science and what constitutes a very fertile imagination!"

This attempt to place the fossil record on a par with written records is also associated with an attempt to discredit the Bible as a legitimate historical account of the origin of the earth and of life. An interesting sidelight in this regard is the use of the terms "prehistory" and "prehistoric." These terms, as innocent as they seem and as universal as their use, reflect evolutionary concepts and are a loading of the dice against Genesis, for if Genesis is legitimate history and tells us of the origin of all things, then there is no such thing as prehistoric life or prehistory. Genesis, itself, would be the historic account of life since its beginning.

There are three methods that are usually used to remove the Biblical account of creation from the history of nature and thus allow for evolution. All of these methods were used a number of times in these debates. The first method is to discredit the historical accuracy of the Bible by pointing out alleged historical or scientific errors in it. If the Bible can be shown to be inaccurate, then its teaching regarding creation and the flood can be questioned. The early chapters of Genesis are thus grouped with ancient creation fables of other civilizations. If these chapters are myths or fables, one does not expect them to be historical records. Also included in this category would be the argument used by a large percentage of the evolutionist debaters that Genesis One and Genesis Two are contradictory accounts of creation. Obviously, if the Bible can be shown to contradict itself, its historical accuracy is compromised.

A second method of removing the Bible from the history of nature is to say that the Bible deals with religious values, while science and evolution deal with nature. Thus, there is no contradiction between the Bible and evolution because they deal with two entirely separate categories of knowledge. In this case, the neo-orthodox theologian and the evolutionary scientist would handle the account of Adam and Eve the same way. Both would claim that religious truth has no relation to historical truth. It is not necessary for the account of Adam and Eve to be historically true for it to have profound religious value. The Bible is thus damned with faint praise. It is almost humorous to hear unsaved evolutionists talk about the wonderful moral and ethical values of the Bible. At the same time they will not allow the God who claims to have created the universe to have anything to say about creation or the events following it.

A third way of removing the Bible from history is simply to claim that the early chapters of Genesis were not intended to be taken literally. This tack is not only used by unsaved scientists, but by saved ones as well—those who are theistic evolutionists. What is so convenient about this method is that once one backs off from the literal interpretation of Genesis, the sky is the limit. There are no restraints. One can make Genesis mean anything he pleases. This method is quite helpful for Christians who are offended by the literal view.

On the other hand, there are those who make the Bible compatible with evolution by claiming that it teaches evolution. In this case an appeal is made to the accuracy of the Bible—in contrast to the other three methods. It is simply claimed that the Bible supports evolution rather than Special Creation. Often two or three of the methods mentioned are used together. What is interesting is that each method contradicts the others. When used together, they create a rather humorous situation. For instance, in the debate at the University of California, Santa Barbara, Preston Cloud claimed that the Bible and science are mutually exclusive areas of study and have nothing to do with each other. Cloud's fellow evolutionist debater, Aharon Gibhor, first stated the same thing. Then he attempted to use Bible verses to indicate that the Bible actually taught evolution. Now, if the Bible has nothing to do with science, how can it be used to affirm a theory such as evolution? Cloud and Gibhor were so intent on criticizing the Bible that they didn't notice the contradictions in their arguments.

The Christian faith is a very unique faith. Although most religions of the world have no relationship to history or historical fact, the Christian faith is rooted and grounded in history. Both the Old and New Testaments are in large part historical documents. The archaeological discoveries confirming the historicity of the Bible are nothing short of miraculous. No book has been attacked more, or stood more solidly as a result of historical evidences, than has the Bible. The central miracle of the Christian faith is the resurrection of Jesus Christ. The Apostle Paul points out that this "was not done in a corner." C. S. Lewis declares the resurrection to be as literal as broiled fish—a reference to Christ's eating breakfast with his disciples on the shore of the Sea of Galilee after the resurrection.

During His public ministry, Jesus Christ made a number of bold and audacious claims. One of those claims was that He is God. His bodily resurrection fully authenticated His claims, and it proved that He is Lord—including the Lord of history. He, himself, had validated the early chapters of Genesis. It is

well to remember that when a person challenges the historicity
of the early chapters of Genesis, he is questioning the
authority of Jesus Christ. Christ was there in the beginning
(John 1:1-3) and they were not. That fact helps us to put
things in proper perspective.

The debate at the University of California, Santa Barbara,
on May 24, 1976, involved both Henry Morris and Duane
Gish. Preston Cloud, one of the evolutionist debaters, is
internationally famous both as a biologist and as a humanist.
His attitude toward creationism and creationists can be
summed up by stories which he told in the course of his
presentation.

Cloud stated that Morris' discussion reminded him of the
story of two Polish communities having a contest to see whose
rabbi was the wiser. The rabbis were brought together to
answer a series of questions. The question which resolved the
dispute was the question of which astronomical body was the
more important, the sun or the moon. The first rabbi felt that
the sun was more important. After all, it provides the energy
to drive all processes uphill—everything that seems to be in
conflict with the second law of thermodynamics. (Note
Cloud's naive answer to the creationist argument which he
cleverly slipped into this story.) But the second rabbi won the
contest. He stated that the moon was really more important
because it shone at night when it was dark, but the sun only
shone in the daytime when it was light anyway.

This reference to the stupidity of creationist arguments
characterized Cloud's presentation. He said that he had
searched for common ground with the creationists, but he felt
that he and Morris agreed on only one thing. "We both like
to put commas before the last phrase in a sequence of
statements."

The literal interpretation of Genesis with its implications
was especially offensive to Cloud, although he was careful to
emphasize that he was not attacking the Bible or Christians.
He claimed that the first two chapters of Genesis contradict
each other and that the creator in these chapters was a
"whimsical builder." Scientific creationism, in his opinion,
was not an alternative to anything, but is really anti-science. It
is the attempt by fundamentalist Christians to push their
particular views upon others. "Like flat-earthism, which

branded pictures of earth from space as frauds, it is of interest only for its historical aspects and as current sociological abberation."

"I'd like to illustrate the problem the evolutionists find with the creationist position," Cloud continued, "by the story of the Armenian and the Turk who were having an argument about whose culture was the older." The Turk said that anthropologists came to his community and dug for a very long time. Finally, very deep down they found a piece of copper wire. "That proves," he said, "that the Turks had the telegraph first." The Armenian said that the anthropologists came and dug in his village also. They dug even deeper than they had dug in the Turk village and they didn't find a thing. "That proves," said the Armenian, "that we had the wireless first!" Since Cloud felt that creationism was anti-science, he did not feel the need to answer the arguments—and he didn't.

Aharon Gibhor, plant physiologist and cell biologist, then picked up the same theme. He first emphasized, as Cloud did, the total separation between science and religion by saying: "It is wrong for a chemist to try to make synthetic holy water, and equally wrong for a preacher to come masquerading in a laboratory coat." Although Morris and Gish both have remarkable scientific credentials, it was not clear if Gibhor was claiming they were just preachers, or if he were referring to creationists generally. He continued: "What are facts to Gish and Morris are fiction to Cloud and me, and our facts are fiction to them." Gish challenged Gibhor's foolish statement by saying that they all agree on the facts. The interpretation of the facts is where they differ.

Gibhor then used some of the most absurd arguments to be found in the entire debate series. Although I have studied the University of California, Santa Barbara, debate many times, I still am not sure if Gibhor was serious—although he appeared to be—or if he was just pulling the legs of his audience. After claiming that there was no relationship between science and the Bible, he then contradicted himself by trying to use the Bible to prove the existence of transitional forms. He told of his ability to change a one-celled plant into a one-celled animal in his laboratory and claimed that this was an evolutionary transitional form. Morris pointed out that it did not involve a change in complexity as is demanded by evolution. Gibhor, however, called this a most fundamental evolutionary change, a drastic mutation. He likened this change from a plant to an animal to the case in Exodus 7:10, where Aaron threw his wooden staff down in front of Pharaoh and it became a snake. He said: "You who are rational believers rather than emotional believers could look upon evolution as a wonderful manifestation of the wisdom and power of God."

Gibhor then turned to the vision of the Prophet Ezekiel. Ezekiel saw the form of a man having wings and calf's feet (Ezekiel 1:5). Calling this a transition between birds and mammals, he called upon the Creation Research Society to intensify efforts to find the fossil of this "missing link." Gish pointed out that mammals didn't come from birds according to evolution. Gibhor concluded by saying that modern-day myths such as science fiction, Walt Disney, and Erich von Daniken will in the future have the same status and respect that the old myths found in the Bible have today.

The major debate with San Diego humanists was held two years later in a public school auditorium on April 12, 1978. Whereas local creationists who seek to sponsor a debate often have difficulty finding evolutionists willing to participate, in San Diego it was the humanists who challenged Morris and Gish. Fred Edwords, a philosopher, was President of the San Diego Humanist Society, and Phil Osmond, a physicist, was Vice-President of that society. The proposition statement of that debate dealt with the scientific evidence. Morris, as usual, stated that the laws of thermodynamics indicate that evolution could not happen. Gish, as usual, demonstrated from the fossil record that evolution has not happened.

Edwords and Osmond, however, devoted their entire time to attacking creationists and the Bible. In later correspondence, Edwords stated that since they had heard Morris and Gish use the thermodynamic and fossil record arguments twice in debates at San Diego State University, they had expected the creationists to use different arguments this time. Hence, he confessed, he and Osmond didn't prepare themselves to meet the arguments Morris and Gish gave. Morris replied that he and Gish always use those arguments and will continue to do so until evolutionists come up with satisfactory answers.

Referring to the number of creationists in the audience, Edwords said that he felt like "a lion in a den of Daniels." He then declared his intentions in no uncertain terms. He and his associates were speaking strictly against the literal six-day interpretation of Genesis. He was especially repelled by the concept of the miraculous and the supernatural in Genesis. Virtually all of his presentation dealt with attacks upon the writings of Henry Morris and Morris' literal interpretation of creation and the flood. In essence, he felt that Morris' writings were unfit for public consumption. He said that the views of Morris and Gish represent not only a small minority of the scientific community, but a small minority of the Christian community as well. In a humorous reply, Morris stated that Edwords and Osmond had an unfair advantage in quoting from his books, because he couldn't quote from the books that Edwords and Osmond hadn't written!

Phil Osmond complained that the creationists had bipassed the scientific community and instead had taken their cause to the general public regarding the matter of creation and evolution in the public schools. He seems to have forgotten that it is the general public who pays the bills. He then launched an excellent attack upon the credibility of the creation and flood accounts in Genesis. Although his objections are answerable, it was obvious that he was quite familiar with creationist literature.

While the content of the University of California, Santa Barbara, debate and the San Diego Humanist debate were totally different, there was a remarkable similarity in their attack upon the Bible. Two thousand years ago, the crowd yelled regarding Jesus Christ: "We will not have this man rule over us." A number of humanists have been participants in this series of creation-evolution debates. Many of them used the occasion to attack the Bible rather than deal with the scientific evidences. The San Diego humanists, Preston Cloud, Job Kuijt (University of Lethbridge debate), Joel Warren (Fort Lauderdale, Florida, debate), and Bayard Brattstrom (first Costa Mesa, California, debate) all said in effect: "We will not have this book, the Bible, rule over us!" One way to escape the rule of the Bible over them is to claim that it is not to be taken literally. However, by the authority of the resurrected Christ, the accounts of creation and the flood are—like the resurrection—as literal as broiled fish.

Chapter 21

Evolved in God's Image

University of Kansas

In all probability, few of you spend sleepless nights wondering if the law of gravity is really a law, or if suddenly you might be flung off the earth because gravity failed. There are many problems in life with which we must cope, but gravity does not seem to be one of them. Thus it may come as a surprise—if not a shock—to learn that in the highest reaches of the philosophy of science, even gravity is not noble enough to deserve the status of a law.

E. O. Wiley, specialist in fossil fishes and Assistant Curator of the Kansas Museum of Natural History, set forth this contemporary thinking in the philosophy of science. "Science strives toward truth," he declared. Yet, science is not capable of finding final truth or final knowledge. Hence, nothing in science can be proven in the absolute sense. Even the basic laws of science are not a proven fact in the sense of real truth. He was following the philosophy of Karl Popper. "Gravity," Wiley said, "is just a tested and unrefuted hypothesis and not a proven fact." It is obvious that if gravity is not a proven fact, nothing is.

Wiley and his associate, Marion Bickford, Professor of Geology at the University of Kansas, were debating Henry Morris and Duane Gish on that campus on September 17, 1976. The 3,500 people who filled Hoch Auditorium represented the largest debate attendance to date. It was also believed to be the largest crowd to attend any creation-oriented meeting in recent history. That attendance figure has since been surpassed by debates at the University of Minnesota and at Liberty Baptist College. Those debates were each 5,000 in attendance.

Although Karl Popper's views have a degree of logic to them, the more one hears the ramifications of his philosophy, the more one realizes that this philosophy which is ruling in science today is an atheistic, anti-Christian one. This is not surprising since Popper, himself, is an atheist who believes that the world is such a mess that a good God could not possibly have created it. It is also not surprising that Popper's philosophy is producing some rather strange and curious fruit.

Since Popper's philosophy recognizes that science can never reach ultimate or final truth, one would expect scientists to gladly search elsewhere for that which is ultimate and absolute. *Not so.* Instead, the philosophy seems to produce a disdain for truth in the absolute sense. In other words, relative truth becomes a virtue and absolute truth a vice. Since in the natural world nothing can be proven, everything seems to be equally possible. Thus, that which is absurd becomes as believable as that which is logical and rational. I do not know that Popper necessarily taught this, but this appears to be the fruit of his philosophy. Hence, Wiley's position could be summed up in the words of a recent book: "Darwinism is dead. Long live evolution!"

Wiley admitted that Darwinism had been falsified. The new theory, punctuated equilibrium, was so new that it hadn't even been adequately tested. "Yet," he said, "we shouldn't march backwards and embrace the falsified theory of scientific creationism." It is obvious that he did not understand creationism. I do not believe that his many misinterpretations and misquotes of Henry Morris' writings were deliberate. He simply failed to grasp what Morris was saying. While admitting that evolutionists believe that life came from nonlife, he stated that creationists believe the same thing. He apparently didn't know that creationists believe in a Creator who is very much alive. Morris corrected him, pointing out that creationists believe that life always comes from life. The living God is the source of all life on earth.

It is hard to believe that Wiley actually said some of the things he said. First, he declared that Darwinism had been

falsified because of the absence of transitional fossils, which
the theory demanded. He accepted the newer punctuated
equilibrium model with its emphasis on controller genes which
allegedly explains why there are gaps or discontinuities in the
fossil record. He then advocated *Archaeopteryx* as a transition
between reptiles and birds, claimed that there was a good
transitional candidate between echinoderms and vertebrates,
and called viruses an intermediate between nonlife and life. In
his rebuttal, Gish picked up on this confusion. He stated that
he couldn't figure out which evolutionary model Wiley was
advocating—the older model which needs transitions, the
newer model which doesn't, or a mix of the two.

However, Wiley's most shocking statement came in relation
to the second law of thermodynamics. Wiley's remark was:
"There is absolutely no data which shows whether entropy
decreases with an increase in complexity." Since, he
continued, the second law lacked this observational and
experimental data, the creationist argument was not scientific.
Henry Morris was amazed! Being a gentleman, he tried very
hard to cover up his amazement so as not to overly embarrass
Wiley. However, he expressed his surprise that such a
statement would be uttered. Morris had no difficulty in giving
a number of authoritative citations stating that there is a very
direct relationship between complexity and low entropy.
Further, the second law probably has the most solid
foundation of experimental and observational data of any
concept in science.

I do not know how to explain the attitude of scientists
toward the second law of thermodynamics—with its richness
of observational and experimental data accumulated over
almost 200 years—except as a fruit of Popper's philosophy.
After all, in spite of all the observational data for gravitation
and the second law of thermodynamics, if there are no
absolute laws in the universe, why should scientists respect or
"obey" them? Thus Steven Stanley (University of Wyoming
panel) was able to ignore the second law because he claimed
that no law is absolute in science. Martin Samoiloff
(University of Manitoba debate) was able to ignore the second
law by arbitrarily saying that it doesn't apply to all physical
systems. He didn't say who decides which physical systems it
applies to, and which it doesn't. Betz and Kessler (Tampa TV

debate) were able to ignore the second law by saying that it
can't be proven. Howard Stains (Southern Illinois University
debate) was able to ignore the second law by saying that
perhaps the universe is eternal—in direct and absolute
contradiction to the implications of the second law.
Thermodynamicist John Patterson (Des Moines Area
Community College debate) was able to ignore all of the data
regarding the second law by saying that perhaps someday it
may be shown not to be a law after all—an act of faith in
evolution if there ever was one. It is no wonder that
creationists decry the sad state of science education in our
nation and are calling for a return to basics.

Wiley made a distinction between theory and process.
"There *is* the process of evolution; many theories have been
proposed to explain the process." In other words, the process
of evolution is true, he believes. Even though the old theory
has been falsified, and the new theory has not yet been tested,
there is no doubt in Wiley's mind that evolution is true. Yet,
twice in his presentation he said: "A prediction without an
adequate explanation is worthless." Since he was applying
that to creation, apparently the same rules do not apply to
evolution.

"Darwinism is dead. Long live evolution!" This is the new
faith which one could see emerging as one followed the
progress of these debates over the ten years of their history.

Marion Bickford, Wiley's associate in the Kansas debate, is
a specialist in geochronology—including radioactive dating
methods. He first stated that the sedimentary rock strata on
the earth, when correlated from all parts of the world and
going from the Lower Pre-cambrian up to the Recent, totaled
approximately 80 miles in thickness. He sought to
demonstrate the fact from the Grand Canyon—which is only
one mile deep. In contrast to the claim of Rae Harris (Texas
Tech debate), Bickford stated that the sedimentary rock strata
are very definitely correlated by the fossils they contain.

Bickford then sought to establish the evolutionary estimates
for the age of the earth and the various geologic periods of
earth history by the radioactive dating methods. He began by
telling how the great Lord Kelvin attempted to date the earth
by measuring how long it would take for the earth to cool
down from an original molten state. He mentioned that

Kelvin's work was invalidated by the discovery of
radioactivity which was an additional source of heat for the
earth. However, like most evolutionists, he did not complete
the story. The full story of Kelvin's work is a remarkable
confirmation that there is simply not enough time for the
evolutionary process to occur. Morris, Gish, and especially
Harold Slusher have often referred to Kelvin's important
work in these debates. Allow me to tell the full story.

There is no way that one can, by scientific processes,
determine the date of creation. There is also a question as to
whether the chronologies of Genesis 5 and 11 can give us a
precise date. However, there is a way in which science can
assist the creationist. There are physical processes going on
presently by which science can set upper limits for the age of
the earth.

When Darwin first published his *Origin of Species,* he
stated that for the process of natural selection he needed
millions and millions of generations. Since mutations are the
raw material upon which natural selection works, and since
these mutations must all be very, very small (large ones are
deadly), vast spans of time involving millions and millions of
generations became the secret of Darwinism.

Challenging this whole idea was one of the truly great
scientists of all time, Sir William Thompson (Lord Kelvin),
who lived from 1824 to 1907. It was Kelvin's brilliant
thermodynamic analysis that gave us the absolute temperature
scale that bears his name. He was a staunch Christian (a
Scotish Presbyterian) and a creationist. Kelvin took issue with
Darwin and with Thomas Huxley regarding the amount of
time available for the evolutionary process. Kelvin is reported
to have said that he didn't think that Huxley knew that
science could put limits on the age of things.

Kelvin demonstrated this ability of science to limit the
time available for the age of the earth. Since the earth is
losing heat, he calculated how long it would take for the earth
to cool down to the present temperature gradient from a
molten condition. Kelvin did not necessarily believe that the
earth was formed in this way, but virtually all evolutionary
theories do postulate this molten origin for the earth. Kelvin
estimated (in 1897) that the earth could only be between 20
and 40 million years old as an absolute upper limit. Using

Kelvin's method and recent data not available to Kelvin, the
great Scotish geologist Arthur Holmes stated that the figures
would now be between 25 and 30 million years.

Because of his stature as a scientist, Kelvin was able to put
a great deal of pressure on Darwin regarding this matter.
Darwin hated Kelvin, calling him an "odeous spectre," but
could not match Kelvin's high-powered differential equations.
The sixth edition of Darwin's *Origin* was greatly changed
because of Kelvin's pressure. Darwin tried to introduce the
concept of jumps or saltations in the evolutionary process
(quite contrary to mutation and natural selection) simply to
cut down the time involved because of the limitations set by
Kelvin. Darwin died a very unhappy man because of this
situation. (There are rumors and printed tracts stating that
Darwin died a believer. Based upon correspondence Darwin
wrote just weeks before his death, my research has convinced
me that there is, unfortunately, no truth to this rumor.)

I do not mean to imply from this argument, nor did Kelvin,
that the earth must be 25-30 million years old. That merely
places an upper limit on things. Other factors place much
lower limits on the age of the earth. Kelvin's limits do,
however, destroy evolutionary theory. Twenty-five million
years is only 1/24th of the time needed by the evolutionist to
go back to the beginning of the Cambrian Period where all
the forms of animal life are already found as fossils in highly
developed fashion. Twenty-five million years is not even
enough time to evolve the mammals from the reptiles.

It is a truth of history that evolution has been aided by
many "facts" and arguments that were not valid. Kelvin's
evidence about the upper limit of the age of the earth was
overthrown about the turn of the century when it was recognized that radioactivity gives off heat. It was then reasoned by
evolutionists that the radioactive material in the earth continually replenished the earth's heat. Thus, Kelvin's arguments
were considered invalid. For almost 75 years, evolutionists
have used radioactivity as a source of heat to refute Kelvin.

However, it has been recently recognized that molten
material extruded at great depth, such as on the ocean
bottom, does not have as much radioactive material in it as
do surface rocks. It thus seems that the bulk of the
radioactive material is limited to the upper regions of the

earth's crust. This would not be enough material to resupply the earth's heat. Kelvin's argument still stands. We are back to square one.

In the third edition (1976) of Leet and Judson's *Physical Geology*, they ascribe much of the earth's heat to the radioactive decay process. In the newer fourth edition, they recognize that the vast bulk of the earth's heat is left over from its formation. Lord Kelvin's reasoning is as sound as ever. It alone is enough to refute evolutionary thinking and the concept of vast ages.

Evolutionists were so relieved to discover in radioactivity an additional source of heat to annul Kelvin's figures that apparently no one thought to calculate how much additional time that would give them. Harold Slusher and his graduate students at the University of Texas, El Paso, have calculated it. Based upon the latest available data, even if radioactive materials were distributed throughout the entire planet rather than just concentrated at the earth's surface, the maximum allowable time for the age of the earth is just 50 million years. This is one-twelfth the amount of time evolutionists need from the base of the Cambrian Period to the present. These calculations show the bankruptcy of evolutionary theory. Bickford didn't mention these things. In fact, he may not have even known about them. It is not unusual for evolutionists to be quite ignorant of any evidence contrary to evolution—even though much of it exists.

Bickford gave a very helpful illustration of the concepts behind radioactive dating. Suppose, he said, that he should promise to drop marbles into a basket at the rate of one marble every 30 seconds. If you should leave the room, upon your return you could easily calculate how long you had been out of the room by merely counting the marbles in the basket and multiplying them by 30 seconds.

He then set forth some of the assumptions that underlie these dating methods. There is first of all the assumption that there were no marbles in the basket at the beginning. Or, if there were, the number of marbles in the basket at the beginning was known. Bickford claims that this problem of daughter elements "in the basket" at the beginning is routinely handled by geochronologists. He oversimplifies the matter. There no doubt were daughter elements present.

Harold Slusher points out that there are seven different models or schemes to attempt to determine how much of the daughter product was present at the beginning. This problem is not solved and some feel that it can't be solved—unless one has the omniscience of God. However, until that problem is solved one does not have a dating system.

Another assumption is that the one dropping marbles into the basket did not change the rate at which he dropped them into the basket while you were out of the room. It is usually assumed that the decay rates have remained constant. Slusher points out that the decay rates of thirteen radioactive elements have been changed in the laboratory under conditions that could have occurred in nature as well.

A third assumption is that the basket did not have a hole in it so that none of the marbles escaped. Rocks are not actually closed systems, although the dating methods demand a closed system for accuracy. Further, some minerals, like uranium salts, are water soluble and can be easily leached out. Not only did Bickford minimize all of these problems, but he claimed that dating with different radioactive minerals gave concordant results. This simply is not true. Slusher quoted authorities in several of his debates to the effect that half of the time the radioactive dating methods date the Precambrian Period younger than the Cambrian. Creationists believe, with good evidence, that these dating methods give dates which have no relation to reality.

Bickford also showed a lack of understanding of the second law of thermodynamics. He stated: "It seems to me to be quite wrong to equate increasing complexity of living forms with decreasing entropy." One can only ask in amazement, "What would you equate it with?" You certainly wouldn't equate it with increasing entropy!

Bickford claimed to possess a unique qualification as a participant in the debate. "I am a Christian," he declared. He concluded his remarks by saying:

> Man evolved in God's image, endowed by evolution with a superior intellect to study and understand. It's a wondrous record of creation and evolution. Why is it necessary to attempt to refute all this evidence and cram earth history into only a few thousand years? Why make creation less than it is?

Chapter 22

Mother Nature Did It!

University of Texas

"Either you gentlemen are ignorant of the second law of thermodynamics or you are dishonest about the second law of thermodynamics, or both." So charged botanist Irwin Speer of the University of Texas faculty. It was during the question period at the end of the University of Texas, Austin, debate on March 24, 1977. But Speer did not explain to the crowd of over 2,000 just where Morris and Gish had gone astray in their use of the second law.

Less than a year before, in the question period after a debate Morris had on the campus of the University of Massachusetts, Amherst, a professor teaching thermodynamics stated that the creationist argument based on the second law was irrefutable. He challenged the evolutionist debaters to answer it. They confessed they were unable to do so. He then challenged anyone in the audience to respond with an answer. None did.

Since each debate seemed to have its own personality—a combination of the setting, the speakers, and the audience— the University of Texas debate could best be described as being like the spoiled brat next door or the neighborhood bully living down the street. It was the most rude, unruly, and boisterous debate that Morris and Gish have ever had. There is reason to believe that there was a plan to disrupt it to keep Morris and Gish off base in their presentation of the scientific evidences for creation.

The evolutionist debaters were Larry Gilbert and Alan Templeton. Both were from the Department of Zoology at Texas. Gilbert referred to himself as a Field Biologist. Both men declared that they had creationist backgrounds and that they had known very little about evolution until they got to college. Their presentations seemed to be emotional reactions against their backgrounds. Gilbert, the more offensive of the two, told of having been spawned on Moody Bible Institute films.

Gilbert began by saying that creationists are quite worried that humans might not be unique. Since he loved nature, it didn't bother him that he might be descended from other primates. "That seems equally as good to me as descending from dust," was his reasoning.

He then stated that he took part in the debate because science, and especially biology, was under attack around the world and more so in this country. He implied that the "big return" to Fundamentalism and the literal interpretation of Scripture had something to do with it. His second reason for debating was that we are in a serious ecological crisis. He felt that the ability of insects to become resistant to DDT was evidence for evolution. This proved that species have evolved and that evolution is a fact. Thus, in dealing with the ecological crisis, we are in deep trouble if we ignore the evolutionary evidence.

Templeton gave a definition of evolution that was in essence: "Change in gene frequency." This allowed him to use present day changes as evidence for evolution. He then accused Morris and Gish of changing the definition of neo-Darwinism from something observable to something that was not observable. Since Morris and Gish always use the definition of evolution given by Sir Julian Huxley, it was not clear what Templeton meant by the charge.

The scientific evidence presented by Gilbert and Templeton left much to be desired. Citing data by Dobzhansky back in 1934, Gilbert claimed that one-fourth of all fruit fly mutations were beneficial. In response to this strange claim, Gish mentioned an occasion in which Dobzhansky was asked to illustrate favorable mutations he had observed in his fruit fly research. He was able to name only two—and these were questionable.

Referring to intermediate forms, Gilbert stated that "there are transitional forms all over the place." Later he said there were "billions of major groups with intermediate forms all along." However, he didn't name any. In light of admissions by leading evolutionists that there are none, his statements seemed a bit enthusiastic.

Templeton took Morris and Gish to task for their use of the thermodynamic argument. He said that the second law applied to closed systems, but that Morris and Gish insist on applying it to open systems where it doesn't belong. He gave the illustration of studies on chickens which prove that they don't lay eggs. However, he said, there are two types of chickens—hens and roosters. The study applied to roosters, but not to hens. In the same way the second law applies to closed systems, not to open systems.

Without question, most evolutionist debaters who speak to the second law argument state that it applies to closed systems, while the earth is an open system. However, a bit of reflection will reveal how totally inadequate that response is. First of all, there are no closed systems in nature (unless one considers the entire universe as a closed system). It is also apparent that most of the evolutionist debaters are using the terms "closed system" and "isolated system" interchangeably. Actually there is a difference. A closed system exchanges energy, but not matter with its surroundings. An isolated system does not exchange either energy or matter with its surroundings. I suspect that when these evolutionists refer to a closed system, they really mean an isolated system.

Morris points out that the only isolated system in the world is when a professor draws a circle on a blackboard in an engineering classroom. The quotations he gives from thermodynamics authorities all refer to open systems. Harold Blum of Princeton writes: "A major consequence of the second law of thermodynamics is that all real processes go toward a condition of greater probability." (*American Scientist,* Vol. 43, Oct. 1955, p. 505.) Morris also quotes R. B. Lindsey to the effect that there is "the general natural tendency of all observed systems to go from order to disorder, reflecting dissipation of energy available for future transformation—the law of increasing entropy." (*American Scientist,* Vol. 56, 1968, p. 100.)

A condition of greater probability, as Blum refers to it, is the same as a condition of greater disorder. It should be noted that Blum speaks of "real processes" and Lindsey speaks of "all observed systems." These are situations in the real world where you and I live. They are talking about open systems and state that the second law very definitely applies to them.

If we say that the second law applies only to closed (isolated) systems and that there are no closed (isolated) systems in the natural world, we are really saying that the second law has no relationship to the real world. Yet, nothing could be further from the truth. It is impossible to make a more unscientific statement. It is obvious that open systems degenerate, decay, run down. The second law definitely applies to open systems. It is one of the very few universal laws of nature.

Because there is so much confusion regarding thermodynamics, allow me to use an illustration dealing with gravitation as an analogy. We are all familiar with gravitation. It is also a universal law. It is possible for an intelligent being to design a system to overcome gravity. An airplane would be such a system. Now, the airplane does not annul gravity. It overcomes it. While the plane is flying, gravity is continually at work. To prove it, all we need do is to shut off the engines. The lift of the wings and the power of the engines utilize other laws of nature to overcome gravity. Notice that this ability to overcome gravity is only a temporary condition. After a time, the airplane must land in order to refuel. It is impossible to build an airplane able to carry enough fuel to fly indefinitely. In other words, gravity eventually wins.

In the same way, it is possible for an intelligent being to design a system to overcome the second law. A refrigerator would be such a system. The refrigerator does not annul the second law. The second law is continually working. The refrigerator is able to overcome the second law as long as electricity is continually fed into the system. Turn off the power and the second law wins. However, just as it is impossible to build an airplane that will overcome gravity indefinitely, so it is impossible to build a machine that will overcome the second law indefinitely. Eventually, the refrigerator wears out, decays, disintegrates. The second law eventually wins anyway.

Just as man is able to design systems that overcome the second law, so God has designed living systems—plants, animals, and man—which are able to overcome the second law. As long as energy, such as food, is poured into the system, it is able to overcome the second law temporarily. Eventually, however, we die, decay, and as Gish puts it, "go to a pile of dust." Eventually, the second law wins.

The crucial word in all of this is the word, "design." It is possible for both God and man to design systems to overcome the second law. But evolution postulates that systems are able to arise naturalistically, spontaneously, that overcome the second law. The whole point creationists are attempting to make is that the second law prevents such systems from arising. Only intelligence can bring such systems into being. This, in a nutshell, is the basic creation-evolution issue.

The need for design by an intelligent being to overcome the second law is a concept that Morris and Gish have been emphasizing for the ten years of these debates. Evolutionists still do not seem to grasp it. Yet, as we have written previously, they continually slip design into the system and try to call it natural and spontaneous. Templeton stated that he had studied entropy himself. One of his first problems was to prove that refrigerators can't exist in closed systems. "But," he said, "we live in open systems." However, the question is not, "Can refrigerators exist in open systems?" Of course they can. The real question is, "How do refrigerators arise in open systems in the first place?" Do they come about spontaneously, naturalistically? No, they are designed. Templeton slips a whole refrigerator into his argument to try to show that life can arise without design.

While Templeton was using faulty scientific arguments, Gilbert was telling his audience about the "sins" of creationists. He associated creationists with the flat earth idea, with geocentricity, with racism, with Jehovah's Witnesses, with a lack of research, and with prejudice. He accused creationists of ignoring evidence that would support evolution. He felt that evolution was so obvious that, in spite of his creationist background, he became an evolutionist just by studying nature. "This is what did it," he said. "Mother Nature did it, I'm afraid."

Chapter 23

I'll Take It All Back Before I Die

Northwestern University

"Stop thinking about the bloody gaps in the fossil record," urged Michael Ruse in the debate at Northwestern University, Evanston, Illinois, on April 4, 1977. Ruse was critical of Gish for dealing only with the fossil record, rather than speaking to all of the evidence for evolution. It did not detour Morris and Gish from concentrating on the two most powerful arguments against evolution—the laws of thermodynamics and the record of the fossils.

Opposing Morris and Gish at Northwestern were Ruse and Donald Weinshank. Ruse is Professor of the Philosophy of Science at the University of Guelph, Ontario, Canada. His books, *The Philosophy of Biology* and *The Darwinian Revolution* have established him in the front ranks of the contemporary philosophers of science. He was one who testified on behalf of evolution in the 1981 Arkansas court case regarding creationism in the public schools.

Donald Weinshank is Associate Professor of Natural Science at Michigan State University. He was a team-teacher with John N. Moore, famous creationist on the Michigan State faculty, in a course entitled "The Creationist-Evolutionist Controversy." That course was a model after which other universities have patterned courses on creationism.

Weinshank began by declaring that it takes a minimum of

ten years to train a scientist. The problem is not so much a matter of learning the theories of science as it is of learning the methodology. If a person has not had that ten-year apprenticeship in science, he is not able to have an informed position on a scientific question. He emphasized further that being trained in one area of science "does not give one the right to shoot off his or her mouth in another area" of science in which he is not well-trained.

Those remarks by Weinshank produced some humorous comments from his fellow evolutionist, Ruse. Without intending to do so, Weinshank—by definition—had disqualified Ruse from speaking on the subject of the debate because Ruse was not a scientist, but a philosopher. Catching the implication of what Weinshank said, Ruse remarked that it was one thing to debate your opponents, but it's really bad when you have to debate your partner, as well.

Weinshank maintained that the order of scientific methodology is: observations, hypothesis, more testing, theory, publication for examination by other scientists, and mention of the work in review articles in science journals. The work is then finally accepted as a "law" in science. "One such 'law' is the modern theory of evolution," he asserted.

It might have been well had Weinshank not ruled his partner out of the discussion so quickly. He could have profited from a bit of time spent with a philosopher of science. Although scientists in their methodology think that they start with observations, Karl Popper has demonstrated quite clearly that this is not the case at all. Further the conventional wisdom in the philosophy of science is to question if anything is really a law. Thus, Weinshank was not quite up to date in these matters, in spite of his ten-year apprenticeship.

By stating that only a scientist can have an informed opinion on a scientific subject, and then only in his own field, Weinshank was setting up a scientific "elite" that can be very dangerous in a democratic society. Gish defends his own speaking in areas not directly related to his chosen field, biochemistry, by saying that he can read and that he has done his homework. The tremendous inter-disciplinary aspect of science today also calls into question some of Weinshank's remarks.

In preparation for his team-teaching at Michigan State, Weinshank stated that he had spent 18 months studying creationism and creationist literature. He picked out, he said, the creationist evidence that he felt was the most damaging to evolution theory. In researching this evidence, he was very disappointed. "I have yet to see a piece of creationist 'research' which comes even close to meeting the ordinary standards of science," he concluded.

Weinshank acknowledged that Gish had previously had a distinguished scientific career at the Upjohn Pharmaceutical Company. But he implied that Gish was neglecting the sound scientific principles in his creationist research and writing that he had followed in his research and writing while at the Upjohn Company.

In contrast to most evolutionists, Weinshank stated that he considered the concept of instantaneous creationism, with apparent age, as completely defensible. He spoke of it as a theological or philosophical position rather than one involving a reconciliation with science or earth history. "But," he said, "scratch a creationist and you instantly find spilling out Noah's Flood, waters above the earth, the canopy, and so on." It was obvious that although Weinshank recognized the concept of creation as being philosophically possible, he had no regard for the Biblical account as respectable history.

Ruse declared that evolution was a well-established scientific theory. After admitting that there are many aspects of it that are not directly observable, he attempted to build a case for circumstantial or indirect evidence. In Canada, he said, they have hanged men on the basis of the same type of evidence that evolution uses to validate itself. If that is the case, one can only wonder about the justice system in Canada.

He asserted that one must consider the entire array of evidence for evolution in order to make one's decision. Besides the progressive nature of the fossil record, he cited evidence from homology, geographical distribution, and embryology. Regarding homology, he felt that the similarities in the hand of man, the wing of the bat, and the flipper of the whale go against what we would expect from an all-wise God. In fact, he believes that homology falsifies creationism. He also thought that one of the strongest evidences for evolution was the geographic distribution of animals.

Morris and Gish then went to work. Morris stated that if the geographic distribution of animals was the strongest evidence for evolution, "I suggest that the theory of evolution is in bad shape." He explained that creationism is compatible with the evidence also. Hence, that material does not discriminate between the creation and evolution models.

Gish zeroed in on embryology and homology. The concept of embryology, Gish demonstrated, had been disproved and rejected by knowledgeable embryologists since the 1930's. However, it is simply impossible to weed it out of the textbooks and out of the minds of evolutionists. Geneticists have discredited homology as legitimate evidence for evolution, also.

During the question period, someone asked Ruse about man's self-meaning and value if he were just the result of time, chance, and the impersonal. Ruse replied: "Man is the function of chance in the sense that there is no divine purpose—in the traditional sense."

In the light of that statement, one of the funniest incidents I have ever witnessed in these debates happened at Northwestern. Ruse was talking about the fossil record not being in accord with what one would expect if a catastrophe like the Flood had been responsible for it. Suddenly there was a very loud, shrill noise in the public address system. It frightened everyone. Ruse exclaimed: "Somebody doesn't like this point." Then he looked up toward heaven and said: "Don't worry. I'll take it all back before I die!"

I hope he does.

Chapter 24

That Mean Ol' Beetle-Eater

San Diego State University

"We are in the minority of scientists in that we feel that the so-called two-model approach might not be all bad." The words are those of William Thwaites speaking for himself and for his fellow evolutionary geneticist, Frank Awbrey—both on the faculty of San Diego State University. That surprising statement revealed that Thwaites and Awbrey had done a bit of evolving themselves in their attitude toward creationism.

It started when Morris and Gish held a debate on the campus of San Diego State University on April 7, 1976. Opposing them were Benjamin Banta, Professor of Zoology, and Hale Wedberg, Professor of Botany—both of San Diego State. The debate was a rather lackluster affair characterized by an incredible absence of scientific evidence on the part of the evolutionists. Wedberg stated that he had been warned by someone that if he got up there, "Morris and Gish will make a monkey out of you!" Wedberg replied that had happened in the opposite direction many years before.

The most exciting part of the evening was the question period. Stanley Miller, world-famous for his origin of life experiments, was in the audience. He was called up to the platform by the evolutionists to answer a question on that subject. Miller made some serious charges regarding arguments used by Morris and Gish on the second law. However, he did not explain how the second law had been misrepresented. His major defense of his experiments was his statement: "If these amino acids can't form on the primitive earth, how come we find them in meteorites?" After Gish explained the falacies of Miller's experiments, he suggested to Miller that they schedule a debate solely on the origin of life. The crowd enthusiastically approved. Miller declined.

Among the 1,400 present on that occasion were Thwaites and Awbrey. Because the evolution position was not well presented, Thwaites and Awbrey accepted the challenge to debate Morris and Gish on that campus again. This they did a year later—April 26, 1977—before an audience of 1,500. Thwaites and Awbrey had spent much time studying creationist literature. They apparently studied well. Morris and Gish felt that they were among the most able opponents they had faced thus far.

The story does not end there. Thwaites and Awbrey then began team-teaching a semester course at San Diego State University on creation-evolution. Later they debated Richard Bliss of the Institute for Creation Research staff. On November 7, 1979, they debated Gish and Gary Parker at Palomar College, San Marcos, California. Parker is also on the ICR staff. It was at the Palomar debate that Thwaites made the statement endorsing the two-model approach in the study of origins. Although he is definitely still an evolutionist, he even stated that he felt that many aspects of the creation model were testable. What is remarkable about his statement is that if a model is testable, it is a legitimate scientific theory. Even Morris and Gish do not make that claim for the creation model. And to think that just a few years before, Thwaites had referred to the creation model as "Alice in Wonderland" mentality.

Thwaites and Awbrey showed considerable understanding of the creation model. Being geneticists, it was natural for them to spend the bulk of their time in both the San Diego State and the Palomar debates on the genetic aspects of the issue. They sought to establish the fact of good mutations and show how good mutations could work through a population. They also sought to overcome Gish's probability arguments against mutations and natural selection.

Thwaites charged that creationists had made up their own version of the second law which was quite different from the second law of science. It is hard to believe that Thwaites was serious, since Morris and Gish always quote evolutionists, themselves, regarding the facts of the second law. As an illustration that one can get order from disorder in opposition to the second law, Thwaites suggested the designs on the surface of a cup of hot coffee on a cold day. This he considered an illustration of increasing order, thus showing that evolution could take place in spite of the second law. Both Thwaites and Awbrey claimed that creationism stifles scientific inquiry and discourages the study of nature. The entire history of science prior to Darwin demonstrates the error of that charge.

A remarkable exchange took place during the question period of the San Diego State debate. Awbrey had claimed, based on the similarity of human and chimpanzee proteins, that if a human and a chimpanzee were crossed, the result would be a viable hybrid. He stated that evolutionists couldn't do such an experiment because it would be unethical. He suggested that since creationists are so sure that man and chimpanzee are different kinds, and that the experiment wouldn't work, they should do the experiment to prove that the evolutionists are wrong.

Awbrey: "It is an hypothesis that can be tested."

Gish: "I consider that suggestion absolutely, totally unbelievable. I can't believe that I have actually heard that statement being made here tonight."

Gish pointed out that a chimp has 48 chromosomes while man has 46, and that the alleged similarities between man and chimp have to do with the structural proteins. There are other genes and proteins that produce significant differences.

Gish: "If I were a betting man, I would mortgage everything I could lay my hands on and bet you'll never produce a fertile offspring between a chimp and a man."

Awbrey: "Well, do the experiment."

Gish: "I'm not going to do the experiment. I don't have to. You do the experiment. You made the statement!"
Thunderous applause from the audience.

Awbrey: "I'm basing my refusal to do it on the probability that I think it would happen, and I think it would be unethical."

Gish: "You have made your prediction on the basis of faith that it would happen. Now, you support your statement with the empirical data, with the actual test."

Moderator: "Let's go to another question."

Questioner in audience to Awbrey: "Would you be willing to have a blood transfusion from a chimpanzee?"

Awbrey: "If it were a tissue match, yes!"

Another questioner to Awbrey: "If we have all evolved from lower forms, what would be unethical about the experiment you talked about?"

Awbrey: "There are many people who don't believe in God who have ethics, and there are many people who believe in evolution who believe in God, and they are ethical people." He never did answer the question as to why it would be unethical.

Awbrey concluded with this statement: "You don't have to reject God to accept evolution; you just have to reject the Biblical account of Genesis as an exact authority."

In the San Diego State debate Gish also told the remarkable story of the bombardier beetle. Although it effectively illustrates the reasonableness of creation and the bankruptcy of evolution theory to explain such marvels of nature, Gish seldom tells it. When he does, the audiences love it.

However, do not let the humor detract from the point of the illustration—that every part of this amazing creature's defense mechanism must operate in unison. One cannot have one part of it evolve gradually, then a second part, and so on. There is simply no imaginable evolutionary scenario to explain the origin of the bombardier beetle. Gish tells it as follows:

"Although he looks like an ordinary beetle, he is really a very unusual beetle. When some mean ol' beetle-eater comes and threatens to eat him, BOOM!—an explosion goes off right in the face of this mean ol' beetle-eater.

"It turns out that this beetle mixes hydrogen peroxide and hydrogen quinone and puts it in a storage chamber. The remarkable thing about this is that it is a very explosive mixture. It would blow up if I did it in the laboratory. But the beetle adds an inhibitor. When the mean ol' beetle-eater comes up, he squirts this solution into twin combustion tubes. At just the right moment, he adds an anti-inhibitor which neutralizes the inhibitor. BOOM! An explosion takes place. Noxious gases are expelled at 212 degrees Fahrenheit right in the face of the mean ol' beetle-eater. That's enough to discourage any mean ol' beetle-eater!

"Let us imagine how this might have happened by evolution. Millions of years ago, there was a little beetle. Let's call him 'Beetle Bailey.' How he got a storage chamber, I do not know. One day he decided to throw in some hydrogen peroxide and hydrogen quinone. BOOM! He blew himself up. You see, he didn't have the inhibitor. But why would he evolve the inhibitor until he had the two chemicals. He would have no use for it. It would have no evolutionary adaptive value. But if he had the two chemicals first, it's too late! He's already blown himself up.

"BOOM! BOOM! BOOM! For thousands of generations little beetles are blowing themselves up. They can't pass the information down to their offspring because they didn't have any offspring. There is no way that evolution could work that out.

"Let's suppose that by some miracle some little beetle gets the inhibitor. You say, 'That's tremendous!' No, absolutely not. What good would it do? It would just soak and sour and corrode his innards. It would do no good. He still doesn't have the anti-inhibitor. Why would he invent the anti-inhibitor until he had the inhibitor to begin with? But why would he invent the two chemicals and the inhibitor first. It does no good. There is no evolutionary rationale for it.

"Let us suppose that finally, by some miracle, some little beetle invents the anti-inhibitor. You say, 'We have arrived.' No, he doesn't have the twin combustion tubes yet. He adds the anti-inhibitor and BOOM! He blows himself up again. There would be no evolutionary advantage to invent the anti-inhibitor without the other chemicals, but if he invents it with the other chemicals, he blows up.

"BOOM! BOOM! BOOM! Again, for thousands of generations little beetles are blowing themselves up. They don't have those twin combustion tubes which are incredibly complex. An amazing genetic apparatus is needed to evolve those twin combustion tubes. Why would they need the twin combustion tubes until they had the two chemicals, the inhibitor, and the anti-inhibitor? But they would have no use for the other until they had the twin combustion tubes. You have to have it all together.

"Let's assume that by a tremendous miracle of evolutionary

mutations or mistakes that some little beetle evolved the twin combustion tubes. 'Now,' you say, 'we finally are there!'

"No, not quite. He doesn't have the communication network. He doesn't have the signal worked out. Can you imagine how embarrassing it would be if his friend, Joe Beetle, comes up, pats him on the back and says, 'Hi, Friend!' BOOM! He will lose a lot of friends that way.

"But, why would he need the communication network and the signal until he had everything else? But everything else without the network does him no good either. You see, you have to have everything complete. You must have the storage chamber, the two chemicals, the inhibitor, the anti-inhibitor, the twin combustion tubes, and the communication network. Then and only then will you have a bombardier beetle. Up until that time you have nothing but disaster. You have no way of getting from one to the other. You must remain little old 'Beetle Bailey.' "

Mean ol' beetle-eaters should be enthusiastic for evolution. It is because of creation that those mean ol' beetle-eaters are not able to eat more bombardier beetles.

Chapter 25

Stop Telling God How to Do Things!

University of Minnesota

> Let me say that I really fear for Dr. Gish on this
> matter of the second law. We have every reason to
> believe that our Creator is tremendously proud of this
> law. Otherwise He would not have made us all obey it.
> Dr. Gish is going to have to meet his Maker just like the
> rest of us, and he is going to have to do some tall
> explaining on the way he has misrepresented the second
> law. Let me quickly add that I, too, will have to do some
> tall explaining when I meet my Maker, but I don't think
> it will be on the question of the second law.

So said Samuel Kirkwood, Professor of Biochemistry at the
University of Minnesota, in his debate with Duane Gish on
that campus on April 29, 1977. The attendance of 5,000 still
stands as a record—equaled only in late 1981 in the debate at
Liberty Baptist College, Lynchburg, Virginia.

Kirkwood then went on to explain how Gish was in error
on this second law question. He posed an experiment in which
he had hydrogen and oxygen gas in a strong container at 5
degrees Celsius. Here was a random system. He then sparked
it, and the result was steam composed of water molecules
which were more highly organized than they were before, he

maintained. He then began to refrigerate the steam. When it got below 100 degrees Celsius it became liquid water. Liquid water is even more highly organized than steam because the water molecules loosely bond together in one huge "super-molecule." He continued the cooling process until the temperature went below 0 degrees Celsius and snowflakes formed. Since snowflakes are crystals of water, they are more highly organized still, he said.

Kirkwood maintained that according to Gish, all of this could not happen because it allegedly violates the second law. Gish, of course, maintains no such thing. Kirkwood teased Gish by saying that Gish could even give probability figures to show that it couldn't happen. The probability that oxygen would arrange itself around hydrogen atoms would be one chance in one jillion. The probability that it would become more complex liquid water is one chance in a jillion jillion. And the probability that hydrogen and oxygen would form even more complex snowflakes would be one chance in ten jillion jillion jillion. "But we know that it does happen," he said. "The assertion that it does not happen might sell in California, but it will not sell in Minnesota!"

Kirkwood, like so many other evolutionists, revealed that he does not understand the basic issue regarding the second law. The assumption that crystallization represents an increase in complexity analogous to the increase in complexity of living systems is in error. Kirkwood has been the seventh evolutionist up to this point to suggest crystallization as evidence of a natural increase in order. Gish and Morris quote knowledgeable thermodynamicists, including Prigogine, to the effect that crystallization has nothing to do with the problems relating to the origin of life. No one denies that in nature water freezes and thaws. But it is obvious that just going from ice to water to ice to water and so on is not going to bring about life.

A crystal is an illustration of perfect regularity rather than increased complexity. When a crystal is divided, the smaller crystals are physically and chemically identical to the original. No information is lost. In fact, the information needed in the formation of a crystal is in the atomic structure of the material. In contrast to this, when organic molecules are divided, the original complexity, together with some of the

information, is lost. The smaller molecules which come from
the break-up have less complexity and less information than
did the larger structure. This increase in complexity and
information in organic molecules is the problem. They do not
form naturally or spontaneously by accident.

In his presentation, Gish referred to the Piltdown hoax.
Kirkwood claimed that paleontologists were not responsible
for it. He further charged that creationists were perpetrating a
hoax of their own in claiming that there are human footprints
in association with dinosaur footprints in the vicinity of Glen
Rose, Texas. Because so many have not heard of the Piltdown
hoax, a bit of review is in order.

Alleged human fossils were found in gravel beds near
Piltdown, England, beginning in 1908. A part-time geologist
and collector, Charles Dawson, was the one who made the
original find. The finds continued over a period of several
years, and involved authorities from the British Museum, as
well as the famous Jesuit priest and paleontologist, Tielhard
de Chardin. The find consisted of a very human skull and a
very ape-like jaw, together with a mammalian fauna of
apparent ancient age.

The Piltdown fossils stood for 45 years as a pillar in the
alleged evolution of man. Sir Arthur Keith, the most
authoritative evolutionist of that era, built his whole theory
regarding the evolution of man around it. Displays of
Piltdown Man could be seen in every natural history museum.
Every public school textbook dealing with the origin of man
had something about Piltdown Man.

In 1953, a bombshell burst upon the entire scientific world
when the Piltdown fossils were discovered to be a hoax. It
was a rather clever fraud involving the skull of a modern
human and the jaw of an orangutan. The bones were altered
in such a way as to make them appear to belong together. The
teeth of the jaw were filed down, and the bones were stained
to make them appear old.

It is rather pathetic to hear evolutionists today try to
explain Piltdown. Kirkwood stated that when the full story of
Piltdown is known, the paleontologists come out "smelling
something like a rose." I don't know what kind of roses
Kirkwood is referring to, but they aren't the roses you and I
know. He claimed that Piltdown was not universally accepted

by the anthropologists and cited as an example the famed University of Minnesota anthropologist, Hoebel. Michael Charney (Colorado State debate) also claimed that Piltdown was not universally accepted and cited Weidenreich's rejection of it. He didn't mention that Weidenreich rejected it only because it did not fit his concept of evolution. Gish pointed out that Piltdown was indeed accepted by the vast majority of the world's leading anthropologists and paleontologists.

Many evolutionist debaters have tried to make Piltdown out as a plus for science. They claim that it demonstrates the self-correcting nature of science, since it was evolutionists, themselves, who discovered the fraud. It is true that science is supposed to be self-correcting. There are a few examples that can be cited. However, since it took 45 years for scientists to discover the Piltdown fraud, it hardly seems to be an example of any self-correcting element in science. It would seem to illustrate that science is not very efficient in self-correcting.

The real facts of Piltdown do not have the fragrance that Kirkwood suggested. Piltdown was kept under lock and key in the British Museum. Even the great Louis Leakey complained that he was not allowed to make a detailed study of the Piltdown fossils (*Adam's Ancestors*, p. VI). On each occasion, Leakey was shown them for only a few brief moments and then was given plaster casts of the fossils to work on. The file marks on the teeth were not apparent on the plaster casts—as they were on the originals.

The only reason the Piltdown fossils were restudied in the early 1950's was because Piltdown had become an embarrassment to evolutionary theory. It did not fit the concepts of that time. Piltdown had a large brain and a small, ape-like jaw. The discovery of the australopithecine fossils caused evolutionists to prefer a theory of early man involving a small brain and a large jaw. It was only because Piltdown had become the "oddball" among the hominid fossils that it was reexamined.

Even then, it was fluorine analysis that revealed Piltdown to be fraudulent. Gish questions why anthropologists for all those 45 years were not able to recognize the jaw of an orangutan. Instead, they saw in it subtle human resemblances. Even though the hoax was discovered in 1953, I saw Piltdown Man displayed in the Harvard University museum as late as

1970. For 45 years, every ounce of evolutionist propaganda was extracted from the Piltdown fossils. Even though they were an embarrassment to evolutionary theory, and even though they were proven to be a hoax, evolutionists hated to give them up, as Piltdown Man had been so valuable in selling evolution to the people.

Seeking to neutralize Gish's argument about Piltdown, Kirkwood referred to the discovery of human footprints in conjunction with dinosaur footprints in the Paluxy River rocks near Glen Rose, Texas. He quoted University of Texas geologist Keith Young as saying: "The human tracks are a hoax, and a very poorly done hoax at that." Actually, while Young did visit the general area, he did not see the evidence that creationists have uncovered and are circulating in the film, *Footprints in Stone.*

The evidence in this film was uncovered by a team of creationists in the early 1970's. It is most convincing. Reports had been circulating in the Glen Rose area since the 1930's about human footprints in conjunction with dinosaur footprints. Evolutionists have either ignored the reports or claimed that the footprints were carved by humans. A creationist team finally went in with heavy equipment to dig under ledges in order to find new footprint trails. Digging under the rock ledges on the river bank, they were able to find three separate trails of human footprints in the very same rock layers as the dinosaur footprints. At one point, a human had stepped inside a dinosaur track when the rock was just a mud flat. By digging under rock and discovering new trails, it was possible to eliminate the charge that these footprints were carved by man.

Evolutionists consistently refused to go down and look at the material creationists had uncovered. When Gish responded to Kirkwood's charge of fraud by defending the legitimacy of the human tracks, Kirkwood suggested that a team from the National Academy of Science go down and investigate them. There is about as much chance of that happening as there is of Pope John Paul becoming a member of the First Baptist Church of Fort Collins. It is much easier to remain aloof and then claim that the human tracks are a fraud, for if these human footprints are genuine, it means that there is a 70-million-year mistake in the geological record.

Gish tells of one evolutionary geologist who did come down to view the human footprints. He first stated that the alleged human tracks couldn't have been made by man because man wasn't in existence at the time of the dinosaurs. When asked what made these very human-like tracks, he could only suggest that there must have been some two-legged animal, as yet undiscovered, living at that time with feet like human feet. This illustrates that evolution is such a deeply held belief that facts to the contrary are explained away—even if one must resort to absurdities.

In the Colorado State debate, Charles Wilber stated: "Supposed human footprints adjacent to or imposed upon dinosaur tracks indicate badly distorted rock strata." He did not explain how rock could be distorted so as to place a human footprint inside a dinosaur footprint and have them both look genuine and undisturbed.

As stated before, Morris and Gish quote extensively from evolutionist writings in the most authoritative journals. If evolutionists refer to this, it is usually to charge that Morris or Gish are misquoting the authors. Kirkwood, however, did something quite unusual. He first confessed that of all the evolutionists Gish quoted—some of them well known in science—the only one he had heard of was Sir Julian Huxley. He then challenged the scholarship of the journals from which Gish quoted. The audience was quite shocked to hear Kirkwood state regarding the journal, *Evolution:* "It, too, publishes a fair share of crappy articles—like the *Ladies Home Journal.*"

To hear an evolutionist speak in such a way of the scientific literature was quite astounding. The only evolutionist in all of the debates who came close to saying anything like that was Roger Cuffey (Pennsylvania State University debate). He tried to counteract the impact of Gish's quotes by stating that the scientific literature is vast and varied. Since, he said, people with weird ideas also contribute to this scientific literature, "It is possible to find in it quotations to support almost anything." With some evolutionists, you can't even quote an evolutionist and get respect.

Kirkwood declared that to him religion was a very important matter, and he got very upset when anyone tried to present the Old or New Testaments as scientific documents.

The question is not whether the Old and New Testaments are "scientific" documents, but whether they are accurate when they speak regarding nature and creation. This, of course, was the very thing Kirkwood was denying.

In the question period, someone asked Kirkwood about the origin of life. Kirkwood replied that science cannot speak about "first origins." He then went on to say: "It is my belief that our Creator did the whole thing and that He chose to do it by evolution, and I think it is a very beautiful process."

Whenever Gish would suggest that the scientific evidence is against evolution and that Genesis is also very much against evolution, Kirkwood would say: "Dr. Gish is telling God how He did things!" Obviously, all debaters are not created equal. Only *evolutionist* debaters have the right to tell God how He did things!

Chapter 26

Nice, But Not Necessary

UCLA and Fuller Seminary

As a child, he was raised in a church that accepted literally the Genesis account of creation. But he had a deep interest in natural history. Even in the third grade he was embarrassed by the dinosaurs. They seemed to contradict what the Bible taught about creation, recalled Henry Hespenheide, Assistant Professor of Biology at the University of California at Los Angeles. On May 10, 1977, he debated Duane Gish on the campus of Gish's Alma Mater. Gish later took graduate work at the University of California, Berkeley. He remarked that UCLA was fun, but Berkeley was a "riot" (a reference to the campus riots of that period). The internationally famous biologist and paleontologist, Everett C. Olson, served as moderator for the UCLA debate. In contrast to some moderators, Olson was extremely fair and impartial.

This debate, and a debate one week later, focused on creation vs. theistic evolution. Although Morris and Gish have debated many theistic evolutionists, these two debates emphasized in a unique way the issues between the theistic evolution position and a literal interpretation of Genesis.

The second debate, on May 17, 1977, was held at the First Congregational Church, Pasadena, California. It was sponsored by Fuller Theological Seminary. The theistic evolutionist opposing Gish was Jerry Albert, research biochemist at Mercy Hospital, San Diego, and an officer of the American Scientific Affiliation.

There was a remarkable similarity in the two debates, although each evolutionist had a unique presentation. Both Hespenheide and Albert are Christians. Both emphasized the redemption provided by God through Jesus Christ. Both men were raised in churches teaching the literal interpretation of Genesis. Both men agonized over the contradictions between a literal interpretation of Genesis and the alleged evidence for evolution that they faced in college and graduate school. Both men accepted theistic evolution as the means of reconciling Genesis and evolution. Both men presented somewhat similar evidences for evolution. Both men also presented similar views on their interpretation of the Bible. Albert listed the techniques he found necessary to bring about this reconciliation. Since these techniques are utilized by most theistic evolutionists, it is well to examine them.

Listed first by Albert as a means of reconciliation was the doctrine of providence. He quotes Richard Bube in his book, *The Human Quest,* as follows: "The universe exists moment by moment only because of the creative and preserving power of God." This idea is amplified by Albert when he states that the original organic material created by God has the inherent ability to self-organize and self-replicate into living systems only because of the creative activity of God.

There is a confusion here of two foundational, but distinct Bible doctrines—creation and providence. Genesis 2:4 states that creation was completed at the end of the sixth day. It is not an on-going process. What God is doing today is maintaining the universe that He originally created. All of God's activity in history and in nature today comes under the concept of providence. It is the difference between building a house and then maintaining it after it is built. The distinction is legitimate. When the house is under construction, we don't say that we are maintaining it. After the house is built, even if extensive alterations are undertaken, we don't say that we are building it. Since the Scripture is clear on this distinction, one can't help but wonder why there needs to be confusion at all. There is a reason. Since evolution is actually a concept of continuous creation, it is obvious that in order to reconcile Genesis and evolution, the concept of creation must be bootlegged into the concept of providence in order that creation might be continuous.

This technique involves a serious error in Biblical interpretation. It is universally recognized that one must allow the Bible to speak for itself rather than to superimpose outside concepts upon it. However, this basic rule of Biblical interpretation is violated. An evolutionary concept is imposed upon Genesis that would never flow from a study of the text itself.

An amusing story illustrates what happens in this resulting compromise. A hunter went into the woods to hunt bear. As he raised his rifle to shoot one, the bear lifted his paw and said, "Wait! Don't shoot!" The hunter was so startled that he lowered his gun. The bear said, "Let's sit down and talk. I'm sure we can work things out. All I want is my lunch." The hunter, after recovering from his surprise, said: "All I want is a bear-skin coat." They continued to talk. Finally, they were able to work out a compromise. The bear got his lunch and the hunter got his bear-skin coat.

This is the type of compromise which theistic evolutionists impose upon the Bible. The concept of evolution remains completely intact—no different from that which is held by atheistic evolutionists. On the other hand, the unique concept of creation taught in Scripture is destroyed.

This confusion of creation and providence has two aspects. The first involves the insertion of creation concepts into the area of providence where they do not belong. The second is the ignoring of the vast amount of activity in the world by God that properly does come under the concept of providence. Theistic evolutionists then often accuse the special creationist of confining all of God's activity in the universe to that which took place during creation week. This is such an absurd accusation that one is hard-pressed to believe that it is made with sincerity. While creation is limited to creation week, there is no special creationist who denies that God actively works in the world today. Yet, Albert states: "Special creationism appears to entertain a Deist view which limits God to only initial supernatural creative acts of Genesis and the natural laws which operate in the universe."

Theistic evolution is a confounding of two doctrines which are distinct. The result is a distortion of both doctrines. It is a matter of utmost gravity to special creationists that theistic evolutionists give so much authority to the concept of evolution and so little authority to the direct teaching of the very Scriptures they claim to accept as the Word of God.

The second technique stated by both Albert and Hespenheide is the distinction between "mechanism" and "meaning." "Where did I come from?" is said to be a scientific question. Biological evolution supplies the answer. "Who am I?" is a theological question. The answer is that God is our Creator in a metaphysical or theological sense. The two questions are on different levels of reality. Both levels are needed for a complete statement of the nature of man, but the two are not in conflict. This dichotomy between mechanism and meaning was earlier emphasized by another ASA theistic evolutionist, George Schweitzer (University of Tennessee debate).

Separating "mechanism" from "meaning" is foreign to the Bible. In fact, it is foreign to all of life. Sometimes we can see the fallacy of an argument by using an analogy from another area. If we say that there is no relationship between "mechanism" and "meaning," we are saying that how we do something carries no message. It is really a version of "the end justifies the means." We are saying that there is no ethical or moral quality in the way things are done. When we put it that way, we see that it is not true. There is a very direct relationship between "method" or "mechanism" and "meaning." There should be harmony between the two, for the "mechanism" does carry a message. The "mechanism" should speak the same language, sing the same song, as the "meaning." The message of the "mechanism" can enhance the "meaning" or it can detract from it.

Separating "mechanism" from "meaning" has serious Biblical implications. Romans One teaches that God has designed the universe and everything in it to witness to the human mind. The mind has in turn been so constituted as to recognize creation, through its design, as the work of a Supreme Being. It is on the basis of this witness that man is held responsible—and is said to be without excuse. His judgment will—in part—be based upon his response to this witness of God in nature. It is thus with a sense of shock and deep concern that we hear Albert say that theistic evolution "removes the unnecessary argument for the existence of God from the design evident in living creatures."

When we understand the importance of creation as a testimony to the wisdom and power of God, to say that God created by evolution is to speak nonsense. The two terms are diametrically opposed. They are contradictory. Creation means concept, design, wisdom, and purpose. Evolution means randomness, without purpose, without design, and without mind or knowledge. To say that the infinitely wise God created by random evolutionary processes is to insult His wisdom.

The third method of reconciliation given by Albert is to interpret Genesis One and Two by a nonliteral method. A literal meaning is properly restricting, for it affirms that there is just one basic meaning to a passage. On the other hand, with a nonliteral interpretation, one is free to interpret Genesis any way he pleases, make it fit any philosophy he desires. The nonliteral interpretation of Genesis can result in some very beautiful, profound, and "spiritual" interpretations. The one question not asked is, "Is that interpretation of Genesis true?"

There is, however, a slight problem with the nonliteral view of Genesis. Although both Albert and Hespenheide called Genesis One a parable and likened it to the parables of Jesus (which we all recognize are stories), they did not even attempt to demonstrate Scripturally that Genesis should be interpreted as a parable. The way Genesis is quoted in the rest of the Bible, including the way Christ quoted Genesis One and Two, would never lead us to the interpretation suggested by them.

Although Albert felt that Genesis One and Two were very definitely nonliteral, he was very emphatic about the literal death and resurrection of Jesus Christ. Salvation depends on it. The problem is that the same logic he used to claim that Genesis is nonliteral could be applied with equal force to the redemption of Christ. By what right does Albert decide that one passage is literal and the other nonliteral, when there is no Scriptural indication that they are to be interpreted differently. Is a person free to make any portion of Scripture nonliteral if the literal interpretation is offensive to him?

Theistic evolutionists deal very shabbily with the creation passages in an effort to circumvent their obvious message. They feel that there is a sophistication and beauty in their interpretation of Genesis One as compared to the crude and narrow interpretation of the special creationist. Yet, if Albert would interpret the Gospel of John or the Epistle to the Romans the way he interprets Genesis, he would be considered a liberal and an unbeliever. Why is that method of interpretation so right in Genesis and so wrong in Romans? There is not the slightest hint in Genesis One—or anywhere else—that the chapter is to be considered a parable.

The plot thickens. Both Albert and Hespenheide introduce something that challenges the historicity and accuracy of Genesis One and Two. Both men emphasized that Genesis One and Genesis Two are two distinct and contradictory accounts of creation, separated in their composition by hundreds of years. Likening Genesis to the plays of Shakespeare or to the novels of John Updyke, Hespenheide said: "We don't require all things to be factually true in order for them to move us." We are able, he felt, to grasp meaning through fiction as well as through fact.

The issue is *not* whether or not fiction has value. *The issue is whether or not Genesis is fiction.* Since Jesus Christ authenticated the historicity of those early chapters of Genesis, this attitude toward Genesis undermines the authority and truthfulness of the very One these two evolutionists claim is the Son of God Who died for their sins. In fact, many unbelieving debaters used the idea of two different accounts of creation to undermine faith not only in Genesis, but in the entire Bible as God's Word. Christians should think very soberly about accepting that idea.

Although both Albert and Hespenheide knew well the theories that question the historicity of the early chapters of Genesis, they did not seem to know well the contents of Genesis. Both men made numerous errors in the factual details of the creation and the flood accounts, indicating that they did not know clearly what the Bible actually said. One cannot help but wonder if there might be a relationship between ignorance of the Bible and questioning the accuracy or the authority of certain passages of it.

Hespenheide had told of his embarrassment over the dinosaurs when he was in the third grade—something that might have had far more influence on his rejecting the literal interpretation of Genesis than he realizes. So Jerry Albert revealed—perhaps unintentionally—that his reasons for

rejecting special creation were not entirely intellectual or
scientific. With him, as with many other theistic evolutionists,
there is a psychological element that may be an important
factor in his attitude toward Genesis.

In explaining his early search for a solution to the creation-
evolution problem, Albert said: "Is my faith subject to a
theological domino theory postulating that a fall in the
historical and scientific accuracy of the first domino of the
creation accounts eventually results in the fall of the historical
resurrection and thus in the fall of my Christian faith?"
Albert was describing his early pilgrimage. What he was
actually saying, although he might not be willing to admit it,
is that he was afraid to put the early chapters of Genesis to a
scientific or historical test. Should they prove to be in error, it
would destroy his faith in the rest of the Bible. So, to protect
himself, he divorced "mechanism" from "meaning." He
removed the creation account from any relationship to
scientific or historical truth. That made it impossible for them
ever to be shown to be in error. It also cancelled the witness
which God had established in nature.

Albert praised a faith which was not dependent upon proof
or empirical evidence. He felt that to be concerned with
historical or scientific proof for the Bible would always cause
one to be unsure and insecure. One would always live in fear
that something would come up to destroy faith in the Bible.
He spoke of a "total trust from our heart which doesn't
demand tangible proof as doubting Thomas did." The
amusing thing is that when doubting Thomas asked for proof,
Christ gave it to him. Rather than rebuke Thomas for asking,
the Lord honored his request. Albert's own words reveal that
his real reason for rejecting special creation is a fear that God
has not given us a creation account that is scientifically or
historically true.

Many theistic evolutionists do not understand the nature of
Biblical faith. The resurrected Christ told doubting Thomas to
touch Him and believe. Christ spent 40 days after His resurrection ministering to the disciples on earth, specifically so
that they could see that He really was the very One Who had
been crucified. Paul emphasized that these things were not
done in a corner, but openly for all to see and verify. The
Bible is rooted and grounded in history. Yet Albert and

Hespenheide apparently think there is something wrong with a faith based on a Bible which is historically and scientifically accurate. Hespenheide spoke of a "leap of faith." He means something which has no relationship to history or nature. As spiritual as that may sound, it is not the faith of which the Bible speaks. With Albert and Hespenheide, faith seems to be more a metaphysical or philosophical hope than it is a response to the God Who stepped into history at creation and beyond.

Although we have mentioned a number of Biblical doctrines and teachings which theistic evolution compromises, this is not the end. Hespenheide has problems with the Biblical teaching on angels, Satan, and miracles. Albert tended to redefine original sin. He felt that it had more meaning if it referred to our individual sins rather than to the sin of Adam and Eve imputed to us—as the Bible teaches. When Gish asked Albert about the Biblical teaching that physical death came upon all human and animal life as the result of the sin of Adam and Eve, Albert responded that he felt that these references were not to physical death, but to spiritual death. As an evolutionist, he felt that physical death was a normal part of the life involving Adam and Eve and their animal ancestors.

Our Lord said, "By their fruits ye shall know them." Although Christ was referring to people, His words apply to philosophies, as well. By this standard, theistic evolution is seen to be not only an improper reconciliation of the Bible and evolution, but a very dangerous one as well.

It is interesting that Hespenheide, a Christian, used the same kind of reasoning as did Fraser (University of Cincinnati debate), an agnostic. There was no doubt in Hespenheide's mind that the world not only has evolved, but that it looks as if it had evolved. Therefore, he said: "If one argues theologically that God could have created the world to look as if it evolved, this argument makes God out to be a cosmic practical joker."

He has no difficulty, however, in going to church and reciting the Apostle's Creed: "I believe in God the Father Almighty, maker of heaven and earth and all things visible and invisible." He feels that he is related to God the Creator in some metaphysical sense. Regarding the inconsistency between Genesis and evolution, he said: "It would be nice if they meshed, but it's not necessary."

Of all the debates in which Gish has been involved, these seemed to be the most bewildering to him. He had no difficulty handling the rather scanty scientific evidence that these men presented to support evolution. What did seem to shock Gish was to debate Christians who handled so irresponsibly the Book which is the foundation of Christian faith.

Chapter 27

But I'm Not a Christian

Bradley, California, and Iowa State

To have life originate by evolution, "All you need is a planetary surface and a flow-through of energy," insisted Harold J. Morowitz, thermodynamicist from Yale University, in a debate on the origin of life at the University of California, Berkeley. Gish responded, "What about Mars?" There is, of course, no answer.

Mars was a perfect test for evolutionary theory. And it failed. Most people are unaware of how significant the search for life on Mars was. Creationists themselves have not grasped the full impact of this actual falsification of evolutionary theory regarding the origin of life.

Creationists have long claimed that evolution is not a valid scientific theory because it cannot be falsified—that is, evolutionists simply will not accept any falsification of it. A comparison of statements made by evolutionists before the Viking probes to Mars and statements made afterward demonstrates that any evidence against evolution will be explained away. No amount of contrary scientific evidence can falsify evolution, since its followers believe it to be a fact. Mars is just the latest example of this.

Before Viking, evolutionists were confident that life would be found on Mars. Gish quoted a number of evolutionists regarding their optimism. *New Scientist* declared that "[Carl] Sagan expects life to loom large on Mars." Harold Kline, one of the scientists in charge of the Viking project, was quoted as saying that if life was not found on Mars, scientists will "have to go back to the drawing board and devise a new theory for the origin of life." These were typical statements made before the Viking probes.

There was good reason for this optimism. All the prerequisites for life, according to evolutionary theory, were on Mars. The necessary chemical elements were there, including water vapor. Mars was not so far from the sun as to render it inhospitable to life. Most important of all, energy from the sun was pouring down upon its planetary surface. Hence, Mars was an open system with plenty of available solar energy. Evolutionary doctrine had long held that this was all that was needed to spark the evolution of life from nonlife. This is exactly the way evolutionists claim that it happened here on earth.

Then came the Viking missions. The failure to find life on Mars was a shock. Now, however, evolutionists say that the absence of life on Mars has no significance. Russell Doolittle, Gish's opponent in an origin of life debate at Iowa State, said that life could well be found elsewhere in the solar system—on one of the satellites of Jupiter or Saturn—and that the failure to find life on Mars doesn't affect the evolutionist argument at all. This type of statement comes very close to intellectual dishonesty. Since Mars was a perfect test, and since we know how much evolutionary propaganda we would have heard had life been found there, it is hard to understand why the failure to find life on Mars doesn't cause evolutionists to ponder a bit.

Three of Gish's debates were specifically on the origin of life. The one at the University of California, Berkeley, was on May 19, 1977. Gish's opponent, Harold J. Morowitz, is Professor of Molecular Biophysics and Biochemistry at Yale University. He is recognized world-wide as an authority on thermodynamics.

The Iowa State University debate was held on October 22, 1980. It was the third time that Gish had faced the world-famous biochemist, Russell F. Doolittle. The other debates with Doolittle were not limited to the origin of life. They first debated on the campus of the University of California, San Diego, in 1972. Doolittle is Professor of Chemistry there. About a year later they debated on the campus of San Diego

State University. Doolittle admitted that Gish won those two debates. Doolittle also debated Henry Morris in the pages of the *San Diego Union* newspaper on September 19, 1975. Doolittle and Gish were to meet again at Liberty Baptist College, Lynchburg, Virginia, on October 15, 1981, in one of the most sensational debates of all. It had an attendance of 5,000 and was scheduled for nationwide TV coverage.

The third origin of life debate was more of a panel discussion than a debate. It was held on June 15, 1974, at Bradley University, Peoria, Illinois. Sharing the panel with Gish were Merrill Foster, Professor of Geology at Bradley University, and Richard Hoffmann, Professor of Chemistry at Illinois Central College, East Peoria. Although the attendance at this panel was the smallest of the three, in some ways this one was the most significant.

In the Berkeley debate, Morowitz recognized that a naturalistic origin of life would be impossible in a system that is in thermodynamic equilibrium. An equilibrium condition occurs when a system has been in isolation and has aged for a very long time. In our day-to-day living, we never meet equilibrium systems. Everything is dynamic. Morowitz's main argument with Gish was that Gish uses equilibrium thermo-dynamics to try to disprove evolution. However, the surface of our planet is very far from equilibrium. It is in a non-equilibrium condition because there is a flow-through of energy from the sun to the earth and then into outer space.

Morowitz confessed that "no evidence has come forth to challenge the second law of thermodynamics" since it was formulated over a century ago. However, he said, the second law demands only that the entropy of the entire system increase. The "system" to which he referred is the solar system involving the sun, planets, and outer space. There can be a local ordering or entropy decrease (on earth) which is offset by a greater entropy increase elsewhere in the system (the sun).

Life is not a property of the universe as a whole, but only of planetary surfaces, Morowitz emphasized. On these far-from-equilibrium surfaces, the sun's energy acting upon the proper chemical elements is able to build up order to produce biochemicals and macromolecules. Thus, there is no conflict between evolution and the second law of thermodynamics. He did admit, however, that at the moment we lack both the theoretical and the experimental basis to talk very much about these nonequilibrium processes in physics. He expressed great optimism that not only will these problems be solved by future scientific investigation, but that the remaining problems in the evolution of life will be resolved also. This hope of his actually constitutes an act of faith.

In 1972, well before the Viking probes to Mars, Morowitz had written an article in which he stated that planetary surfaces *must* be organized because they are the intermediate stage in the flow of energy from the sun to outer space. He thus predicted that when we are able to examine the surface of another planet, we will find some kind of molecular organization on the surface. This, he felt, would be true anywhere in the universe.

Here we have a very definite prediction based upon evolutionary theory regarding thermodynamics. The idea that life forms—or at least biological molecules—are bound to evolve whenever conditions are right is the view held by most evolutionists. This view was refuted and falsified by the Viking probes to Mars. Gish used Morowitz's own words against him in the Berkeley debate. Gish pointed out that all of the necessary building blocks were there—carbon, nitrogen, oxygen, and hydrogen. Here was the perfect natural laboratory for an origin of life experiment. It failed. It demonstrated that a naturalistic origin of life is impossible in open systems or nonequilibrium systems, as well as in equilibrium and closed systems.

This was not the only time in the debate that Gish used Morowitz's words against him. Morowitz had calculated that the improbability of the existence (and hence its origin by naturalistic means) of a relatively simple form of life was one over one followed by 100 billion zeroes. Gish emphasized, as he does in all of his debates, that the proven principles of thermodynamics, kinetics, and probability all demand that life was created by a Designer. Gish used Morowitz's own probability figures to show the impossibility of life arising naturalistically.

In an effort to counter this very damaging probability argument, Morowitz made an incredibly bad logical error. He confused intelligent processes with random processes. The origin of life is a totally random process according to evolutionists. Yet, Morowitz likened a naturalistic origin of life to a human being with intelligence dialing a telephone number. He said that the combinations of numbers involved in dialing a long distance telephone number exceed a hundred billion trillion. Yet, he had dialed such numbers many times successfully. The illustration is totally out of order. Gish expressed amazement that Morowitz would use such an argument. It proved, said Gish, that only a highly intelligent being using deliberate action in dialing could overcome such incredible odds. If monkeys had done the dialing, the calls would never have been completed. In the same way, an intelligent Designer was the only logical answer to the problem of the origin of life.

Morowitz cited the origin of life experiments by Stanley Miller. Repeatedly, Gish must respond to this argument. In the late 1950's Miller placed into an apparatus various chemicals that were thought to duplicate the early earth's atmosphere—ammonia, methane, water, and hydrogen. The gases were circulated through the system and sparked. After some time, some very simple amino acids were obtained. Since amino acids are the basic building blocks of proteins, this was considered to be evidence that life could have arisen naturalistically. It made Miller famous.

Gish points out that Miller had a trap in his apparatus. It was only by trapping out and removing the product (amino acids) from the energy source that he was able to preserve it. Had the product been exposed again to the energy source it would have been destroyed. Actually, Gish emphasized, the rate of destruction is far greater than the rate of synthesis. Hence, the experiment did not fairly duplicate alleged primitive earth conditions.

Gish dramatically explained to the audience that the evolutionist is on the horns of a dilemma. To build up amino acids into proteins requires energy. However, to expose these amino acids to the necessary energy destroys them. To suggest that there was a trap on the primitive earth which would protect them is the end of the road. Without energy, they can't go further up the road to become proteins. "Either way, you're dead!" says Gish.

I am convinced that in every origin of life experiment

devised by evolutionists, the intelligence of the experimenter is involved in such a way as to prejudice the experiment. It no longer becomes a true simulation of naturalistic conditions. I am also convinced that in every illustration used by evolutionists regarding the origin of life, the illustration involves an intelligence factor that once again renders it invalid as a true illustration of naturalistic conditions. The trap in Miller's experiment and Morowitz's illustration of dialing a long distance telephone number are cases in point.

Morowitz stated that he was opposing creation science because he felt that it inhibited legitimate scientific inquiry. He also declared that Gish tries to use science to support a rigid fundamentalism. (I suspect he means a literal interpretation of the Bible.) "He can't do this," Morowitz maintains, "without distorting the science to the point where it is not recognizable." Morowitz does not want creation science taught in the public schools because it is "bad science."

I have never known Gish to be as frustrated as I perceived him to be in the Iowa State University debate. The reason for his frustration was the "science fiction" that Doolittle was passing off (in the name of *science*) to the 1,500 assembled students. Doolittle first listed the fundamental forces of nature. He then said: "Give me these forces, and one little eminence and I will create life on earth for you—not only on earth but on other planetary systems." He then went through the entire evolutionary scenario from the "big bang" to the origin and development of life on earth. He explained his impossible scheme by saying that we are not talking about life as it exists today. We are talking about primitive organisms that evolved at the beginning. Of course, this places it outside the realm of empirical science—as Gish has constantly maintained.

Part of Doolittle's system consisted of *starting* with certain complex biological materials—such as a protein enzyme—rather than with the more simple elements. This is just another way of bootlegging order or intelligence into the system. He also claimed that these early systems were quite sloppy in contrast to the incredibly precise and exact chemical and genetic systems in the cell today. He likened it to a sculptor who starts by taking big chunks off a block and gradually gets down to very precise work. Doolittle thus compared the work of a sculptor having intelligence to the process of evolution which is totally random. Another case where intelligence is used to improperly illustrate a process having no intelligence.

Probability also suffered under Doolittle. He tried to deal with Gish's probability arguments by claiming that if one calculated the odds that all 1,500 who were in attendance would be there that night, the odds would seem to be impossible. But here we are! Gish struck back. "He has made my point. We are here by design—each of us deliberately." Gish went on to say that this was the fifth time in these debates that an evolutionist has used the attendance argument to try to disprove probability.

Doolittle then tried to show that things that seem very improbable aren't improbable after all. He said that there are 365 days in a year, and there are 26 people sitting on the first row. I'll bet Dr. Gish one dollar that two people in the first row have the same birthday. Each person then called out his birth date, and two people did have the same one. Doolittle said it was the easiest dollar he ever made. It did seem impressive until Gish explained why it was not a fair test of probability. Doolittle later admitted that it was an old statistical trick.

Gish then gave them a lesson in real probability. He said that he would pick out 17 students from the audience. He would write their names on a piece of paper in a certain order. He challenged Doolittle. "I'll give you $10,000 if they line up in the order I have listed on the paper, and you give me $10.00 if they don't." Doolittle wisely refused. Gish said that they could line up in 355 trillion different ways. He uses this illustration to show the many different possibilities of the amino acids that must be in precise sequences in the proteins of life. If any one of the thousands involved is not in precisely the right order, there is no biological activity.

The Bradley University panel revealed one of the most astounding evidences for creation that has ever come out of this debate series. Although Gish was aware of it, it was not brought out by him, but by chemist Richard Hoffmann. It is surprising to me that Gish has used it so seldom. In fact, I do

not recall Gish using this argument until the debate at
Western Washington University in 1980. Since it seems to preclude the possibility of life arising naturalistically, it is never
mentioned by evolutionists. Morowitz did not mention it as a
problem, nor did Doolittle.

The argument has to do with the fact that amino acid
molecules are not symmetrical. They have what is called
"handedness." Look at your two hands. They are very much
alike, yet different. One cannot be superimposed on the other.
A right-handed glove does not fit on the left hand. Our hands
are what are called mirror images of each other. In the same
way, amino acids can have a right-handed configuration or
twist or a left-handed configuraton or twist, like right-handed
or left-handed corkscrews. They, too, are the same—yet
different. If you were to cook up amino acids in the
laboratory, the result would always be fifty per cent left-
handed and fifty per cent right-handed. In any origin of life
experiment, such as Stanley Miller's, the resulting amino acids
are always a fifty-fifty mixture of right and left-handed
molecules.

Right-handed amino acids and left-handed versions of the
same amino acids are not the same substances. They are very
different in their biochemical and biological activity. What is
of the greatest importance is that the *amino acids* in living
systems are exclusively of the *left*-handed variety. The *sugars*
in living systems are exclusively of the *right*-handed variety.
However, there is simply no mechanism nor process in nature
nor in the laboratory that can steer left-handed amino acids so
that they alone go into living systems. Nor does anyone
understand why living systems have only left-handed amino
acids and only right-handed sugars.

This arrangement is so basic to life that if you had a cell
with 2,000 amino acid molecules in it, and all were left-
handed but one, all biological activity would cease because of
that one "deviant" amino acid. If you should be on another
planet in which all the organisms had right-handed amino
acids and left-handed sugars, no matter how much you ate of
that food, you would starve to death. Our enzymes are not set
up to handle that type of diet.

As we stated before, there is no mechanism known in
nature or in the laboratory to direct the molecules with the

proper handedness into living systems. When you cook them up, they are always a fifty-fifty mixture. The problem, and an insurmountable one it is, is to explain how life could evolve naturalistically when there is no way for only molecules of the proper handedness to get into the system. Miller's origin of life experiment is continually cited as producing amino acids which are the building blocks of proteins. Yet, it is never mentioned that these amino acids were a random mixture in handedness, and they would never work in living systems. It is intellectually dishonest for evolutionists to withhold this important aspect from nonscientists and make them think that the evolution of life is a rather feasible theory.

What is also remarkable is that Richard Hoffmann, who brought out this amazing design aspect of living systems, said: "I perhaps share some of the creationist's point of view, but I'm not a Christian." With that amazing insight into the Creator's works, one can't help but feel that he will be someday.

Chapter 28

I Was Invited

Utrecht, The Netherlands

"There is light enough for those who want to see." With
these words from the great Christian philosopher, Pascal, Dr.
W. J. Ouweneel, moderator, concluded one of the most
unusual debates in the series. Ouweneel, a geneticist, is one of
the leaders of the creationist movement in The Netherlands.

The debate was actually three debates in one. It was held in
Congress Hall in Utrecht, The Netherlands, on October 1,
1977. It featured creationists Duane Gish, Harold Slusher,
and Donald Chittick. Chittick is Professor of Chemistry at
George Fox College, Newberg, Oregon. The first of the three
debates was between Gish and biologist M. Sluijser of the
Dutch Cancer Institute. Harold Slusher's opponent in the
second debate was Carl Koppeschaar, astronomer and science
journalist. Chittick then debated Cees Laban, a geologist with
the Geological Service of Holland.

Although the sessions covered the usual evidences for
creation and evolution in the areas of biology, biochemistry,
geology, and astronomy, the most unique feature was the
emphasis placed on the question of whether or not creation
science should be taught in the public schools. Moderator
Ouweneel had each of the six participants give their personal
and professional views on the subject. There are probably few
reasons for or against the teaching of scientific creationism in
the public schools that were not mentioned by these six
participants.

The first one to address the question of the teaching of
creation science in the public schools was Duane Gish. He
stated that the dictates of academic freedom, religious

freedom, good science, and good education all demand that
the creation model be included along with the evolution model
in the study of origins in the public schools. He emphasized
that it was just good science education to make students
aware of (1) the absence of transitional forms in the fossil
record, (2) the sudden appearance of the various types of
animals and plants in the fossil record, and (3) the
implications of the second law of thermodynamics that the
universe is running down and that there is no self-ordering
principle in the natural world. These also happen to be the
three basic points of the creation model.

Gish went on to state that a two-model approach—teaching
by comparison and contrast—causes students to think and to
weigh the evidence for themselves. To teach only the evolution
model, he said, is nothing short of indoctrination in a
materialistic, naturalistic philosophy. We would expect that
type of approach in the Soviet Union, China, and Cuba, but
it is totally out of place in a democratic society, such as The
Netherlands or the United States. The only fair and
democratic approach is to give the students the scientific
evidence on both sides of this important question of origins
and allow them to decide for themselves.

Biologist Sluijser spoke next. He reasoned that the Dutch
people were probably not aware that in the United States
there was a resurgence of religious fundamentalism, and that
it was these people who were trying to get their religion into
the public schools. This, of course, is the way the issue is
usually presented. The argument is that to bring creationist
religion into the public schools would be a violation of the
principle of the separation of church and state. In fact, a
number of evolutionists stated that they took part in these
debates because of their concern over the public school issue.

It is obvious that evolutionists have not been listening or
thinking. Had they been listening to what creationists are
saying, they would have known that creationists want only the
scientific evidence for creation presented in the public schools,
not the religious aspect. The three points of the creation
model which Gish presented can all be established
scientifically. They do have religious implications, however.
Here is the rub. Evolutionists are very aware—fearfully
aware—of the religious implications of creation. They seem to

be very dull, however, regarding the religious implications of evolution.

If evolutionists would think about it, they would realize that the last thing creationists want is to force public school teachers to teach Genesis. Many public school teachers would do an excellent job, but many others could teach it in such a way as to do far more harm than good. It doesn't take a great deal of intelligence to realize that this is not what creationists are after. Yet, one continually hears it said that creationists are trying to bring their religion into the public schools.

Sluijser then referred to a document entitled, "A Statement Affirming Evolution as a Principle of Science." This statement was drafted by the American Humanist Association and signed by about 500 scientists, educators, and religious leaders. It was then sent to major school districts in the United States. Signers who were involved in debates with Morris and Gish were Preston Cloud (University of California, Santa Barbara, debate) and Everett C. Olson (Moderator of the UCLA debate). This statement declared that evolution was established and verified, that creationism is not scientific but is purely religious, that there are no alternative theories to the principle of evolution, and that school boards, teachers, textbook publishers, and concerned citizens should resist every effort to have creationism included in the public school curriculum.

Emphasizing that many famous scientists, including Nobel Prize winners, had signed this statement, Sluijser stated that this was his answer to the question of whether or not creationism should be taught in the public schools. It was nothing but an appeal to authority—something that scientists say they do not do. Harold Slusher answered well in his response to Sluijser. He said, amid much applause, that we don't get our science by majority vote. We get it by careful investigation of the universe.

Sluijser further claimed that to teach public school children the creation theory is very wrong "because it is an irrational theory and the schools are for rational education." Gish jumped on that one. He declared that just the opposite is true. It is irrational to teach children that the universe could create itself and order itself when everything in science tells us just the opposite. It is an irrational approach to say that an

isolated system can start out in a disordered state and end up
in an ordered state.

Sluijser's last comment was that if one were going to teach
creation in the public schools, one would also have to teach
Buddhism, Hinduism, Confucianism, and the "crack
theories" of all of these other religions. This objection is
given by many sincere people out of a sense of fairness in our
pluralistic society.

First, this idea does not comprehend the fact that creation
science can be presented in a nonsectarian manner. Second,
this idea also fails to grasp the fact that virtually all of the
non-Christian religions have an evolutionary concept of
origins. Details vary, of course. But Gish pointed out that
there are only two basic models of origins. Either organisms
appeared suddenly, as creation would imply, or they appeared
gradually according to an evolutionary scenario. Either the
fossil record has systematic gaps, as creation would imply, or
there are transitional forms, suggesting an evolutionary origin.
Either the universe is running down, as the creation model
postulates, or it is becoming more ordered, as evolution
demands. All of the creation and evolution schemes can be
fitted into these two models. The approach is truly nonsectarian.

Astronomer Koppeschaar remarked that he could see good
points on both sides. He felt that the problem could be solved
by having those students who want creationism taught go to
private schools and those who wanted a "clear view not
spoiled by creationism" go to the public schools. In The
Netherlands, private schools are in the majority. However, in
the United States, if a person goes to a private school in order
to avoid evolutionary indoctrination, he or his parents are still
taxed to pay for the public schools. This is hardly an
equitable solution.

Koppeschaar also felt that creation theory "spoils one's
thoughts" because it means the end of all scientific research.
"All questions are already answered," he declared. This
objection, although heard repeatedly, is the most mistaken of
all. It is held by many sincere scientists, but it reveals a tragic
ignorance of the history of science. Before Darwin, the major
paradigm of science was creationism. That era has been
labeled by historians as "the golden age of science." Slusher

mentioned Newton, Kelvin, and Boltzman as just a few of the great scientists who were creationists and who were tremendously productive in research. Rather than stifle research, creationism encourages research and opens up new vistas for research.

Harold Slusher continued by saying that evolutionists are concerned that creationism would bring religion into the schools. But as it is now, religion is already being taught in the public schools—secular humanism. This is what evolution is in the long run. Evolutionists seem to desire a preferred frame in which to operate—one in which they have a total monopoly. Thunderous applause followed his statement: "If the evolutionist is right, why is he so worried about an opposing viewpoint?" He concluded by quoting the great English writer, G. K. Chesterton, as saying that the reason evolution is so controversial is that it has powerful ramifications in morals, ethics, and man's viewpoint regarding his fellow man.

Professor Chittick affirmed that both models should be presented in the public schools. His observation was that students appreciate being treated with enough respect to be allowed to make up their own minds on the matter of origins. He stated that not only were the foundations of good science laid by creationists, but that students learn better when challenged with the two-model approach. Studies have shown that in the two-model approach, students actually learn the concepts of evolution better than when they are taught evolution alone.

Cees Laban was the last speaker. Although he is an evolutionist, he openly advocated the two-model approach to origins. He confessed that evolution has many unsolved problems. To teach creationism is to make the students aware of those problems. He concluded by saying that he had learned in this debate that creationism is not as cut and dried as he had thought. Therefore, he expressed the hope that the schools would offer both models. There was much applause.

Although Laban's statement is a remarkable one for an evolutionist to make, he was far from alone in making it. At least 16 evolutionists stated publically in these debates that the scientific evidence for creation should be presented along with evolution. At least six of these 16 are actually doing that in courses which they are teaching on the university level.

In at least four of the debates, Gish asked for a show of hands from the audience as to how many people would prefer that both the creation model and the evolution model be taught in the public schools. In each case (Racine, Wisconsin; Des Moines Area Community College; University of Nebraska, Lincoln; and North Dakota State University, Fargo) the audience preferred the two-model approach by about 95 per cent. If science is really self-correcting, and if evolution is really true, then the best way for evolutionists to destroy creationism would be to allow it to be exposed to widespread scrutiny.

Several incidents took place in the Utrecht debate that are of interest. In Slusher's confrontation with Koppeschaar, he asked him how one gets the age of a star. Koppeschaar replied that it came from the concept of stellar evolution. When Slusher later asked him how one arrived at the concept of stellar evolution, he replied: "From the ages of the stars." This is just one of the many cases of circular reasoning that one finds in evolutionary thought. Koppeschaar apparently did not catch the flaw in his reasoning.

When Sluijser was asked if there was purpose in the physical universe, he replied, citing the second law: "Matter has the purpose of obtaining as much entropy as it can." In other words, the purpose of the universe is to run down and wear out as fast as it can. This is a new twist in the concept of purpose in the universe.

The most remarkable exchange came when Gish stated that the chance that amino acids would spontaneously form biologically active protein molecules was practically zero. In an attempt to discount the probability argument Gish had used, Sluijser said that if someone had asked him on the day of his birth to calculate the probability that on this day in Utrecht he would be having a debate with Dr. Gish from San Diego, that probability would also be practically zero. "Am I therefore to understand," he said, "that you are not Dr. Gish from San Diego?"

The reaction from the audience when Gish replied showed that they realized that Sluijser had made a crucial error in logic and had actually confirmed that random chance processes could not accomplish that which demands purposeful action by intelligent beings. Gish replied: "I am not here by chance. I was invited!"

This incident must have tremendously impressed Sluijser. Years later, he read in the British Journal, *Nature,* that Sir Fred Hoyle had said that for higher forms of life to have emerged by chance is comparable to the chance that a tornado sweeping through a junk yard will assemble a Boeing 747. Sluijser then wrote to *Nature* and told them about his probability exchange with Gish. His letter was printed in the January 21, 1982, issue.

Chapter 29

Toward "Truth" — Whatever That May Mean

University of Wisconsin

A dog was milling around the platform of the Stock Pavilion, known affectionately as Cow Palace, on the campus of the University of Wisconsin, Madison. I wondered what—if anything—should be done about him. As John T. Robinson began his defense of evolution against Duane Gish, on February 20, 1978, he welcomed the 3,300 who were expectantly gathered there. He also greeted the dog. The crowd was obviously partisan. No effort was made to determine the attitude of the dog.

Robinson, Professor of Zoology at Wisconsin, is one of the world's best-known evolutionary paleoanthropologists. He is a leading authority on the South African australopithecine fossils. Gish expected Robinson's research in this area to comprise a major part of his presentation. It seemed quite normal for a person to speak on the results of his own unique research when it was so directly related to the evolution of man. All of us were quite surprised—a bit of an understatement—when Robinson did not even allude to that material. Gish emphasized the work of Lord Zuckerman on the australopithecines. Zuckerman's fifteen years of research led him to the conclusion that the australopithecines did not walk upright and were not in the direct lineage of man. Even this did not draw Robinson out, though he sharply disagrees with

Zuckerman's interpretation. One can only speculate as to why Robinson did not respond—even in his rebuttal—on a subject in which he is acknowledged to be one of the world's leading authorities.

What Robinson did talk about was his conviction that special creation is not a legitimate scientific model, and that special creationists are not well-fitted to handle scientific matters. He quoted much from the writings of Henry Morris to show that Morris and Gish are strongly influenced by a literal interpretation of Genesis in the building of their model. This was not the issue. The issue was whether or not the scientific evidence is supportive of the model.

Next Robinson emphasized that the only authority allowed in science is that of well-documented facts. No person or book has any authority to dictate what a scientist must believe. In contrast to this, Robinson pointed out that Morris and Gish believe in the absolute inspiration and authority of the Bible—literally interpreted—in all matters. Robinson's conviction was that a person cannot function in a creationist framework according to the rules of science. No matter what the experiments show, he declared, a creationist is not allowed to believe anything that is inconsistent with the literal interpretation of the Bible. He is not free to follow where the facts lead, but can "believe only that which his inflexible authoritarian religious system allows him to believe."

Robinson gave the impression that creationists were unfit as scientists because of their belief in the authority of the Bible. The implication was that all qualified scientists believe in evolution and do not make appeals to authority. A study of these debates reveals that more than half of the evolutionists who debated Morris and Gish appealed to authority—usually the authority of the scientific establishment. Morris and Gish, however, never appealed to the Bible or cited Scripture in their debates except in some of their rebuttals. Even then it was only to respond to a slanderous attack on the Bible by an evolutionist opponent.

Robinson was a gentleman. He repeatedly emphasized that he was not being critical of either the Bible or of the religion held by Morris and Gish. He was speaking strictly to the nature of science. He stated that he wasn't even speaking as to which view was ultimately the better one—creation or evolution. He was only seeking to point out that a scientific case for creationism was not valid because Morris and Gish—and members of the Creation Research Society—were following a religious definition of what constitutes science. Further, their criteria for what constitutes science lay outside of science itself. As logical as Robinson's argument seems, it reveals an ignorance of the history of science. Before Darwin, science was based entirely upon creationist postulates and was very productive and fruitful. Hence, history demonstrates that Robinson's main argument in this debate is not valid.

Robinson seemed quite sincere in his conviction that creationism was not a valid scientific model. However, it was obvious that Robinson—together with most evolutionists—did not hear what creationists were saying. It's like the story Lemmon (Sacramento State debate) told about three hard-of-hearing men on an English train. As the train slowed down, the first man said, "Is this Wedley?"

"Oh," said the second man, "I thought this was Thursday."

"So am I," said the third man. "Let's get off and have a drink!"

There is no doubt that Morris and Gish believe in creation as taught by the literal interpretation of Genesis. However, what they and other creationists are saying is that if one considers the laws of thermodynamics, the laws of probability, and the evidence from the fossil record, one can build a creation model from the scientific evidence alone. The fact that this scientific model is compatible with Genesis is not at all surprising to Christians because the God Who wrote the Word is also the God Who created the world.

It is interesting that this idea of unity between the Word and the world is used with different conclusions by theistic evolutionists, such as Thomas H. Leith. Leith is a Christian and a member of the American Scientific Affiliation. He is Professor of the Philosophy of Science at York University, Toronto. In his debate with Gish in November, 1974, Leith developed his case for evolution using alleged evidence for an old earth and a repugnance for the concept of apparent age. He ignored the probability arguments against an evolutionary origin of life. By assuming evolution to be the way God brought the universe and life into being, Leith then reasoned that there should be compatibility between the scientific study of the world and our interpretation of Genesis. Genesis, therefore, should be understood as allowing for evolution so that there might be agreement between the Word and the world.

Robinson accused creationists of presenting the creation-evolution issue as one in which there were just two options. Either one believed in a literal six-day creation or one believed in an atheistic materialistic view of evolution. Robinson protested that these were not the only two options. Although Robinson believes evolution to be a fact, he said: "I do not accept an atheistic, materialistic point of view of the universe."

Robinson maintained that evolution is strictly a biological theory. It is entirely neutral as far as any philosophical or theological concepts are concerned. He said that atheism and materialism are not scientific viewpoints. They are philosophical viewpoints. They may incorporate into their system what science knows about evolution, but they go well beyond science into metaphysics.

Here again is the separation between "mechanism" and "meaning" advocated by Schweitzer, Albert, and Hespenheide. In spite of what they say, there does seem to be a relationship between "mechanism" and "meaning." For instance, it is hard to imagine a creationist who is an atheist. The two terms seem mutually contradictory. On the other hand, it would be difficult to find an atheist who is not an evolutionist of some sort. One can find creationists who later accepted evolution as a way of harmonizing the Bible with their view of science—Albert and Hespenheide would be examples of this. However, it is far easier to find teen-aged creationists who have had their Christian faith entirely destroyed by evolutionary theory. Their number is legion. In contrast to this, it would be very difficult to find someone who was brought to God or Christ as a result of evolutionary theory.

What this means is that there are powerful latent implications in evolutionary theory that point toward naturalism, atheism, and a mechanistic view of nature. The idea that evolution is just a neutral, innocent scientific theory seems to be held only by certain types of Christians—those who were Christians before they became evolutionists and have accepted evolution in order to reconcile their Christian faith with the contemporary world view.

In seeking to separate the "scientific" theory of evolution from the atheistic philosophy of evolution, Robinson's own words were used against him. Gish had quoted Huxley and Simpson. Robinson claimed that the atheistic views of Huxley and Simpson had nothing to do with their science. However, Robinson claimed that creationists cannot be objective scientists because of their creationist views. He did not explain why creationist views prejudice a scientist, but atheistic views do not. In his rebuttal, Gish quoted from one of Robinson's books (*Early Hominid Posture and Locomotion*) as follows: "The conceptual framework within which a student works shapes the viewpoint from which he approaches the material being studied and powerfully influences the conclusions that he draws." Robinson writes far deeper truth than he speaks.

A chance remark by Robinson revealed one of the basic flaws in the contemporary philosophy of science. All scientists agree that the goal of science is to gain an understanding of the natural world. Although admitting that science contains errors, Robinson stressed the self-correcting nature of science. He stated that science "proceeds by a method which uncovers its own errors, and therefore tends always to produce a closer and closer approximation to 'truth'." He then added, almost under his breath, the little phrase, "Whatever that may mean."

Here is the enigma which science faces. It is striving to arrive at "truth." Scientists are humble enough to state that science will never arrive. They thus claim that they are searching for "relative truth." But, as these debates have aptly demonstrated, those same scientists have shown an aversion bordering on hatred for the idea of "absolute truth." The main reason for their rejection of the Biblical message and their desire to remove it from all areas of science is because of its claim to absolute truth.

Although science rejects the concept of absolute truth, it believes that it is capable of finding relative truth. Yet, one looks in vain in the philosophy or the methodology of science for a definition of "truth." The closest they come is the idea that a theory is "true" in some sense if it fits or explains all the facts. But they never know for sure that they have discovered all the facts. It is also possible that two different theories could both fit the known facts equally well. Which one then is "true?"

Science is thus in the unenviable position of searching for something that it has never defined. How, then, does it know in which direction to go? How does it know then it has arrived? There seems to be the unwritten assumption in science that when it discovers truth, it will be able to recognize it. In other words, that truth will be self-evident. But isn't this in itself a subtle testimony to the fact that some absolute Being or standard has created both the universe and the mind of man? Isn't science saying that at the bottom line there is Truth or unity or rationality? Even though the scientific community believes in a universe allegedly produced by random evolutionary processes, in its search for truth it seems to be saying: "We really know better." Perhaps this is what Romans One means when it says that man is without excuse. However, until the individual scientist recognizes the One who is The Truth, he will say as Robinson did of "truth," "Whatever that may mean!"

Chapter 30

I Give Up!
Racine, Wisconsin

The 1,000-seat Memorial Hall on the shore of Lake Michigan in downtown Racine, Wisconsin, was filled to capacity on Monday, May 1, 1978, for the creation-evolution debate between Duane Gish and Vincent T. D'Orazio. D'Orazio is an industrial chemist in Racine and has been in active opposition to the teaching of the creation model along with the evolution model in the Racine Public Schools.

It is difficult to remember a debate in which less positive evidence for evolution was presented than was presented by D'Orazio. Instead, he devoted almost all of his time to challenging the credentials and the integrity of creationist scientists, as well as the quality of their work. Not only did Gish comment on the lack of scientific evidence presented by D'Orazio, but one of the questions from the audience during the question period was directed to D'Orazio asking him why he chose to handle his portion of the debate in that fashion.

It is a well-known axiom in debate that if you feel that you have a strong case, you should build it; if you feel your case is weak, it is better to attack the opposition relentlessly while ignoring your own position. One thus hopes to gain victory by revealing the weaknesses of the opposing position rather than by systematically building a positive case for your own position. Since the question to be debated was: "Does scientific evidence adequately support the theory of evolution?", D'Orazio's reason for using this technique remains a mystery. Yet, his failure to present rigorous evidence for evolution did not go unnoticed by the audience.

Gish began his initial presentation by stating that evolution contradicts well-established natural laws, whereas these laws are in accord with the concepts of special creation. He defined the evolution model and the creation model and cited the logical expectations or predictions based upon each one. The evolution model would predict that the matter-energy of the universe would be conserved, but also that it would be integrated into more complex forms as time progresses. The creation model would likewise predict the conservation of the matter-energy of the universe. However, since creation implies a Creator, and this Creator would have created the universe in a perfect condition, any change in the initial condition would be a degenerative or downward change rather than an integrative change. Thus, the second law of thermodynamics is strongly supportive of the creation position.

Since mutations are random and, according to probability theory, cannot account for the complexity we see in the universe, Gish then pointed out that natural selection is raised to the status of a deity by evolutionists. According to current concepts of evolution, it is natural selection which takes the raw material of mutations and utilizes them in creating all of the design and order and complexity we see in the biological world. Since natural selection does all that the Scriptures state that God did, natural selection thus becomes the god of evolution. It literally takes that which is impossible and makes it certain. Evolution is thus not without its own miracles of faith. In this sense it is fully as religious as is creation.

Gish's third area of emphasis was the fossil record. He demonstrated that the history of life gives no evidence that the transformation from one kind of plant or animal to another kind of plant or animal of higher complexity has taken place. Instead, complex living things appear abruptly without ancestors or transitions.

After giving a very brief statement as to how science operates, D'Orazio used almost the entire time in his initial presentation to challenge the work of creationist scientists. Citing recent articles in the ICR "Impact Series," he claimed that Henry Morris had misquoted thermodynamicist Ilya Prigogine and that Gish had misquoted geologists Stephen Jay Gould and Steven M. Stanley. D'Orazio cited letters from each of these men to the effect that they had been misquoted. This was a rather unusual procedure, for it is hardly necessary to write to a man to ask him if a written statement of his had been taken out of context. All one need do is to study the original work cited and then make a determination as to whether or not the quotation taken from it is used accurately. Nor is it surprising that evolutionists would claim to be misquoted when their statements are turned against their own position. In all of this, D'Orazio did not actually demonstrate that these men had indeed been misquoted.

Using as his source an article by Gish ("A Decade of Creationist Research," *Creation Research Society Quarterly,* Vol. 12, June 1975), D'Orazio then questioned the quality of work done by geologist Clifford Burdick regarding the Grand Canyon pollen fossils, the work of physicist Thomas Barnes regarding the decay of the earth's magnetic field, and the legitimacy of human footprints found *in situ* with dinosaur footprints in the Cretaceous deposits of the Paluxy River, Glen Rose, Texas. He further challenged the accuracy of the film, "Footprints in Stone," produced by Stanley Taylor. Creationists who are familiar with these research projects detected many errors in D'Orazio's statements.

D'Orazio claimed that he had spent time with Dr. Aureal T. Cross, a distinguished palynologist from Michigan State University. Going over Burdick's work, Cross concluded that the fossil pollen grains of gymnosperms (conifers) and angiosperms (flowering plants) that were found in the Precambrian Hakatai Shale of the Grand Canyon were actually contamination from present-day plants, that the work was very sloppy, and that many of them were mislabeled. However, anyone who is familiar with Burdick's work knows that all of the pollen grains found in the rocks at the very bottom of the Grand Canyon were of extinct species—which would rule out entirely the possibility of contamination by present-day forms and might also account for Cross' thinking that many of them were mislabeled. D'Orazio did not mention that similar finds have been discovered elsewhere by evolutionists since the 1950's and reported in—of all places— the journal, *Evolution.*

D'Orazio made many references to the work of Prigogine, claiming that Prigogine had been awarded the 1977 Nobel Prize in chemistry for having solved the problem of how evolution can take place in spite of the second law of thermodynamics. At one point, he held up a thick file which he said contained Prigogine's articles on the subject. Yet, D'Orazio never explained what Prigogine proposed or how the contradiction between the second law and evolution had been resolved. One had the haunting feeling that D'Orazio, himself, did not understand it and that his continued references to Prigogine were more rhetoric than substance. Later on, Gish clarified the fact that Prigogine had not solved the problem of evolution vs. the second law, but had just worked on the problem, and that he was given the Nobel Prize for " . . . his contributions to nonequilibrium thermodynamics, particularly the theory of dissipative structures" (*Science* 198:716).

It was only at the very end of his hour-long statement that D'Orazio introduced some positive "evidence" for evolution. He attempted to deal with the gaps in the fossil record which most evolutionists themselves recognize as very real. He cited the famous horse series and then referred to transitions between reptiles and man, especially dealing with the jaw hinge and the palate. In this sense he abused the term "transitional form," for neither evolutionists nor creationists use the term to span such a wide gap as that between reptiles and man. His illustrations were theoretical rather than actual.

He closed his presentation by claiming that *Archaeopteryx* was actually a feathered reptile. Apparently, what D'Orazio was attempting to do in making *Archaeopteryx* a feathered dinosaur was to claim that both dinosaurs and birds had feathers and in this way establish an evolutionary link between the two. Of course, there is not a shred of fossil evidence to support this contention.

In the rebuttal period, after defending the credibility of creationist scientists and his own use of quotations, Gish dealt with the work of Prigogine and the second law of thermodynamics. Gish pointed out that Prigogine's solution was strictly a theoretical, mathematical model that could not and did not work in the real world. It was in essence a "bull in a china shop" proposition where Priogogine suggested that if a system had enough disorder and was far enough away from equilibrium, there was the possibility of some order emerging. However, this explanation has yet to be demonstrated in the real world and could in no wise explain the origin of life from nonlife.

   D'Orazio, in his first rebuttal, chided creationists for not publishing their findings in established scientific journals. D'Orazio exhibited a very naive attitude toward the scientific community when he said that one could literally get anything published if one had the facts to support his conclusions—even that the moon was made of green cheese. Creationists know that there is a massive evolutionary establishment that seeks to suppress all creationist research and publication. Gish gave several illustrations of this in response to D'Orazio's claim that if creationist research were respectable, the scientific journals would publish it. D'Orazio then concluded his first rebuttal by asking Gish if he would accept evolution if the facts, without equivocation, supported it. Gish replied that as a scientist he would accept the facts and follow them where they led.

   Gish, in his second rebuttal, directed a question to the audience. Since D'Orazio had been so opposed to the teaching of the creation model in addition to the evolution model in the Racine Public Schools, Gish asked the audience how many would like to continue the practice of having only the evolution model taught in the public schools. Approximately 12 people in an audience of 1,000 raised their hands. Gish then asked the audience how many of them would like to have both the evolution model and the creation model taught with full discussion, such as was being demonstrated that evening. Virtually everyone raised their hands. The effect was clearly impressed upon D'Orazio.

   Gish then turned to D'Orazio and issued a challenge to him. He said, "Dr. D'Orazio, if you have read Prigogine's works and if you feel he has solved the problem of evolution vs. the second law, would you please explain to this audience exactly what Prigogine has proposed?" D'Orazio evaded the issue, stating that Gish's time was up and that it was necessary for him (D'Orazio) to make a concluding statement. Gish then offered D'Orazio as much time as he needed. D'Orazio continued to evade, saying that Gish was merely trying to keep him from making a concluding statement. Gish then responded by saying, "I am prepared to explain Prigogine's work in five minutes—are you?" D'Orazio persisted in saying that he had to make a concluding state-ment, but that he would explain Prigogine's work later. The "later" never came. Whether D'Orazio was able to explain Prigogine's work we will never know. The effect on the audience, however, was that D'Orazio did not really understand as much about the second law of thermodynamics and Prigogine's alleged solution as he claimed he did. From a strategic point of view, it would have been far better for D'Orazio had he at least attempted to answer Gish's challenge.

D'Orazio concluded his second rebuttal by stating that he was against creation being taught in the public schools only because creationism was poor science. He then went on to state that there was no problem in discerning scientific truth. All one had to do was to consult the experts in any given field and they would give one that truth. The session concluded with Gish asking D'Orazio if he believed that the universe was an isolated system. D'Orazio responded that he did. Gish then asked him if he believed that this isolated system was ordered without God and contrary to the second law. D'Orazio refused to answer the question on the grounds that they had previously agreed to rule out anything religious in the debate. Gish responded that when one deals with origins, one is outside of science and is in the area of religion.

Twice in July 1979, D'Orazio debated Gish again, once in Fort Wayne, Indiana, and once at North Central College, Naperville, Illinois. The North Central debate was specifically on thermodynamics and its relationship to evolution. The attendance of 100, the smallest attendance of any of the debates, was limited to scientists and educators with a background in that field. In contrast to his first one, D'Orazio had very little criticism of creationist scientists in these two debates.

As would be expected, thermodynamics loomed large. Attempting to show that natural processes can give rise to increasing organization and complexity, D'Orazio cited sun spots and tornadoes as evidence. He also claimed that the sun will experience a tremendous increase in organization before it dies. How he could be so sure of this he did not say.

D'Orazio again brought up the work of Prigogine. He seemed shocked when Gish claimed that he knew more about biochemistry than does Prigogine. Although D'Orazio took it as a very audacious statement, Gish is a Ph.D. in biochemistry, and Prigogine is not a biochemist. It would be rather strange if Gish didn't know more about biochemistry than Prigogine.

The Fort Wayne debate was held in a church. As he began his presentation, D'Orazio asked the audience how many of them believed in creation. Apparently, almost every hand went up. Somewhat taken aback, D'Orazio laughingly said: "I give up!"

But he didn't. He made it known that he was open and available any time and anywhere to debate creationists. Have briefcase—will travel!

Chapter 31

All in the Family

Wheaton College

The confrontation at Wheaton College, Wheaton, Illinois, on May 2, 1978, was different. Whereas the other debates were on the creation-evolution issue, the Wheaton panel addressed a problem within creationism regarding the age of the earth and its Biblical implications. A similar "family" discussion was held on the Wheaton campus in 1974 on the topic of flood geology.

Discussing the subject, "Does a Proper Interpretation of Scripture Require a Recent Creation?", were Duane Gish, Marvin L. Lubenow (the author), Walter C. Kaiser, Jr., and David L. Willis. The author is the Senior Pastor of The First Baptist Church, Fort Collins, Colorado. Kaiser, one of the nation's distinguished Old Testament scholars, is Professor of Old Testament at Trinity Evangelical Divinity School. Willis is Chairman of the Department of General Science, Oregon State University, Corvallis. Gish and Lubenow represented the literal six-day creation position, while Kaiser and Willis opted for long periods of time in the Genesis account.

At issue was the interpretation and meaning of Genesis 1-2, especially involving the question of how much time the Biblical text would allow. The truthfulness, verbal inspiration, and the authority of the Bible were not at issue, as all of the panelists stated that they held to these doctrines. The purpose of the panel was to discover the doctrinal and theological implications of the alternate views of the Genesis text— especially as far as the time issue is concerned.

Gish began by stating that whatever position one takes regarding the age of the earth, it must be properly fitted into

the Biblical record of earth history as set forth in Genesis
1-11, including the events of creation, the fall, the flood, the
dispersion at Babel, and the genealogies of Genesis 5 and 11.
Gish said that attempts to reconcile Genesis with the
geological column lead to numerous contradictions, even if
one rejects evolution.

Some of the questions Gish insisted must be answered are
as follows. If the rock strata constitute the record of hundreds
of millions of years, where is the record of the Biblical Flood?
If man is several million years old, why was it that post-flood
man developed agriculture and animal husbandry only a few
thousand years ago when, according to Genesis, these skills
were known from the very beginning? Further, why did it take
so long to generate the population explosion when studies
show that a population increase of one-fourth the present rate
will generate our present population in just 5,000 years?
Another concern is whether the genealogies of Genesis 5 and
11 will allow time gaps involving millions of years. Gish concluded by questioning the wisdom of sacrificing the Biblical
record of earth history to accommodate a naturalistic time-
scale, which is actually an evolutionary time-scale—though it
is held by many evangelicals who would deny evolution.

Kaiser emphasized that although there can be only one true
meaning of Scripture, our interpretations are many. On the
one hand, he called for evangelicals to do their homework in
the text and to dedicate themselves anew to inductive,
exegetical study of the details of God's Word. Yet, six times
during the course of the evening he insisted that we cannot
arrive at conclusive knowledge regarding the time element of
Genesis 1. Our interpretations are just that—interpretations by
sinful fallible people. He urged humility and respect for those
with differing views on creation.

He then made reference to an essay by R. John Snow.
Snow argues that all of the events recorded in Genesis 1 and 2
which transpire on Day Six are simply too time-consuming to
have happened in one 24-hour period. This, he feels, constitutes internal evidence that these days were not to be taken
literally.

Kaiser felt that Genesis 1-11 showed tremendous com-
pression of time and of sequence that is incompatible with the
literal position. He stressed the gaps in the chronologies of

Genesis 5 and 11, but was not prepared to state how much time Genesis 1-11 would allow. The important message was that God had created, He had done it "In the beginning," and it was done by the Word of God.

In my own presentation, I stated that the determination of the time element in Genesis 1 depended upon the nature of creation and the length of the days. I stated that the term, "evening and morning," used once for each of the six days in Genesis 1, reflects the normal Hebrew reference to a literal day which, for the Jews, began at sundown. Recognizing that both the term "day" and the parts of a day, "morning and evening," can legitimately be used for a long period of time (Genesis 2:4; Psalm 90:4-5), I pointed out that when these terms are used in other than their literal meaning, the context gives ample evidence of that usage. Comparing Genesis 1 with Psalm 90:4-5, both probably written by Moses, I demonstrated that the same Hebrews who used the expression, "evening and morning," when referring to a literal day reverted to the usage "morning and evening," when speaking figuratively of a period of time. Thus, the phrase "evening and morning" constitutes powerful evidence that literal days are intended in Genesis 1.

The meaning is made doubly clear by linking the days of creation week to our normal week of work and rest (Exodus 20:9-11). I expressed the belief that the confusion over the time problem in Genesis 1 was not so much the result of ambiguity in the text as it was the result of pressure and intimidation by the scientific community.

In what proved to be one of the more controversial issues of the evening, I stated that Biblical creationism involves two elements: (1) instantaneousness or suddenness—a massive acceleration of time over normal processes; and (2) a massive increase in complexity. Even when God starts with something, such as starting with dust to make man, or starting with water to make wine, this vast increase in complexity is characteristic of Biblical creationism.

Relating creation to the miraculous rather than to the natural, I illustrated the point from the miracles of our Lord in the Gospels. All 35 of the miracles of our Lord show evidence of being very sudden, and many of them are declared to be so. Many of them are also miracles of creation. One of these miracles of creation was the turning of water into wine (John 2:1-11).

The fact that our Lord started with water should not detract from the fact that it was a genuine miracle of creation. Our Lord took H_2O and turned it into $C_6H_{12}O_6$ (fructose, the sugar found in wine), as well as the many other products found in wine. There was not only the direct creation of billions of carbon atoms, but also the arranging of all of these atoms into the highly complex molecules in wine. None can deny that it was sudden.

Referring to Genesis 1:1, I stated that the original creation had to be instantaneous with a tremendous increase in complexity. One might argue as to whether God started with nothing and created something relatively simple or whether He started with nothing and created something quite complex. However, when one starts with nothing, in either case, the order of magnitude for the increase in complexity would be staggering. Further, it had to be instantaneous. One cannot go from nothing to something by degrees.

The miracles of the feeding of the 4,000 and of the 5,000 involving the instantaneous creation of both animal and plant material certainly casts light on the creation of the animals and plants in Days Three, Five, and Six of Genesis 1. Although Genesis 1 does not explicitly state that Adam was created suddenly, Christ's raising of Lazarus (John 11) illustrates this matter also. Because the decay process involves the breakdown of complex biological compounds into simple ones, every cell in the body of Lazarus had to be recreated and restored to its original complexity. That it also was sudden none can deny.

Perhaps the most remarkable analog to the original creation of Adam "of the dust of the ground" is the resurrection of the bodies of believers at the return of the Lord. Here God will literally recreate their bodies from the "dust" of decay, and the Scriptures state that it will be "in a moment, in the twinkling of an eye" (I Cor. 15:52). The future resurrection of believers is an almost "instant replay" of the creation of Adam. It remains for those who disapprove of instantaneous creation to demonstrate even one Biblical miracle or act of creation that involves a long process of time.

I concluded by stating that time is not philosophically

neutral. It is the one common denominator of all evolutionary systems and, in the form of philosophic gradualism, is the essence of almost all non-Christian religions. Further, there is hardly a Biblical miracle that could not be destroyed or compromised by injecting time into it.

There is a direct relationship between the amount of time one can insert into a miracle and the difficulty one would have in demonstrating to others that it was a miracle at all. There comes a point at which, if enough time is inserted into the miracle, it becomes possible to explain it by normal processes, and the miracle is totally destroyed. To inject even 24 hours into the miracle of the stilling of the waters of the Sea of Galilee would enable one to say that a low pressure cell moved off the scene and a fair weather high pressure system moved in to take its place. To inject even a few days into many of our Lord's healings would enable one to argue that the person recovered naturally or normally without miraculous intervention.

If the purpose of a miracle is for God to demonstrate something to man, *time is everything.* Finally, I called upon evangelicals to understand what time can do the miraculous elements of the Bible and suggested that the doctrine of creation, with its apologetic value, is compromised by injecting vast quantities of time into the creation account.

Willis, in his presentation, stressed our need to learn from the history of the Bible-science controversy. While the text of Scripture has remained constant, interpretations have changed greatly. He stated that all of us hold positions that would have been considered heretical in the past. He cited the heliocentric system of Copernicus as opposed to the older geocentric system of Ptolemy, and the conflict involving the church—both Catholic and Protestant—at the time of Galileo. Such texts as Psalm 93:1 ("The world also is stablished, that it cannot be moved") were used to give Biblical support to the Ptolemaic system. Willis expressed concern that evangelicals today not fix themselves upon a certain interpretation of Genesis 1 and, in their rejection of the ideas of modern scientists, find themselves as foolish from history's standpoint as those who fought Galileo.

The issue introduced by Willis is one which evangelicals must squarely face. It concerns the degree of authority scientific findings should be accorded in the interpretation of Scripture. It is essentially a hermeneutical problem. However, there has been a great deal of confusion because the crux of the problem has not always been well-defined. There is no Bible-science conflict if one regards the domain of science to be the investigation of present-day phenomena. Although some evangelicals have not recognized this fact, the Bible-science controversy is limited to the interpretation of the *past*. It is really a conflict between the generally accepted "scientific" interpretation of earth history as opposed to the Biblical record of earth history.

In the rebuttal, Willis' use of the illustration of Galileo was challenged by Gish. Gish declared that the incident of Galileo has been totally misunderstood. It is normally presented as a case where the Bible and the church obstructed science because of dogmatism. However, Ptolemy was a Greek, not a Jew or a Christian. His geocentric system was not based upon Biblical teaching or evidence. His system became the scientific dogma of the establishment of that day. When Copernicus and Galileo suggested that the geocentric system was wrong, they found themselves fighting the establishment. The establishment then used the Bible and the church to exert pressure upon Galileo to renounce his scientific beliefs. The geocentric theory was not based upon the Bible. Christians had allowed the Bible to be accommodated to the current dogma in science. Gish concluded: "Is that what we are trying to do today—trying to fit the Bible to a worldly scheme of things?"

After Willis' reference to Galileo, he then proceeded to demonstrate that the Hebrew word for "day" does occasionally refer to a period of time (Genesis 2:4). Actually, no creationist questions that occasional usage (always so indicated by the context), and I had previously stated it. Willis seemed to share the attitude of some evangelicals that because "day" does occasionally refer to a period of time, that meaning can then be injected into Genesis 1 without any attempt to justify that usage by the text or the context.

Willis appealed to evangelicals to "hang loose" in their interpretation of Genesis 1. He quoted several orthodox theologians to the effect that the days in Genesis 1 can be long periods of time. Actually, there is an error in logic here.

The ability to quote a few orthodox theologians who agree with a position does not prove that this is the teaching of Scripture. Willis felt that the reason there are divergent viewpoints on creation is that the issues are not settled or settleable on the basis of our current knowledge. Since the Scriptural revelation is complete, he apparently had reference to the ability of science to cast light upon Genesis 1 and the concept of creation.

The question of the relative priority of science vs. Scripture and whether or not science is able to cast light on creation was highlighted in what was the most dramatic moment of the evening. Gish was commenting on the very cavalier manner in which the words "creation" and "creationist" are used by people who mean something quite different from the traditional meaning of those words. In an effort to clarify what the members of the panel meant by those words (for all had described themselves as creationists), Gish turned to Willis and said: "Dr. Willis, the Bible says that God took the bone and flesh of Adam's side and made woman. Do you believe that is literally what God did in the creation of woman, or would you entertain the possibility that this term 'creation' might allow the evolution of man and woman from some lower creature?"

Although Kaiser had previously stated that the Genesis record clearly demands that Adam had not been alive or in existence at all until he was created by God as man, Willis responded to Gish's question as follows: "I would not have a specific answer for you, Duane, in this regard. I think it's clear to everyone that there is considerable difficulty with the scientific record to take the literal view of the creation of Eve as the Scripture gives it. I'm willing to take it. The question I would have is: 'Is it required?' "

Gish then responded: "How do you make that decision, Dr. Willis? Are you basing your decision on what the Scriptures say or what the world has to say—the current dogma in science?"

Willis responded, but did not really answer Gish's question. The truth is that there is no answer to Gish's question until one first settles the question of which source of information regarding creation will be given the higher priority—science or Scripture. As is obvious from many of their writings, this represents an unsolved problem among progressive creationists. Willis later clarified his position on the creation of Eve by saying: "I believe what the Scripture says. I don't understand it."

The question of whether or not science can cast light on creation reflects yet another problem. If creation is still going on, as all theistic evolutionists and some progressive creationists believe, then the distinctions between creation and providence, the supernatural and the natural, become obliterated. If creation has ceased, as Genesis 2:4 indicates, then one cannot use science to cast light on past supernatural acts of creation. Here, of all places, Scripture must have the highest priority and it *alone* must be the final authority.

Often those who believe that Genesis 1 involves a long period of time seek to make creation—at least certain phases of it—a process rather than a sudden event or series of events. It should be realized that in the account of some miracles, the time element is left out. In other cases, there may have been a period of time between the announcement of the miracle and the moment when it took place, but it was sudden—not a process—when it did take place. I then emphasized that suddenness was not only characteristic of Biblical miracles— including creation—but it was the very essence of the apologetic element. It was that which largely separated the miraculous from the natural—and creation from providence. Kaiser declared: "I think there is the whole essence of our problem—the definition of miracle as being in every case a sudden, instantaneous interruption into the natural order."

Kaiser then referred to *miracle* as a divine intervention of a higher natural law rather than an instantaneous intervention of an entirely different category. To illustrate, he cited the plagues of Egypt (Exodus 7-12). He referred to their "seasonal pattern" and stated that these plagues were a combination of direct intervention and the normal forces of nature.

Yet, even a casual reading of the text reveals that all of the plagues were direct divine interventions totally beyond anything having to do with the seasonal pattern. There is simply nothing "natural" about them. Further, all of them were very sudden—many of them happening when Moses or Aaron lifted their staffs in the air, prayed, or struck the water. Five of them, including the three days of darkness, happened in

Egypt, but not in the land of Goshen nearby where the
Israelites lived. Several of them are of such severity as to be
beyond anything that had ever happened in the whole history
of the land. One looks in vain for anything "natural" or
"seasonal." They are declared to be signs to show God's
power and judgment. It is for this reason that they had to go
beyond the natural and the seasonal.

The appeal to Snow's argument that there was not enough
time in a 24-hour day to accomplish all the things mentioned
on Day Six, although innovative, is questionable at best. It is
based on faulty logic. Snow assumes that because there would
not be time enough today, according to present-day processes,
to accomplish these things, that there would not be enough
time for God to accomplish them on Day Six of creation week
either. This is extrapolation with a vengeance! Other than the
details given in Genesis 1-2, there is only one thing we know
about conditions during creation week, and that is that they
were quite different from what they are today. The absence of
sin and the curse would guarantee that fact. A reading of
Snow's article reveals that it is largely wishful thinking rather
than solid exegetical evidence. It requires far more omniscience than I suspect Mr. Snow has to state categorically that
24 hours is not enough time for the things to take place that
God says took place on Day Six.

Considering its divisive nature among evangelicals and the
importance of other doctrines of Scripture, Willis suggested
that there may be too much emphasis on creation. His words
were: "The aspect of creation, for example, is covered in two
chapters in the book of Genesis. Twelve chapters alone are
devoted to the life of Abraham and other individuals and
their walk with God. I think we may be over-emphasizing the
importance of creation." Actually, as I pointed out, this is far
from the truth. One of the three major themes of the Book of
Psalms is the doctrine of creation. When one assembles all of
the passages on the subject in both the Old and New
Testaments, the total amount is staggering. If one is judging
on the basis of sheer bulk or volume alone, it can be
questioned if any doctrine—other than the doctrine of salvation—is given more extensive coverage than the doctrine of
creation.

Willis also questioned whether the purpose of God was to

give us "a detailed, point-by-point, blow-by-blow description of how God brought things into existence." He suggests that the purpose of God was not to give all of the details of creation to a scientifically inclined age, but that instead the purpose was primarily "religious" in setting forth the Creator-God as a deterrent against the very common Old Testament problem or idolatry. While it may not have been Willis' motivation, this ploy of making the purpose of Genesis 1 basically "religious" is often used by those who would prefer not to deal with the historical accuracy of that chapter. When one considers all of the things that must have taken place in creation, it is obvious that there are a great many details left out. The question is not whether or not God intended to give us all of the details of creation. Obviously, He did not. The real question is how historically accurate are the details that are given. The fact that Genesis is "pre-scientific" does not alter the question. Nor need the fact that Genesis 1 is a document of exquisite beauty from a literary point of view detract from its historical nature. We would expect the God of creation to be able to combine literary beauty with historical accuracy.

The topic for the evening was: "Does a proper interpretation of Scripture require a recent creation?" Gish and I argued fervently for a literal six-day creation. Kaiser and Willis argued eloquently for a longer span of time in Genesis. Kaiser mentioned a total of at least 3,100 years in the gaps in Genesis 5 and 11. Actually, we could grant Kaiser all of that (I am inclined to do so, anyway) and even grant him (for the sake of argument) that each creative day was a thousand years in duration. That would still make him a recent creationist, for it would add only about 9,000 years to the date of creation.

The issue today is not "Does Genesis 1 refer to six literal days or would it allow for thousands of years?" The main reason one would opt for more time in Genesis 1 is to some-how make it compatible with contemporary scientific thinking. Presently, these demands are 4.5 billion years for the age of the earth and upward of 20 billion years (and counting) for the age of the universe. Anything less than that simply will not do. The real issue is: "Does Genesis allow for that kind of time?" One gets the impression that some of those who advocate a degree of time in Genesis 1 feel that if they can just establish the fact that the days in Genesis were not literal, they then have the license to dump all the time necessary into Genesis 1 to make it fit contemporary scientific thinking. One cannot help but question the ethics of using quotations from Augustine and Luther—who thought in terms of thousands of years at the most—as an excuse for dumping billions of years into the text of Genesis 1.

I warned that while progressive creationists claim to hold to Biblical inerrancy in doctrine, some of them (in their writings) have come perilously close to denying it in actual practice. I feel that evangelicals must decide how far the Scriptures can be accommodated to the time demands of the modern scientific establishment before the very concept of Biblical inerrancy is violated.

The issues are real, and they are vital. Evangelicals are divided, not because of personalities or organizations, but because of the legitimacy of the issues in Genesis. Nonetheless, it is an issue that is "all in the family."

Chapter 32

In the Image of A Chimp

North Dakota State University

Vincent Sarich has a better idea. He recognized that many of the alleged evidences for evolution can be a problem— especially the fossil record. Regarding human evolution, he confessed that if you deal only with the fossil evidence for man and the other primates, "you are in a lot of trouble."

With his extensive background in both chemistry and anthropology, Sarich helped to pioneer what he feels is a new category of evidence for evolution. It is said to confirm the evidence upon which evolution was first developed—anatomical similarities and their supposed evolutionary relationships. This new evidence is based upon comparisons of the DNA, proteins, and other molecules of life. It is called molecular taxonomy.

Sarich, who is Professor of Anthropology at the University of California, Berkeley, has debated Gish four times. The first debate was in a high school auditorium in Morgan Hill (San Jose), California, on November 9, 1978. Some months later, on April 28, 1979, I was one of the 1,500 in attendance at his debate at North Dakota State University, Fargo. One month later, Gish and Sarich met again. This time it was at De Anza College, Cupertino, California. There were 1,600 who witnessed that exchange. The last debate was televised in Kansas City, Kansas, on March 7, 1980, for nationwide showing on *The 700 Club, The PTL Club,* and other Christian programs.

In each of these debates, Sarich first gave a statement on
the philosophy and methodology of science. He called science
sort of a game. "We have a faith game and a science game."
He was far more honest than many of his fellows, for he
admitted that science is itself a new kind of faith. It is a faith
in which man believes he can gain a greater understanding of
the world around him. Sarich pleaded guilty to being a
humanist—believing that the mind of man alone is sufficient
to make sense out of the world. He confessed that a faith that
is rooted in our fallible selves is more difficult to maintain
than faith in an Infallible Being because "we know how dumb
we are."

Sarich felt that science is a superior faith because it is self-
correcting and self-testing. Other faiths do not have this self-
correcting mechanism built into them. They are dogmatic.
People doing science can be dogmatic, he recognized, but if
they are, it is because they have forgotten what science is all
about. It is a never-ending search for answers. "The game of
getting to the answer is a lot more interesting and more
exciting than the answer itself," he said, adding that he was
interested only in the big questions. He would leave the little
questions to others.

Although science, according to Sarich, is not dogmatic,
there was no doubt in his mind that evolution was a fact. The
similarities of life molecules demonstrated this organic relationship. The minor dissimilarities in the molecules are the
result of mutations.

Utilizing these minor dissimilarities, one can develop a tree
of relationships. The molecules, maintained Sarich, are the
best way to do this. We can measure the differences in quanti-
tative and reportable terms—which is impossible with other
types of evidence for evolution. We can then generate a scale
of similarities and differences that apply to all forms of life.
Thus, one is able to reconstruct the evolutionary history of
life.

Gish challenged Sarich right across the board. First, he gave
numerous examples where the molecular data was inconsistent
with any possible evolutionary relationship. In other words,
this method of determining evolutionary relationships works
only with certain data. One must be very selective. If
evolution were true, we would expect all of the data to

conform to some degree. Much of it does not conform at all.

Further, although Sarich had stated that the molecular data was an independent confirmation of evolution, Gish showed that it is no such thing. Originally evolution was developed on the basis of comparative anatomy. However, the genes code for the proteins of the body and its anatomy. Thus, the molecules are very closely linked with comparative anatomy and are not independent of it at all. It is really just the argument from homology on the molecular level. That argument has been shown by Sir Gavin deBeer to be faulty.

Gish went on to show that the molecular evidence is at best circumstantial. It does not prove evolution. Instead, it assumes evolution to be true. There is another explanation for the molecular data that is as satisfying—that is that a Divine Creator created both the similarities and the differences. Gish put it this way. If the Creator, being a good engineer and biochemist, had worked out the best metabolic process in the conversion of sugar to carbon dioxide and water, with the attendant release of energy, why wouldn't He use it in all of the animals? The animals and man live on the same planet, breathe the same air, drink the same water, and eat the same types of food. It would be normal for the Creator to work out the best process for metabolism and then use it—with minor variations—in all of His creatures. Why does the evolutionist insist that a Creator incorporate a totally different and unique process for each type of animal?

Sarich was quick to admit that many paleontologists and anthropologists did not accept his data because it conflicted with the time scale worked out from the geological record. However, he felt that his data was more accurate than the fossil record. In fact, when dealing with hominid evolution (man and his ancestors), there was so little primate fossil data with which to work that the molecular data was the only way a satisfactory account of human evolution could be achieved.

The chimpanzee is man's closest primate relative, Sarich maintains, because their DNA is 98%-99% alike. However, this 1%-2% difference does represent 10-20 million mutational differences. In great contrast to estimates made from the fossil record, he believes that the transition from quadruped to biped took place approximately 3.5 to 4 million years before the present. Also in contrast to those who hold to slow and gradual evolution, Sarich feels that the actual transition took place rapidly, perhaps in only 10,000 years. This is because the alleged transition between a quadruped and a biped would be a very unstable, high-energy situation that Sarich feels would either move on quickly to bipedality or fall back to quadrupedal locomotion again.

Rapid transition from quadruped to biped in a small, localized population also explains the absence of transitional forms in the fossil record. The chances of finding them would be extremely remote. However, Sarich believes that the gaps in the fossil record are actually filled in by the molecular data.

Gish pointed out that in the absence of transitional forms, Sarich's scenario is entirely hypothetical. Further, although evolution is supposed to be the "evolution of the fit," Sarich is actually proposing "evolution of the unfit." The alleged reason for the rapid transition from quadruped to biped is that the assumed intermediate would be very "unstable" or "unfit."

Man's early ancestors, Sarich claimed, were small bipedal chimpanzees. The fossils allegedly demonstrate this. Sarich mentioned the very human-like footprints found by Mary Leakey in Tanzania that were dated at about 3.75 million years before the present. He further cited the famous australopithecine fossil, Lucy, found by Donald Johanson in Ethiopia. Lucy's skull, jaw, and teeth are almost exactly like those of a chimpanzee. Yet, Owen Lovejoy, an anthropologist from Kent State University who worked closely with Johanson in interpreting Lucy, declared that the knee joint and the pelvis proved that Lucy walked upright. Current evolutionary thought is that bipedal locomotion came first in man's evolution and the larger brain and human dentition came later.

Gish emphasized two points. First, there is not a shred of evidence that the very human-like footprints found by Mary Leakey were made by an erect-walking australopithecine. The more logical assumption is that they were made by erect-walking humans. We know that humans are bipedal. We don't know that the australopithecines were. This was Gish's second point. He cited Sir Solly Zuckerman and Charles Oxnard, both of whom have done extensive multivariate analysis of the australopithecines, to the effect that they did not walk upright. Their mode of locomotion was of the hanging, climbing type most similar to the orangutan. Gish stated that these men had used extensive measurement and computer analysis compared to the visual assessment of Lovejoy and others.

There followed a most fascinating exchange on this topic. Gish told of his attendance at a recent seminar on human evolution with Richard Leakey, Donald Johanson, and other famous anthropologists. Owen Lovejoy was demonstrating with various manipulations how the knee joint of Lucy "proved" that she walked upright. He then showed a computer multivariate analysis of Lucy's knee joint. The computer analysis contradicted what Lovejoy said about the joint. The computer analysis showed it to be far removed from man and right in the middle of the apes. Lovejoy declared that he didn't know what to make of that data and discarded it in favor of his visual interpretation.

Sarich then quoted anthropologist Sherwood Washburn as saying that some anthropologists do not have an eye for anatomical form and function and must resort to measurements and computers. He implied that these were an inferior breed of anthropologist using inferior techniques. Further, he challenged the value of multivariate analysis, quoting the expression, "garbage in, garbage out."

Gish replied that it was not a case of an anthropologist with an "eye" for form vs. another one using a computer. It was Owen Lovejoy's "eye" vs. his own measurements and computer analysis. Further, that when the two were in conflict, Lovejoy discarded the computer analysis based on extensive and objective measurements and chose instead the subjective evaluation based solely on his visual analysis. Zuckerman had stated that it was a myth to believe that one could just look at the pelvis of the australopithecines and determine whether or not they walked upright.

Sarich showed a picture of Lucy's pelvis compared to a human pelvis. The two looked quite similar. Gish revealed that in only one orientation (from only one angle of view) did Lucy's pelvis appear human-like, and that was the orientation which Sarich showed the audience. In all other orientations, the pelvis was extremely ape-like.

Toward the close of the North Dakota State debate, Sarich

gave an illustration that caused one to wonder how much he really understands aboaut genetics. Gish—emphasizing the absence of transitional forms—had mentioned the "hopeful monster" mechanism proposed by Goldschmidt. He added that Stephen Jay Gould of Harvard had recently predicted that Goldschmidt would be vindicated in the 1980's because of the need to propose very rapid changes in evolution to explain the absence of transitions.

Sarich cited the caterpillar/butterfly metamorphosis as an evidence of genes producing rapid change—implying that this was an evolutionary change. Gish was quite taken aback by this improper analogy. He showed that the caterpillar/butterfly metamorphosis was not an evolutionary change at all. The entire caterpillar/butterfly sequence is programmed in the genes of this organism and is passed on from generation to generation. There is no mutation or natural selection involved. If the caterpillar genes mutated to produce the butterfly, then those mutated genes would have been so changed that they would never be able to produce another caterpillar. To have the genetic program already there for the caterpillar/butterfly sequence is one thing, and to have the caterpillar genes mutate to produce a butterfly is quite something else. Only the second situation would be an evolutionary change, but that is the way it *doesn't* happen. As I witnessed Sarich's reaction, I honestly question if he understood the difference.

At the conclusion of Gish's rebuttal at North Dakota State, he asked the audience whether they would prefer to have only evolution taught or if they would rather have both the creation model and the evolution model presented in the public schools. Of the 1,500 present, all but about 15-20 declared that they preferred having both models presented in the public school classroom.

In the Morgan Hill debate, Sarich asked this question: "If you are the product of special creation, then why were your genes created in the image of those of a chimpanzee?"

The answer is simple. They weren't. If our genes were created in the image of a chimpanzee, we would look like a chimpanzee. However, most people have no difficulty telling the difference.

Chapter 33

Gish Will Massacre You!

Leeds, Reading, Sussex

"I agree with Gish wholeheartedly that I cannot see how the concept of evolution can be shown to be consistent with a belief in God or the creation." These words were spoken by paleontologist E. G. Halstead of Reading University, England, in a debate he had with Gish on February 9, 1979. Halstead declared himself to be an atheist. Since a scientist must challenge everything, admit to no authority, and take nothing on faith, Halstead felt that every scientist worthy of the name must be an atheist—or at least a skeptic. He placed the attitude of the scientist and the attitude of the believer in stark contrast.

After reading publically the Biblical account of the Fall of man, Halstead stated that it was the most inspiring part of the whole Bible. He declared that the hero of the plot was the serpent because it gave good advice. Man's obedience to God and submission to His authority is something against which we all should fight. Adam and Eve, he felt, did the right thing in disobeying God that they might gain the knowledge promised by the serpent. In criticizing the idea of obedience and submission to God, Halstead asserted that "the kingdom of heaven is being like a good dog."

Citing the book of Job as "one of the most disgusting bits of writing that one could ever hope to read," Halstead claimed that religion came from the Near East where there are many sudden natural catastrophes. This would account, he felt, for the Old Testament concept of a vengeful, cruel God. The concept of slow change and gradualism which led to evolution came originally from Egypt where the annual overflowing of the Nile River was both predictable and welcome.

Halstead considered the Genesis account of creation just one of many creation legends of ancient man. He concluded his attack upon the Bible by reading Henry Morris' list of fifteen contradictions between Genesis One and evolution.

Although Halstead repeatedly emphasized that a scientist will not believe anything unless he sees the evidence, he, himself, accepted many things "by faith" without any evidence—such as his belief that there is no God, that the Bible is not true, and that life and man evolved.

He illucidated his faith by giving a rather unique explanation for the origin of the animal phyla. Since he conceded that there are no transitional forms between phyla, he assured us that none are needed. The various phyla originated when a single-celled animal mutated in many different directions—all without a shred of fossil evidence. He further admitted that the fossil record tells us that "evolution always takes place somewhere else." Yet, he was confident that evolution had taken place, though we may never be able to explain the mechanisms. He did not seem aware of the inconsistency in his many statements of faith in evolution and his scorn for faith in the Bible and creationism.

The Reading debate with Halstead was one of three which Gish had in English universities in early 1979. On February 1, he debated J. Alexander, Professor of Zoology at Leeds University. On February 12, Gish faced the world-famous evolutionary biologist, John Maynard Smith, at Sussex University.

At Sussex, Gish used an illustration he has used many times since—including the debate at the University of Nebraska, Lincoln, one month later. Gish held aloft a copy of Maynard Smith's book, *The Theory of Evolution,* with a picture of an evolutionary tree on the cover. He emphasized that this evolutionary tree, to be a legitimate scientific theory, must be a continuum from the roots to the ends of the branches without a single gap anywhere. Gish then went on to demonstrate that the only part of the tree that does exist is the tips of the branches—the tiny twigs that represent present-day life.

Gish first declared that a tree must have a seed. He likened this seed to the first single-celled organism in the evolution of life. He then demonstrated that a naturalistic origin of life was simply out of the question based on known principles of kinetics and thermodynamics.

A tree must also have roots. These Gish compared to the alleged mechanisms of evolution—mutations and natural selection. By the laws of probability, Gish showed that mutations are not able to increase the complexity of a system. He also pointed out that many evolutionists are now questioning if natural selection does anything at all—let alone whether it can overcome the tremendous odds which evolution places upon it. Quoting Julian Huxley, Gish gave the odds for getting a horse from a single-celled organism by mutations alone—without natural selection—as the number one over one followed by three million zeroes. This is a number so large that it would take three large volumes just to print. Huxley recognized the impossibility of this number, but claimed that since we do have horses in the world, evolution must have produced them. Thus, natural selection is able to overcome such impossible odds in the evolutionary process. Gish showed that a force so powerful, able to overcome such odds, is nothing short of a god—a naturalistic deity.

The trunk of the tree was likened by Gish to the ancestors of the Cambrian animals. All of the animal phyla are found in the Cambrian. Nowhere in the lower rocks have their alleged evolutionary ancestors ever been found. This is one of the foundational points which Gish always emphasizes.

The transitions between phyla are analogous to the branches of the tree. Evidence for the alleged transition between the invertebrates and the vertebrates, said to have taken 100 million years, is totally lacking. When Halstead admitted that there are no transitions between phyla, Gish claimed—with good reason—that Halstead had virtually conceded the entire debate.

All of the evolutionists—Alexander, Halstead, and Smith— tried to establish transitional forms from the fossil record. Alexander spent a great deal of time on the evolution of the horse. Gish rammed home the point that it is foolish to talk about the subtle changes in the toes of horses, which are nothing more than the twigs of the evolutionary tree, when you can't establish the seed, the roots, the trunk, or the branches.

Although Maynard Smith is considered one of the most influential evolutionists of the Twentieth Century, he often resorted to humor or sarcasm rather than to factual data in dealing with Gish's arguments. He said that if Gish would write out his probability arguments, he would submit them to his second-year students. "If two-thirds of my students can't see the fallacy of it, I will be greatly disappointed." However, Smith never did explain just what the supposed fallacy was.

Regarding Julian Huxley's calculations on the probability of a horse, Smith said that he was willing to yield at once to Dr. Gish that there was no probability whatsoever of a horse suddenly appearing on the platform in front of them. "If it does," Smith continued, "I will accept creation on the spot."

Smith had given the australopithecines as an example of a bipedal intermediate form in the evolution of man. When Gish countered with the 15-year research of Sir Solly Zuckerman showing that they were neither bipedal nor intermediate, Smith replied: "If I had to choose an anatomist to rely on, Solly Zuckerman would be the last person I would choose." Continuing the theme of human evolution, Smith stated: "The main difference between us and the apes is our buns, not our brains."

Evolution is falsifiable, Smith maintained, whereas creation is not. Smith then used an illustration several debaters have used. "I want to present a new theory—God created the world at 9:00 a.m. this morning, with all of us having built in memories." He defied anyone to refute it. Although this idea is often given as an illustration of the creation concept, it is far from it. Smith then claimed that to create the world to look as if it had a past means that God created one enormous lie.

Gish not only accused Smith of setting up a false and ridiculous concept of creation to attack and knock down, but claimed that neither evolution nor creation were refutable scientific theories—although both have elements of scientific data in them. Smith then protested saying that he had given certain criteria whereby evolution could be falisified. If the deeper rocks (allegedly older rocks) had more species in them belonging to existing genera than the more recent rocks have, Smith stated, evolution would be falsified.

Smith: "Would you not accept that as a falisification of evolution?"

Gish: "No, and I don't believe you will either, because on that basis I can falsify your theory."

Gish then gave evidence that the prosimians, when they first appear in the fossil record, are far more diversified than they are in the present or in the intermediate stages. Prosimians first appear in 50 different genera involving many more species than exist today.

Gish: "On the basis of your own criteria, Dr. Smith, you must falsify your theory. It cannot be true."

Smith: "It simply isn't relevant. Why shouldn't it be true that the prosimians were more diversified then than they are now."

Gish, somewhat taken aback, repeated the statement Smith had made regarding the falsifying of evolution.

Smith: "You said that. I didn't say that."

Gish: "That's just what I said in the first place. You can't falsify the theory of evolution because he won't accept it. Nobody will accept it."

Smith then contended that he gave a criteria for falsification of evolution, but the observations support evolution.

Gish: "That's precisely what I said. You can't falsify the theory. It doesn't make any difference what the data is."

In this exchange, it never was clear what Smith thought was wrong with the data Gish gave regarding the prosimians. It was obvious, however, why Smith couldn't accept it.

In the light of the recent challenges to evolutionary theory, Smith made a distinction between the doctrine of descent (the *fact* of evolution) and neo-Darwinian mechanisms. Smith maintained that those who are saying that neo-Darwinism is not a scientific theory are not saying that evolution is not a scientific theory. "They all believe that evolution has happened."

Here we see the new direction evolutionists are taking. Whereas for a whole generation evolution and neo-Darwinism have been synonymous, evolutionists are now saying that neo-Darwinism may be wrong, but evolution is still a fact.

"Darwinism is dead. Long live evolution!"

Halstead revealed a remarkable incident in the Reading debate. In speaking on the fossil record, Halstead stated that he had talked to someone the day before at the British Museum. That person—unnamed—said: "Don't talk about fossils or Gish will massacre you!"

Gish's response to that incident is a classic. "That man at the British Museum doesn't know me. I don't think that he has ever heard me speak. It's just his knowledge of the fossil record that was the note for the warning."

Chapter 34

Speak Up, John!
Des Moines Area Community College

John Patterson is a thermodynamicist. John Patterson teaches thermodynamics at Iowa State University. John Patterson has been highly critical of the way creationists use thermodynamics as evidence for creation. John Patterson had an opportunity to publicly demonstrate in open debate how wrong creationists are. John Patterson was rather quiet.

It wasn't that John didn't say anything. He said a great deal—but not about thermodynamics. In fact, he has been saying a great deal about creation and evolution for several years. Although by his own admission he is an atheist—or the next thing to it—he was responsible for establishing a seminar at Iowa State on the creation-evolution issue. It proved to be the most popular seminar on campus until a higher power at Iowa State axed the course. Patterson was most unhappy about it because he does believe in confronting vital issues. Later, he tried to arrange a creation-evolution debate at Iowa State. After writing many letters to those higher powers, he stated that somebody at Iowa State "is very busy not answering."

Patterson's opportunity to confront creationists himself came in January 1980. He had two debates with Duane Gish. The first one was on the campus of Des Moines Area Community College, Ankeny, Iowa, on January 16. The second one was at Graceland College, Lamoni, Iowa, the following day. Because of the very small attendance at both debates, and because both institutions are relatively unknown, I had not originally planned to devote space to them. However, they are two of the finest debates that have been held in grappling with some basic issues. They were confrontations in the finest sense of the word.

Although Patterson is a thermodynamicist, and although thermodynamics is one of the strongest creationist arguments, Patterson avoided it. He devoted most of his time in both debates to the philosophy of science, maintaining that creationism is outside the realm of science and cannot be considered a scientific theory. This is exactly what Morris and Gish say. They readily admit that creationism is outside the domain of science because it deals with the matter of origins. They further emphasize that evolution is in the same category. What *can* be done, Morris and Gish explain, is to consider both creation and evolution as conceptual models or frameworks for the correlation and integration of scientific data. While neither creation or evolution can be proven scientifically, evidence can be collected and a level of credibility established for one model or the other.

Patterson declared that creationism is not falsifiable, whereas evolution is. Since creationism involves a supernatural Creator, "there is nothing that the Almighty power can't do." In other words, anything can be explained by invoking the power of God. Whereas one might think that this would make it good theory, just the opposite is true. There is no way to test it or to falsify it. This, of course, creationists readily admit. However, what evolutionists can't see is that evolution is also beyond falsification. As Gish puts it, "The theory of evolution is so plastic that it can explain everything and anything."

Gish emphasized that there are a number of different types of evolution that demonstrate its all-inclusive nature. Normally in evolution we would expect that similar characteristics come from a common ancestor. However, there are many cases where organisms share similar characteristics that were not inherited from a common ancestor. An illustration of this would be the duckbill platypus. Although it is a mammal, it has a duck bill, webbed feet, and lays eggs. One would think that it would be related to birds, but according to evolutionary theory mammals did not evolve from birds. This would be an illustration of what is called "convergent evolution."

There are cases where animals did supposedly evolve from a

common ancestor, but only much later developed similar characteristics. This is called "parallel evolution." When characteristics are thought to be the result of adaptation to the environment, rather than due to mutations, it is called "adaptive evolution." When characteristics are thought to be the result of something other than the environment, it is called "nonadaptive evolution." There is a brand of evolution to explain everything.

Actually, as Gish delights to point out, the major tenets of evolution have been falsified. Yet, its disciples go marching forward as doggedly as ever. This indicates that evolution is not a scientific theory, but a philosophy. It is a belief system. The three major factors of evolution have been the fossil record, mutation, and natural selection. The newer "punctuated equilibrium" model which does not require transitional forms and which deemphasizes the role of natural selection is a tacit admission that the fossil record has failed evolution and that natural selection is not an adequate mechanism. The crisis in homology, based on the work of Sir Gavin deBeer, is actually a falsification of the concept of mutations as a means of explaining the evolutionary process. However, even though the major elements of evolution have been found to be deficient, evolution is as firmly believed as ever. Evolution truly is as nonfalsifiable as creation because it is philosophy, not science.

Patterson then stated that creationism is not science because creationists are "committed to the very position they are trying to do research on." He then read the doctrinal statement of the Creation Research Society to which its members must subscribe. He challenged the right of any creationist to teach in the areas of science or history if they sign the CRS statement of faith. This commitment, he felt, made it impossible for them to do science, because "creationists can't change their mind." Yet, he began his own presentation by saying: "I am committed to the scientific world view." (By "scientific" he meant "evolutionary.")

Gish pointed out that if evolutionists or atheists were allowed to join the Creation Research Society and gained a majority, all research on creationism would cease. Adherence to the doctrinal statement is essential to the very existence of the organization. Further, these debates have demonstrated that evolutionists are as fully committed to evolution as creationists are to creation. The idea that scientists are non-committed and totally objective is a myth. If evolutionists can do science while committed to an evolutionary world view, creationists can do science while committed to creationism. For 200 years before Darwin, creationism was the prevailing world view. Newton, Maxwell, Faraday, and many others testify that one can do science very well and be committed to creationism.

Patterson, a follower of the philosophy of Sir Karl Popper, quoted Popper to the effect that, "Science is very anti-authoritarian." Patterson stressed that science is a method of successive approximations and progress toward truth, but is not in the business of discovering final and unchangeable laws. The contrast between the attitude of science toward truth and the attitude of the Bible toward truth was another reason why Patterson felt that the two were incompatible. The absolute nature of Biblical truth—including creationism—was stifling to science, he declared.

It was the enunciation of the contemporary philosophy of science by John Patterson that brought out in bold relief the fact that the present philosophy of science—largely the result of Karl Popper's work—is actually anti-Christian. Patterson made a remarkable and true statement when he said: "There has been a change in the last 50 to 100 years in what we mean by science." It is becoming more and more obvious that the contemporary philosophy of science is anti-Christian. It is not necessary for a philosophy of science to be anti-Christian, but the contemporary one certainly is.

Gish zeroed in on this element in Patterson's presentation several times. Referring to Patterson's aversion to the super-natural, he said: "We don't have to invoke the supernatural to do science today. But in the light of the natural laws, to exclude the supernatural regarding origins is to demand that we all be atheists." Later, Gish put his finger on this absurdity when he pointed out that if creationism cannot be considered by scientists—just because of the element of the supernatural—then it means that even if everyone knew that creationism were true and that evolution were false, the public schools would still have to exclude creation and teach evolution. That is atheism with a vengeance! If the present philosophy continues, the outlook for our schools is bleak, indeed.

One of the most surprising elements of many of these debates was the failure of scientists with expertise in areas directly related to the creation-evolution issue to utilize data from their own fields in their presentations. John Patterson was no exception. Although in both debates Gish emphasized the laws of thermodynamics as evidence for creation, Patterson, who had a total speaking time of about 3½ hours in the two debates (counting the question and answer periods), spent all of ten minutes on the subject of thermodynamics.

Even then, the subject of thermodynamics came up in a rather strange way. Toward the end of his first presentation—at Des Moines Area Community College—Patterson produced a letter from Dr. Sheldon Matlow. Gish had debated Matlow at DeAnza College, Cupertino, California, on August 29, 1974. The attendance of 2,300 made it the largest debate that had been held up to that time. The letter from Matlow said in essence that Gish did not understand the concepts of thermo-dynamics and did not even recognize some of its basic mathe-matical formulas. Patterson then said that it was Matlow's letter that had first caused him to become interested in the creation-evolution controversy.

When Gish heard what Matlow had written, he came on like gangbusters. He criticized Patterson for introducing hearsay evidence into the debate, told how poorly Matlow had done in the DeAnza debate, and stated some of the ridiculous evidences that Matlow had presented in an attempt to get around the impact of the second law of thermodynamics. It was obvious that Patterson had committed a serious tactical blunder. In his debate with Gish the next day, he uttered not a word about Matlow or about thermodynamics.

Patterson's failure to respond to Gish's arguments on thermodynamics was so noticeable that in the question period following the first debate a student made the following remark to Patterson. "Gish's second law argument seems to be very strong. I thought that that was your special area as a professor. In my opinion, you have given absolutely no defense [he meant refutation] of it, and it seems to be an established fact. That is hurting your argument for science." When Patterson asked the student what his question was, the student asked if there was anyone in the auditorium who could refute Gish's arguments on the second law. Patterson's amazing response to that was: "Well, let me pass on that. How do you answer a question that isn't a question?"

But it *was* a question, John! Speak up!

Chapter 35

Homo sapiens—
The Wise Guy
Princeton University

As Duane Gish stepped to the podium on April 12, 1980, he could say that he had "arrived." His debates and his campaign for scientific creationism had taken him to one of the most prestigious universities in the world—Princeton. It was the first time that Gish or Morris had debated at an Ivy League school. (One year later, Henry Morris debated on another Ivy League campus—Brown University.) Opposite Gish that evening on the Princeton platform was Ashley Montagu, author of 65 books and recognized as one of the world's leading anthropologists.

In spite of the auspicious occasion, Gish's basic game plan did not change. In his hard-hitting, homey eloquence he presented the evidence for creation from thermodynamics, the fossil record, and probability studies concerning the origin of life. Because of his training as a biochemist, Gish is at his very best on the subject of the origin of life. He quoted Julian Huxley to the effect that to go from a single cell to a horse by mutations alone was impossible. Yet, natural selection supposedly made it happen. However, Gish emphasized, to go from nonlife to that first cell is a greater step than to go from a single cell to a horse. Here the process must be accomplished without the aid of natural selection because there is no selection on the molecular level—although many evolutionists have implied that there was. By emphasizing the impossibility of a naturalistic origin of life, Gish "cuts the evolutionist off at the pass."

Montagu began his presentation by telling a story said to come out of the famous Huxley-Wilberforce debate 100 years ago. A bishop who had attended the debate told his wife that the horrid Professor Huxley had claimed that man had descended from the apes. "Descended from the apes!" his wife exclaimed. "My dear, let us hope that it is not true; but if it is, let us pray that it will not become generally known."

Ashley Montagu is one who is responsible for evolution becoming generally known. As an older scholar, he presented the more traditional neo-Darwinian position with the mechanisms of mutation and natural selection. He claimed that "we have a great many transitional forms." Since the punctuated equilibrium model was presented often by a new breed of evolutionists in the recent debates, Montagu's arguments seemed painfully out of date. In building his case, he depended more on his reputation and the authority he has built up over the years than on solid evidence.

Montagu is an arrogant, witty, sarcastic Englishman. In dealing with the second law, he claimed that it was discovered by Willard Gibbs, a member of the Princeton faculty. Montagu continued: "He then went to Yale, thus elevating the intellectual stature of both institutions."

Admitting the reality of the second law, Montagu claimed that evolution was dependent upon it. He stated that entropy (disorder) was the very material of evolution. Evolution could not take place without it. Later, however, he affirmed Julian Huxley's definition of evolution which Gish had quoted. Huxley was right, he said. Evolution had indeed gone from simplicity to complexity. He did not explain the contradiction between the uphill movement of evolution and the downhill movement of the second law and did not seem to be aware that he had uttered contradictory statements. It is this contradiction between the concept of evolution and the laws of science that Morris and Gish have been exposing during the decade of these debates. The students seem to see the problem more clearly than do the professors.

In response to a statement by Gish, Montagu admitted that the theory of embryonic recapitulation was destroyed in 1922 "since when no respectable biologist has ever used the theory of recapitulation because it was utterly unsound." Gish agreed that it is utterly unsound. He revealed, however, that half of the evolutionists he has faced in debates still use it. Further, on almost all of the campuses he has visited, students tell him that their professors are still teaching it as evidence for evolution. Montagu replied: "That only goes to show that many so-called educational institutions called universities are not educational institutions at all, but are institutions for mis-education."

Gish mentioned the argument used by evolutionists based on so-called vestigial organs, such as the tonsils. Whereas a few years ago the tonsils were removed indiscriminately because they were thought to be worthless, we now realize that they play a part in fighting germs. Montagu replied that tonsils were removed because "medical men are not interested in health, but only in disease, and they do not understand health or the human body."

Mutations were exposed by Gish for what they actually are—mistakes. Man, with a brain consisting of 12 billion cells with each cell having 10,000 connections, is supposed to have evolved by a series of mutational mistakes from an organism that had no brain at all. Montagu replied that when he contemplated the state of most people, "I have no doubt that there is some metaphorical truth in the statement that we are the result of mistakes." He took sharp issue with Gish, however, on the idea that evolution comes about by mistakes. Most mutations are mistakes, he admitted—probably 99% of them. "Evolution does not develop by the preservation of mistakes, but by the death of mistakes." It is the good mutations that are preserved and advance evolution. He insisted that these good mutations are not mistakes. However, since they are also errors in the copying process of genes, he did not explain the difference. If good mutations are not mistakes, then the only other explanation is that they are the result of some plan or design. But Montagu would not like that idea either. Creationists strongly challenge the idea that there are any "good" mutations.

As a neo-Darwinist, Montagu emphasized the fossil record. Gish had quoted many evolutionist authorities to the effect that the fossil record revealed *no* transitional forms. Although their statements were quite clear, Montagu insisted that these men were saying that there are not as many transitional forms as we would like. He called the famous horse series "one of the best demonstrations that we have." Gish has debunked that series many times.

Since Montagu is an anthropologist, it is to be expected that he would seek to establish transitional forms from his own area of expertise—man. He listed a sequence of transitions beginning with *Australopithecus,* then *Homo habilis, Homo erectus,* the Solo men (Java), the living Australian aborigines who he said were "very closely related to the Solo group," and concluded with ourselves as modern man. He considers the Australian aborigines, among whom he had worked for some years, a transition because of their smaller brain size— 1,300 c.c. as compared to an average of 1,440 c.c. for modern man. Because the Australian aborigines are black, Montagu took great pains to point out that their smaller brain size did not make them mentally inferior. Brain size in humans is not related to intelligence. "The heaviest brains on record happen to belong to an idiot (2,800 c.c.) and a United States Senator," he declared.

There are several problems with Montagu's scheme. First, the Australian aborigines are living today. So they in no wise qualify as a transitional form. They are true men in every sense of the word. By Montagu's own admission, the Solo men, though fossils, are virtually identical to the Australian aborigines. Hence, they are not transitional either.

The other forms which Montagu mentioned—*Australopithecus, Homo habilis,* and *Homo erectus*—have all been found together at several locations in the fossil record. Since they were contemporaries, it is quite artificial to put them in an evolutionary sequence and try to make one ancestral to the other. It is well known that any set of objects can be arranged in an evolutionary sequence from simple to complex or primitive to advanced. The fact that objects can be arranged that way does not constitute any proof at all that they evolved. Even objects made by intelligent beings, such as shoes, cars, airplanes, and furniture can be arranged in an evolutionary sequence. If objects made by man can be put into an evolutionary sequence—even though they did not evolve—it should not surprise us that objects created by God can also be placed in an "evolutionary" sequence. However, it is an artificial sequence having nothing to do with evolution.

During the question period, Montagu was asked a question about human transitional forms. He cited a series of Neanderthal and Neanderthaloid forms from Europe and Israel, *Homo sapiens neanderthalensis,* grading into modern man, *Homo sapiens sapiens.* "And what better transitional forms you could have than that," he said, "I do not know."

Gish knew more about the human fossils than Montagu thought he did. As Gish pointed out, all Neanderthals are classed as *Homo sapiens*—true man. Montagu cited only subspecies which are the result of genetic variation, not genetic mutations. These are not illustrations of legitimate transitional forms for evolution at all. We are not concerned, said Gish, about how we got various varieties of humans. "The issue," Gish continued, "is how we got a human from something that was not human!"

Montagu seemed a bit shaken when Gish revealed that the Neanderthal fossils in Israel were not in the order Montagu implied. There, the more "advanced" forms are earlier in date than the more "primitive" forms. Apparently Montagu didn't expect Gish to know that. He admitted that Gish was right, but stated that they were legitimate transitions because they were somewhat different from modern man. Gish had the final word. "There is more difference," he snapped, "between a seven-foot Watusi and an African Pygmy than there is between the forms Montagu was talking about."

Two statements made by Montagu reveal both his prejudice against creation and his faith commitment to evolution. Referring to Gish's argument about the gaps in the fossil record, he said: "Of course it *looks* like special creation, but that doesn't necessarily mean that special creation was operative." If science is based on what we see in terms of tangible evidence, we can't help but ask, "What then do the gaps in the fossil record mean?" They certainly don't mean evolution! Later, in his summary statement, Montagu said: "We know that there must have been transitional forms." Tell me, Ashley, is that a statement of evidence or a statement of faith?

The inconsistency in evolutionary logic was pointed out by Gish. If we were to find an arrowhead, we would all assume that it was formed by an Indian. Even though it is relatively simple, we know that natural processes alone could not have caused it. Yet, the Indian, who is infinitely more complex than the arrowhead, is supposed to have been formed by time, chance, and natural processes alone.

No one seemed more surprised than Gish when Montagu endorsed the two-model approach. He declared that he welcomed the criticism that Gish was offering of evolution because it served as sort of a whetstone upon which evolutionists must sharpen their wits. "He [Gish] has offered very serious challenges which are worthy of very serious consideration."

Montagu then spoke of his spiritual pilgrimage. Unfortunately, it was a pilgrimage in the wrong direction. He was far from the first evolutionist in these debates to declare that he "was brought up to believe in God and in supernaturals." (Montagu had previously defined religion as "the belief in supernaturals.") However, when he grew up and went to the university, he was faced with a choice—a choice between science and belief. He continually contrasted the scientific approach with faith in God and the supernatural. "A scientist," he said, "believes in proof without certainty; other people believe in certainty without proof."

It was obvious that Montagu considered religious answers quite inferior to the answers provided by science. With the evolutionary scenario, he felt it is possible to formulate how things came into being. Regarding an appeal to the supernatural, "We can leave this," he said, "to so-called primitive peoples." Every people has its creation myths. The Genesis creation account is just one myth among many. Gish, he said, subscribes to one of these primitive creation myths in a modern form "dressed up in the language and terms which are borrowed from science." It is very easy, he felt, to fall back on these supernatural explanations. Although he admitted that large numbers of people will accept the answers Gish is giving, it is only because they are not willing to do the hard work of studying the evidence scientists are producing. "I do not think," he said, "that the method of Dr. Gish stands a chance of having a long history on the earth."

Gish struck back. "Evolution is a nature myth which man has invented to explain his origin without God. It is Twentieth-Century mythology." Montagu had given Gish ample reason for putting it that way. Although the evidence for evolution is crumbling rapidly, and the fossil record is worse from the standpoint of evolution than it was in the days of Darwin, Montagu had declared evolution to be "probably the best authenticated scientific theory available to us in the present time." Further, Montagu had said that "evolution is the maximization of the improbable." If something in nature is improbable, it is not likely to happen. Here we have the expression of Montagu's faith. Evolution makes the impossible happen. Montagu has merely exchanged belief in "supernaturals" for belief in "naturals." But it is a faith nonetheless.

Throughout the debate, Montagu's caustic humor sparkled. He referred to man as *Homo sapiens* or "the wise guy." ("Sapiens" is Latin for "wise.") In the light of man's track record, he felt that for man to apply the term "wise" to himself is the most arrogant and offish thing that man has ever done. Man, he said, really deserves no better term than *"Homo sap."*

Chapter 36

I Am Really Bored With Ferns

University of Arizona

Kenneth Miller is a very able man. In fact, he is the most able man that Morris or Gish have ever debated. Further, Miller thinks that debating creationists is really a fun thing. On February 12, 1982, when Miller and his fellow biologist, David Milne, debated Morris and Gish at the University of Arizona, they were not strangers. Miller had already debated Morris twice—once at Brown University where Miller is on the faculty, and once in Tampa, Florida. One month later, he debated Gish at Tampa.

Milne had debated Gish at Evergreen State College, Olympia, Washington, where he is a faculty member. Milne, too, has made debating with creationists a serious study. In the May 1981 *American Biology Teacher* he authored an article entitled, "How to Debate with Creationists and Win."

Although observers feel that Morris and Gish have "won" most of their debates, it can be said to their credit that their main concern is to build the creationist position on solid scientific evidence and to present that evidence as clearly and lucidly as possible. As a result, a Morris/Gish debate is a genuine educational experience.

Because evolutionists became tired of losing, Milne's advice was welcome. Milne's focus was not on education but on winning. Milne counseled evolutionists to use a series of "one-

liners." He advised them to present to their opponent "a
barrage of examples he could not hope to refute within the
allotted time." Thus, education was to be sacrificed on the
altar of debating technique.

Miller utilized Milne's advice to the hilt. He also mixed in
his own natural gifts in an impressive way. His speech was
rapid-fire. He was well-versed in the creationist literature and
in the debates of Morris and Gish. The result was that he
often gave the creationist argument and then attempted to
refute it even before Morris or Gish had opportunity to
present it initially. Psychologically, it was quite effective.
Miller was also an insulting debater, but he had a way of
mixing it with charm and warmth, as well as with a few
compliments. That technique, too, was impressive. In all, the
strategy was to constantly keep the creationists on the
defensive. It was also calculated to draw them away from
their original game plan. But it was not as successful as Miller
and Milne had hoped.

Declaring himself to be a Roman Catholic, Miller often
referred to himself as a Christian and a creationist. This
emphasis was obviously to try to overcome the atheistic
stigma of evolution. "You don't have to turn your back on
St. Peter to embrace Charles Darwin," he declared. He
sought to distinguish between creationism, as such, and the
special creationism of Morris and Gish. As it turned out, he
felt that anyone who believed in God was a creationist. From
his own statements, however, it appears that Miller's religious
position could best be described as that of a deist.

Not only were Miller and Milne impressive debaters, but
there were also some distinguished moderators involved. The
Evergreen State College debate was moderated by the
honorable Robert Utter, Chief Justice of the Supreme Court
of the State of Washington. Moderator for the Tampa debate
on September 19, 1981, was Ralph Turlington, Florida's State
Commissioner of Education. The second Tampa debate on
March 20, 1982, was moderated by William Poe, a former
mayor of Tampa.

A humorous incident occurred in the Evergreen State debate
at the expense of Chief Justice Utter. In dealing with the
absence of transitional forms in the fossil record, Gish
pointed out that the whale is believed by evolutionists to have

evolved from some land mammal similar to a pig, cow, or buffalo. He then asked people to imagine how this unlikely transition might have looked. A friend of his had drawn some possibilities of this alleged cow-whale transition which Gish then projected on the screen. Pointing to the lower rear portion of the animal, Gish remarked: "We could say that a failure in this area would be an 'udder failure'." Realizing what he had said, Gish turned to Chief Justice Utter and assured him that no implication was intended.

In their debates, Miller and Milne spent a great deal of time in criticism of the creation model and very little time in establishing evidence for evolution. They understood the creation model to have three aspects: (1) The entire creation is 6,000 to 10,000 years old; (2) everything was created at the same time; and (3) all of the geologic formations are the result of the Noahic Flood. Although the first and third points are not a part of the basic creation model Morris and Gish present, Miller and Milne addressed themselves to refuting those points.

Miller attempted to show that the universe must be older than 10,000 years by showing pictures of galaxies that are believed to be millions of light years away. To explain this obvious inconsistency, Miller continued, "the creationist must say that the Creator made all of the photons in midstream." Referring to a supernova thought to be 100,000 light years away, he then accused the Creator of making up events that never occurred. "What a devil," he joked, "that Creator must have been!"

Miller explained how God *should* have done it if the universe really were recent in age. "If every day a new star appeared that was one light-day further away, every astronomer would be on Dr. Morris' side." If God had done it that way—created the stars but not the light in transit—two problems would present themselves. Ancient man would not have had enough stars to help him determine the times and the seasons. That is one of the reasons why the stars were created in the first place.

Also, if each day a new star appeared as its light finally reached the earth, it would seem that these stars had just at that moment been created. Since it is only in this century that many of the details of astronomy have become known, the peoples living before this century would not think in terms of the starlight finally arriving at the earth, but would think that new stars were continually coming into being. The idea of a finished creation would be lost. It would appear that the universe is being continually created. That is the very idea God did *not* want to give to his creatures.

Nothing could better explain why God not only created the stars, but the light in transit to the earth at the same time. Only in this way could He present to people of every age a complete creation to bear witness of Himself. When the things God did are seen in the light of His purposes, they do not appear to be so strange after all.

Miller also used radioactive dating to demonstrate that the earth is very old. The problem with radioactive dating techniques is that the dates given are so vast that there is no nonradioactive method to check it, to act as a control. The basic assumptions of the method are also beyond verification. There is, however, an approach which creationists have been investigating. It is to radiometrically date rocks—such as lava flows—that are of known age, verified by historical records. Morris pointed out that when this is done, rocks known to be only hundreds or a thousand years old at best give radioactive ages of hundreds of millions of years. It is for this reason that creationists challenge radioactivity as a dating technique.

Milne and Miller both insisted that the fossil record demonstrates evolution. The various categories appear, they said, in the fossil record in an evolutionary sequence with man appearing most recently. As time goes on, things go from simple to complex—just as evolution would predict. Further, the diversity of life increases as time goes on. If creation were true, they maintained, all of the various categories of life would appear at the beginning. The greatest diversity and complexity would also appear at the beginning—probably the Cambrian. Then, because of extinctions, the diversity would decrease rather than increase.

As convincing as that argument appears, there is a flaw in it. The flaw is that the fossil record—the geologic column— was originally arranged on the assumption of evolution—that is, simple to complex. People think that because the geologic column was formulated before Darwin's time, evolutionary concepts were unknown and that the geologic column is an independent confirmation of evolution. Nothing could be further from the truth. What is so remarkable is that even though there is a built-in bias toward evolution in the geologic column, the fossil evidence for evolution is less impressive today than it was in the days of Darwin.

The gulf between the objectivity that people expect in science and the evolutionary prejudice that is really there was set forth dramatically by Miller. He was emphasizing that if creation were true, the flowering plants would be found at the bottom of the fossil column—the Cambrian. Instead, they are found 400 million years later, as evolution would predict. Speaking of the absence of land plants in the Cambrian, he said: "If paleontologists could find any, they wouldn't hide them—they would shout about it. Why? They all want to be promoted. They all want to win the Nobel Prize. They all want to be on the *Today Show*."

Later, Miller put it this way: "If I were to go out into the Cambrian or Precambrian rock and pull out a fossil acorn, I would get down on my knees and thank the Lord because that would be my ticket to success in the scientific world." In Tucson, he said it differently. "Evolution is falsifiable, and finding an acorn, an oak leaf, a dandelion in any of the geological ages before we believe the angiosperms evolved could falsify the concept of biological evolution. Evolution is absolutely disprovable."

There is no reason to doubt that Miller is sincere. Yet, as Morris and Gish pointed out many times, these types of discoveries have been made by evolutionists and published in evolutionary journals since 1935. Did it falsify evolution? Did it bring fame and success to the discoverer? No! The reports were ignored and forgotten. Evidence that would disprove evolution is not welcome. The scientific community is not nearly as objective in its search for truth as it thinks it is.

Miller and Milne both spoke forcibly against a world-wide catastrophic flood. They declared that there was simply no evidence for it. Gish expressed amazement that on planet earth, with 355 million cubic miles of water covering 70% of the earth's surface, evolutionists deny the possibility of a world-wide flood. Yet, they claim that many of the surface features of Mars, which, as far as we know, does not have a drop of liquid water, were formed under conditions of vast flooding.

Many geologists, Morris pointed out, are now recognizing that the sedimentary layers of the earth were laid down rapidly under catastrophic conditions. He emphasized that since there is no world-wide unconformity in the sedimentary rocks, one can start at the bottom of the geologic column and by zigzagging back and forth work one's way clear up to the top without a break in sequence. This can be done anywhere in the world. It indicates that the bulk of the sedimentary rocks were laid down in one gigantic catastrophe. The fact that this can be done also challenges the various ages ascribed to individual sections of the geologic column.

The idea that many of the organisms of nature are not as "perfect" as they might be served as a reason for Milne's preference for evolution over creation. "Either you must accept a degree of evolution or believe that God did an incomplete job." Milne named several animals, the cormorant and the flying fish, that he thought needed improvement. Like Darwin, however, the eye impressed him. "The eye is a marvelous organ and almost demands a creationist explanation."

Milne's argument was that since there are imperfections in life, this implies evolution. Evolution does not build perfect things. It builds things that work—that are "good enough." "We would expect," Milne said, "the 'perfect' signature of creation rather than the 'good enough' signature of evolution." Milne overlooked part of the creation model which emphasizes that the universe and life are running down. Things now are not as they were created by God at the beginning. The imperfections are the result of the fall and the curse.

Since life looks as if it evolved, Milne felt that there were ways that God could have impressed us with creation if things actually had been created. He suggested that there are things that are createable, but not evolveable, such as the wheel and the axle. If such a wheel and axle organism could be found in nature, Milne felt confident that many, if not most, evolutionists would give up the theory of evolution.

The second law of thermodynamics was not neglected in these debates. It was obvious that Miller, a cell biologist, was not really familiar with thermodynamic concepts when he debated Morris on his home turf, Brown University. Twice in that debate Miller associated high entropy with high order. Entropy is a measure of disorder and high entropy would be associated with low order. However, by the time Miller got to Tampa five months later, he had become an authority. The charges he leveled against Morris' integrity and his use of the second law were by far the most insulting of any debater Morris has faced.

"Dr. Morris is bearing false witness against the second law of thermodynamics and he's attempting to deceive you," Miller began. He claimed that the second law Morris presented to them was an imposter. "The first thing Dr. Morris did, unfortunate to say, is to fib to you about the second law." He then suggested crystallization of snowflakes as an illustration of an increase in order without the plan and the control mechanism Morris had stated were necessary. Calling a hurricane an increase in order, he said it doesn't violate the second law. "It violates Dr. Morris' cheap imitation."

It is hard to believe that one would say, in Tampa, Florida, of all places, that a hurricane is an example of increased order. Gish, in his Tampa debate, made the most of it. After telling the people that they were probably happy to learn that a hurricane was going to generate order and complexity, he said: "The next time one comes along, get a lot of bricks and lumber and pile it on your lot and it will assemble a house for you!"

Regarding snowflakes, Gish continued, "If Dr. Miller doesn't know the difference between forming a snowflake and evolution, I can't help him any." They go in the opposite direction, he explained. A crystal goes to a lower energy state, a more probable state. It is less ordered than the solution from which it came.

At Brown University, Miller acknowledged that although the universe was running down, it started in a highly ordered state. What was that highly ordered state? The Big Bang!

"The most ordered state that ever existed was that Big Bang." It shows how desperate evolutionists are to find an answer to the thermodynamic problem. Before the Big Bang exploded, that "cosmic egg" was supposedly in a state of equilibrium. An equilibrium state is a state of maximum entropy, disorder. One thing we can be sure of is that the order of the universe did not come from the Big Bang.

Gish had a few things to say about the Big Bang himself. If the universe allegedly started with a "cosmic egg" exploding, the question is, "Where did the cosmic egg come from?" Gish suggested that perhaps it was laid by the cosmic chicken. Hydrogen is supposed to be the first element made in the explosion of the Big Bang. From that eventually came all of the elements, structures, and life in the universe. Gish defined hydrogen "as a colorless, tasteless, odorless gas which if given enough time will evolve into people."

The public school issue was also present in all of the Miller/Milne debates. Miller had said that if creation were taught, in fairness, every other philosophy—including atheism—would have to be taught also. Creationists reply that an incipient atheism is being taught now. Morris revealed that recent polls by Associated Press and others indicated that 86% of the American people want the creation model presented when origins are discussed in the public schools.

Morris noted the number of prominent intellectuals who are questioning evolution or declaring that they believe in creation by a Supreme Being. One person Morris mentioned was the former atheist and cosmologist, Sir Fred Hoyle. Morris also mentioned the famous British philosopher and man of letters, Malcolm Muggeridge. Muggeridge has not only become a Christian, but a creationist. He has stated that evolution "will be one of the great jokes in the history books of the future."

In the Brown University debate, Miller mentioned that a number of people had approached him during the intermission and told him that his attitude toward Morris had been rather insulting. He declared that he did not mean it quite that way. He really had tremendous respect for Morris. In questioning established ideas, "Morris does an enormous service to science." Later, in the second Tampa debate he characterized Gish as "bright and articulate and a terrifyingly good debater."

In all four of Miller's debates, he acknowledged that the analysis by Morris and Gish of the gaps in the fossil record was correct. Although he did suggest a few transitional forms, he opted for the newer punctuated equilibrium model of evolution. He was especially impressed with the sudden appearance of the flowering plants. "They appear so suddenly that it looks like the Creator said: 'I am really bored with ferns!' Poof!"

Pointing out that this is exactly the way the creation model would predict the appeareance of flowering plants, Gish replied: "How could the fossil record be so cruel to evolutionists?"

Chapter 37

Our Sideshow This Evening

University of Michigan

The Morris/Gish debates this past decade have been a slice of the historical controversy involving man's origins. How our own species arose is of great intrinsic interest to all. In fact, several evolutionist debaters have insisted that evolution would not be a controversial issue with the general public if it were not that the evolution of *Homo sapiens* is involved in the theory.

Out of a total of 136 debates to date, 19 different anthropologists have been involved in 23 of them. Five of the 172 different evolutionists in these debates were women. (This includes Madalyn Murray O'Hair, who is not a scientist.) Of these five, three were anthropologists. Only two of the 23 debates involving anthropologists were specifically on the origin of man—the second University of Oregon debate and the University of Washington debate.

The anthropologists in these debates were quite varied in the material they used to defend evolution. Although James Gavin (University of Missouri, Columbia, debate) and John T. Robinson (Wisconsin debate) had both written extensively on primate evolution (Gavin authored a textbook on it), neither one used a shred of evidence from his own area to defend evolution. On the other hand, Ashley Montagu (Princeton debate) and C. Loring Brace (University of Michigan debate) used the human fossil evidence extensively because they feel that herein lies the very best evidence for evolution.

When we see artists' representations of our alleged hominid
ancestor, the small gracile form known as *Australopithecus
africanus,* we invariably see it portrayed as being bipedal—
walking erect. This is the conventional wisdom in current
anthropology. It is not only assumed that it had to be bipedal
in order to be our ancestor, but that if it were bipedal, it
would be conclusive evidence that it was indeed our ancestor.
This major issue in anthropology was clearly brought out in
the course of these debates.

Back in 1974, anthropologists William Pollister (North
Carolina debate), George Gill (Wyoming panel), and Evelyn
Kessler (Tampa TV debate) all claimed these australopithe-
cines to be our evolutionary ancestors. Pollister alleged it to
be bipedal. In 1975, Elizabeth Baldwin (Western Michigan
University debate) declared the australopithecines to be inter-
mediate and bipedal. In 1976, Paul Aiello (Ventura College,
California, debate) did the same. Paul Simonds (second
Oregon debate), Donald Gordon (Fort Lewis College,
Colorado, panel), and Michael Charney (Colorado State
debate) all declared, in 1977, the australopithecines were intermediate and bipedal.

In 1978, John T. Robinson (Wisconsin debate) held the
same view. Vincent Sarich, in his four debates from
1978-1980, likewise insisted that these australopithcines were
intermediate and bipedal. Most recently, Ashley Montagu and
C. Loring Brace, who have coauthored a book on human
evolution, declared the australopithecines to be transitional
between ape and man. Brace opted for an upright stance.
Every anthropologist who mentioned the australopithecines
declared them to be the "missing link."

Against this solid wall of evolutionist opinion, Gish—who
dealt more with the fossil record than did Morris—could offer
names of only two evolutionists who disagreed—Sir Solly
Zuckerman and Charles Oxnard. Zuckerman was for many
years the Professor of Anatomy at the University of
Birmingham, England, and devoted 15 years of study to this
problem. Oxnard is Professor of Anatomy and Dean of the
Graduate School at the University of Southern California. In
contrast to others, these two investigators have used
multivariate statistical analysis with computers. Both men
declare emphatically that the australopithecines were neither

intermediate nor transitional between ape and man, and that they were not bipedal in the human manner.

Although some, such as Simonds and Sarich, had questioned the value of such computer analysis, Gish has steadfastly maintained that the work of Zuckerman and Oxnard was more objective, more precise, and more scholarly than the approach used by others. After studying the work of Zuckerman and Oxnard carefully, I am convinced that Gish is right. Yet, anthropologist Elizabeth Baldwin confessed that she was not familiar with the work of Zuckerman or Oxnard. Anthropologist Donald Gordon had not even heard of either one. In a fit of anger, Gordon insisted that anyone who claimed that the australopithecines were not intermediate had not looked at the material or was nuts!

C. Loring Brace attempted to discount the work of Zuckerman: "Many of us have done much more work with the australopithecines than has Zuckerman, and I myself have." Brace further charged that Zuckerman never studied the original material. His work was all done, Brace continued, on "a cast of one-half of the pelvis of a single specimen." Brace concluded by charging that Zuckerman "made no effort to correct for the distortion that the fossil had undergone in the last two million years in the ground."

Brace has quite misrepresented the work of Zuckerman. In his book, *Beyond the Ivory Tower,* Zuckerman states that at first his study was based upon just one specimen. However, there was a good reason for this that Brace neglected to mention. This one specimen was the only complete pelvis of an *Australopithecus africanus* that had been discovered. The other specimens were only fragments.

The specimen studied was the South African pelvis from Sterkfontein, known as Sts 14. The technical literature describing this fossil states that the right hip (innominate bone) is virtually complete, whereas the left hip was badly damaged. It was obviously for this reason that Zuckerman used only the half of the pelvis that was complete. This is no problem to anatomists, because the left hip would be a mirror-image of the right hip. Yet Brace, who had accused creationists of dishonesty, was trying to create the impression that Zuckerman was not a careful scholar and had not used all of the available evidence.

The literature made no mention of the Sts 14 fossil being distorted. There is a pelvis of *Australopithecus robustus* from Swartkrans, South Africa, known as SK-50. This pelvis is in a poor state of preservation and is distorted. However, the robust australopithecines are not even considered by most evolutionists to figure in the evolution of man. Both of these fossils are kept in the Transvaal Museum, Pretoria, South Africa. John T. Robinson has been involved with both. Hence, when Brace charged Zuckerman with not making a correction for distortion, it is possible that Brace himself was confusing these two fossils or he was counting on the fact that his audience would be quite ignorant of the details regarding them.

No one had made such serious charges against Gish (and other creationists) of misrepresentations and out-and-out lies as did Brace. Yet, no evolutionist debater was as "tricky" as was Brace in playing upon the ignorance of his audience regarding the human fossils. His charge that Zuckerman merely used a plaster cast of the pelvis rather than the original fossil material is another case in point.

The truth of the matter is that *all* anthropologists use plaster casts in studying the human fossils. The hominid fossil material is so scarce and so priceless that it is kept under lock and key. Did Brace mean to give the impression that anthropologists the world over all work on the original fossil material? There would not be enough material to go around. Zuckerman emphasized that great care was done in measuring the original to insure that the casts with which he worked were accurate.

Gish's debate with C. Loring Brace on the University of Michigan campus on March 17, 1982, was by far the most significant debate involving the human fossil evidence. It was also Gish's most recent debate with an anthropologist, except for the debate with Michael Park at Central Connecticut State College on April 1, 1982. Brace is one of the world's leading authorities on the human fossil material and represented the most serious challenge which Gish faced regarding his own interpretation of the human fossils.

Gish has always maintained that the fossils which have been classified as *Homo erectus,* especially the Peking Man fossils, were not true men, but were instead extinct apes. Gish based

his conclusion, in part, on the work of the great French
paleontologist, Marcellin Boule, who published his writings on
Peking Man from 1929 to 1946.

I have always felt that Gish was wrong in his assessment of
Homo erectus. Gish has properly pointed out some problems
with the interpretation of Peking Man. However, the many
subsequent discoveries of *Homo erectus* fossils—some of them
quite similar to Peking Man—seem to justify the inclusion of
Peking Man in the *Homo erectus* category. Virtually all
evolutionists recognize that *Homo erectus* was true man. The
differences between *Homo erectus* and "modern man" are
confined to the skull. They can easily be explained as
illustrations of the large degree of genetic variation that is
known to exist in the human family. Hence, I have been
mystified as to why Gish maintained his position that *Homo
erectus* was just an extinct ape. I feel that this has weakened
Gish's otherwise very solid defense of creationism, and it
has—over the years—gotten him into a bit of trouble.

Boule was the one responsible for the very incorrect
restoration of the famous Neanderthal skeleton from La
Chapelle-aux-Saints. This poor old man was suffering from
arthritis and other bone diseases. Boule was one of the
world's foremost paleontologists. Yet his reconstruction of
this Neanderthal skeleton was so badly done as to border on
deliberate fraud. It served as the basis for the "cave man"
impression that we were given of the Neanderthalers for many
years. We now know that it is very wrong.

Gish pointed out Boule's errors regarding the Neanderthal
restoration, but defended Boule's interpretation of Peking
Man. It was only a matter of time until someone asked the
question that anthropologist Paul Simonds asked in the
Oregon debate: "Could you explain why you think Boule was
so good in Peking and so bad in Paris?"

It was the *Homo erectus* stage of the alleged evolution of
man that Brace chose to emphasize in his debate with Gish. It
was Brace's area of expertise. It was Gish's area of greatest
weakness. Since the facts were not entirely on Brace's side, he
chose to attack Gish as a man and as a scientist. In no other
debate has the integrity, honesty, morality, and Christian
character of Gish been as viciously attacked. Brace did it with
great eloquence, but it was obvious that he was punching

below the belt. It was Gish's worst hour, but also his finest hour. He responded as a Christian gentleman. This was the best defense Gish could have made, for it defused Brace's attack and demonstrated Gish's integrity.

It was to Olduvai Gorge in East Africa and the work of Louis Leakey that Gish turned for evidence that man does not really have any evolutionary ancestors. In Bed II at Olduvai Gorge, Leakey reported finding *Australopithecus* (the robust form known as Zinj), *Homo habilis* (which many now consider *Australopithecus africanus*), and *Homo erectus*. These three forms were apparently living as contemporaries. Hence, it is difficult to see how one could be ancestral to the other.

Moreover, at the very bottom of Bed I, the lowest bed at Olduvai, a circular stone structure was found that could only have been constructed by true man. This object, 14 feet in diameter, is considered to be the world's oldest man-made structure. Mary Leakey discovered it during the 1961-62 digging season on the very lowest and oldest of the occupation sites or living floors at Olduvai. She quickly recognized that there was a pattern in the distribution of these stones, an intentional piling of stones on top of each other. The stones themselves are lava rocks that are not indiginous to what was a lakeshore when the structure was built. The several hundred rocks were brought from some distance. Other stones on that occupation site are scarce and haphazardly scattered.

What is this structure? Nobody knows. Is it a habitation hut, a hunting blind, a weapons pile, or a shelter of some kind? What is known is that people of the Okombambi tribe in Southwest Africa construct such shelters today. They make a low ring of stones with higher piles at intervals to support upright poles or braces. Over these are placed skins or grasses to keep out the wind. Turkana tribesmen living in the desert country of northern Kenya also make similar shelters.

What is staggering is that the living floor where this structure was found is thought to be two million years old by evolutionary standards. Also found was the usual stone and bone waste, as well as Oldewan tools. These tools were considered to be extremely primitive. However, Mary Leakey reports that a similar type of stone chopper is used today by the remote Turkana tribesmen in order to break open the nuts of the Doum palm. Actually, these stone choppers are very efficient for certain tasks.

When Gish's opponents are faced with the evidence of three different forms living as contemporaries, and with the circular stone structure at a lower level, their responses are rather interesting. Evelyn Kessler (Tampa TV debate) claimed that the stones were just a windbreak built by australopithecines. We do know that man builds this kind of structure. But, since man was not supposed to be on the scene, and since in Kessler's view the australopithecines were man's evolutionary ancestors, it is "obvious" that they must have built it. This is sound evolutionist logic.

Brace had a better idea. He claimed that the structure was not the result of human activity at all. "I went there myself, saw it, and it's the result of just erosion down on the bottom of that area." Brace stated that Louis Leakey made a number of claims that were questionable. No one challenges the fact that Louis Leakey became overly enthusiastic at times. However, it was Mary Leakey who discovered and described this stone structure. Although in one sense she has come into her own only since the death of her husband, those working in archaeology have long known that Mary Leakey is one of the most respected, accurate, and reliable workers in the entire field. No one challenges her authority because of her careful scholarship. If anyone could recognize the work of man, as opposed to the "work" of chance, Mary Leakey could.

Referring to the fact that *Australopithecus, Homo habilis,* and *Homo erectus* were all found in Olduvai Bed II as contemporaries, Elizabeth Baldwin (Western Michigan debate) claimed that this was not surprising since these forms do overlap in time. Further, she stated that Bed II is not just a single time period, but probably covers one million years. Baldwin is quite wrong. Bed II was never thought to cover more than half a million years, and is now thought to be of even shorter duration. She may have confused it with Bed I which originally was thought to span one million years. Recently, data has come to light which indicates Bed I may span as little as 25,000 years by the evolutionary time table. This compaction of time makes the fossil associations in Bed II and the stone structure at the base of Bed I even more significant.

Brace took sharp issue with Leakey's claim of three hominids living at the same time in Bed II. The exchange during the question period went like this:

Brace: "As for the three different hominids in Bed II, name them! I can assure you that there are not three different hominids living contemporaneously."

Gish: "Were they all australopithecines?"

Brace: "No." (Everyone expected Brace to tell what they were, but he didn't seem anxious to continue the conversation.)

Gish: "What were they?"

Brace (hesitates): *"Homo erectus."*

Gish: "No australopithecines?"

Brace: "Yes, there was a large australopithecine in Bed II." (Zinj, the robust form.)

Gish: "How about his [Leakey's] *Homo habilis*?"

At this point, Brace doesn't answer the question. Instead he asks, "What is *Homo habilis*?"

Gish: "As many of your colleagues would say, it's simply an australopithecine." (Gish here means the gracile or *africanus* form.)

Brace then emphasizes that no one is sure what *Homo habilis* is.

Now, in this case it doesn't really matter what *Homo habilis* is. Certainly it is distinct from *Homo erectus*, as well as Zinj, and it certainly was in Bed II at Olduvai. Brace could not deny it. Further, after claiming that there definitely were not three different forms living as contemporaries in Bed II, Brace admitted that *Homo erectus* and a large australopithcine was there. That, together with *Homo habilis,* seems to make three. And yet, several times Brace accused creationists of double-talk.

The fact that these three forms were found living at the same time is very significant. According to evolutionary theory, *Homo habilis* (or *Australopithecus africanus,* if you please) became extinct because it slowly and gradually evolved into *Homo erectus.* Hence, you cannot have them living together at the same time. As Gish put it, "How could the fossil record be so cruel to evolutionists?"

Brace tried to make creationists out as the enemies of science, claiming that creationists consider science to be of the devil. The rise in popularity of creationism was as dangerous to science, he felt, as was the Islamic revolution in Iran. Further, he charged, creationists practice the "big lie" technique of Joseph Stalin. The idea is that if you tell a big enough lie, and tell it often enough, people will believe it.

Brace claimed that the debate was not an intellectual event, but just a sideshow. It was. But it was Brace, not Gish, that made it so.

Chapter 38

How Am I Going to Face My Wife?

Liberty Baptist College

Isaac Asimov is America's most popular science writer. He has written over 200 books on science and other subjects. Yet, his attitudes reveal that he is a very ordinary atheist. Since hard-core atheists are a small minority in our nation, logic would seem to dictate that they should champion the rights of all people. Freedom for everyone in the marketplace of ideas would ensure their own freedoms as well.

However, in this case, logic does not rule. Asimov, like Madalyn Murray O'Hair, is particularly militant against Biblical Christianity and creationism. He has been active in raising money for the American Civil Liberties Union to fight creation laws in Arkansas and Louisiana. In his money-raising letters he calls creationists "religious zealots" who "neither know nor understand the actual arguments for—or even against—the theory of evolution." Yet, in these same letters he makes absurd charges against creationists. He obviously does not understand what creationists believe or want taught in the public schools.

These attitudes are also seen in Asimov's debate with Gish in the October 1981 issue of *Science Digest*. Asimov, a contributing editor of that magazine, continually tries to make the issue one of religion vs. science. This is even seen in the title of the *Science Digest* debate. Although Gish deals entirely with scientific arguments and does not even mention the Bible or Genesis, the debate is entitled, "The Genesis War."

The 1981-82 academic year was the tenth anniversary of the Morris/Gish debates. It was a fitting anniversary year. First, a total of 22 debates were held—second only to the 1976-77 academic year when 26 debates were held. Second, two of these debates were unique—having a coverage as large as all of the other debates put together.

The first of these unique debates was the Gish/Asimov debate in the pages of *Science Digest*. At that time, *Science Digest* had a monthly circulation of 542,000. How many people actually read the debate is impossible to determine. If we assume that only one-fourth of those who subscribe to the magazine actually read the debate, that alone would involve 135,000 people. It should be remembered that this magazine goes to virtually all public libraries, college and university libraries, and many high school and junior high school libraries where just one copy of the magazine could be read by many people.

The other extraordinary debate was held at Liberty Baptist College, Lynchburg, Virginia, on October 13, 1981. Five thousand were in attendance, which tied the attendance record set in 1977 at the University of Minnesota. However, the local attendance was incidental. The one-hour debate—one of the shortest of them all—was actually a television special which was recorded for rebroadcast nationwide throughout 1982. It was sponsored by *The Old Time Gospel Hour* with Dr. Jerry Falwell serving as moderator. Russell F. Doolittle, Professor of Biochemistry, University of California, San Diego, was Gish's opponent. This was Doolittle's fifth debate with either Morris or Gish.

A lack of anticipated finances restricted the showing of this Gish/Doolittle debate from what was originally intended. However, during Spring and Summer of 1982, it was shown in the following metropolitan areas: Dallas/Fort Worth, Louisville, Philadelphia, Kansas City, Little Rock, Spokane, Clearwater (Florida), and elsewhere. In the Fall of 1982 it was televised nationwide on the Christian Broadcasting Network and the Christian News Network. Although coverage estimates are difficult to calculate, it has become the most widely seen and heard creation-evolution debate in history. A conservative, but *very tentative* estimate is that two million people have viewed this debate in 1982.

When it comes to substance, both Asimov and Doolittle were disappointing. Asimov stated flatly that "Scientists have no choice but to consider evolution to be a fact." His major evidence, however, was that living organisms can be arranged in an evolutionary tree of life and that they can also be classified in discrete categories. He seems unaware that almost any class of objects—living or nonliving—can be arranged in an evolutionary sequence—even though their origin had nothing to do with evolution. I once arranged my tools in an "evolutionary" sequence—that is, primitive to advanced or generalized to specialized.

Although Asimov mentioned Aristotle's attempts to classify living things, he did not mention the greatest classifier in the history of science—Carl Linnaeus, who died in 1778. Since Asimov used the classification scheme as a major evidence for evolution, it would not have helped his cause to mention that the founder of the modern scheme of animal and plant classfication, Linnaeus, was a man of deep Christian faith with a high regard for the Holy Scriptures. In fact, in working out his classification scheme—which is still used today—Linneaus was attempting to delineate the original Genesis "kinds." He was a staunch creationist. More hardly needs to be said regarding the absurdity of using the classification of living things as evidence for evolution.

After touching briefly upon the fossil record, genetics, and radioactive dating, Asimov concluded with this incredible statement: "Evolution is a fact and it cannot be upset without discarding all of modern biology, biochemistry, geology, astronomy—in short, without discarding all of science." It is difficult to respond to that statement because it is so utterly and totally wrong. In fact, there are only three reasons why such a statement would be made. None of the reasons are very complimentary to Asimov.

Is it possible that a man of Asimov's stature is so ignorant of the history of science that he doesn't know that for hundreds of years, a period known as the golden age of science, the only model of the "establishment" was the creation model? Under creationism, science wasn't discarded—it was established! Does Asimov not know that Kepler, Galileo, Newton, Linnaeus, Faraday, Agassiz, Mendel, Pasteur, Maxwell—to name just a few—were all

creationists? It seemes incredible that he would not know.
Yet, if he were aware of that, his statement is nothing short
of deception.

There is a second possibility—that is that Asimov made
such an absurd statement to instill fear of creationism in the
minds of those who would read his article. This would also
explain why he charges that creationists are attempting to
force the teaching of the Bible in the public schools. One has
only to read the bills passed by the Arkansas and Louisiana
legislatures—as well as those proposed in other state
legislatures—to know how false that charge is. Unfortunately,
because this false charge is made so often by evolutionists,
many people believe it.

There is yet a third possibility. Ignorance of the history of
science seems to be out of the question. Deceit is a difficult
charge to make because only God knows the heart and
motives of a person. The only other possibility is an intense
prejudice against creationism as a result of spiritual
blindness—a prejudice so total that Asimov is incapable of
dealing with the history and facts of creationism, even though
these facts are literally staring him in the face. Asimov is not
alone in this prejudice.

The Doolittle debate, according to evolutionists themselves,
was a disaster. Whereas Gish gave an excellent summary of
the evidence for creation from the areas of thermodynamics,
probability theory, and the fossil record, Doolittle simply did
not time his presentation well. He spent two-thirds of his
precious eighteen minutes telling about a fifth and sixth grade
public school teacher in Livermore, California, who was
teaching the Biblical concept of creation in the science
classroom without approval. As Gish pointed out in his
rebuttal, all of this was wasted time because creationists
themselves do not approve of what that teacher was doing.
Creationists want the scientific evidence, not the Biblical
account, taught in the public schools.

With only about five minutes left, Doolittle finally got into
his evidence for evolution—which was the subject of the
debate. He mentioned the organic molecules in outer space
and emphasized the time question based on the size of the
universe and the ages obtained from radiometric dating. He

felt that the age of the moon rocks confirmed the age of the solar system that had been deduced from earth rocks. Since both were achieved by radioactive dating techniques, creationists do not feel that it is really an independent confirmation.

Doolittle was just getting into his evidence when he realized that his time was up. He was shocked and began to panic. The closing words of his presentation were as follows:

> I want to hear Dr. Gish say tonight how old he thinks—Whoo! Thirty seconds. I'm running out of time. It's incredible. Well, I have to very quickly go here. May I, in fact, quickly now just go through my slides. I just saw what I think is a thirty-second flash here. These have been the fastest 18 minutes of my life. And as I'm now on my last slide—Oop! I've been squeezed out. My last slide just went by. I'm out of gas, and I think that . . . .

At that point he was told that his time was up.

In his rebuttal, Doolittle attempted to deal with Gish's evidence that a naturalistic origin of the universe was impossible. Gish had suggested that the only viable option for the origin of the universe was a supernatural one. Doolittle called this "illogical logic." He then gave a common evolutionist argument. "Just because we can't explain something now doesn't mean we won't be able to explain it in the future." After commenting on the marvelous accomplishments of science in the last 100 years, he continued: "So I think that there's no doubt that we will explain all this and any of the questions that he's raised to everyone's satisfaction eventually."

Since evolutionists state this idea so often, it is important to understand what Doolittle is actually saying. First, such a statement is really a confession that there are solid creationist evidences for which evolutionists have no answer as yet.

Second, such a statement is an affirmation that there is nothing in the universe that the unaided human mind will not fathom. The universe is not a witness to God's power, wisdom, and glory. The mind of man is sufficient to comprehend it all. Hence, this is an atheistic statement. I am not pressing Doolittle's words too much. Other statements made by him confirm that this is his thinking.

But most important of all, such statements are not statements of science, but statements of faith. Doolittle is saying that his faith commitment to evolution is so strong that even though there is much evidence against it now, he believes that eventually evolution will be vindicated and the needed evidence will be supplied. A person who makes such a statement is denying a basic tenet of science. Scientists pride themselves in claiming to follow where the evidence leads—no matter what. Doolittle is saying just the opposite. He will not accept creation, even though there is strong evidence for it. Instead, he will trust in evolution hoping that the needed evidence will be supplied in the future. Nothing could more clearly indicate that evolution is a faith—not science.

That type of thinking characterized Darwin himself. Darwin recognized that the fossils needed to support evolution were missing. However, he expressed faith that they would be found in the future. From that day until now, evolutionists have been placing great faith in the fossils they hope someday to find to support their theory. This kind of talk has been so common that creationists have allowed it to pass without pointing out what it actually is.

Because of his poor showing, Doolittle confessed after the debate, "I'm devastated." According to the *Washington Post,* he remarked: "For the $5,000.00 fee, they could pay some numbskull to come in and make a fool of himself. As it turns out, that's exactly what they got." Doolittle has reportedly written to many of his colleagues apologizing for his poor presentation.

The November 6, 1981, issue of the journal, *Science,* reports that both the National Academy of Science and the National Association of Biology Teachers were concerned about how to overcome the bad publicity for evolution that the debate would cause. Some are saying that it was the scientific community that let Doolittle down, rather than the reverse, because, "We let him go there with virtually no help in preparation for the debate and no support once he was there." This attitude is rather humorous. First of all, Doolittle is a grown man and fully able to take care of himself. Since he is one of the world's leading biochemists, he really shouldn't have needed much help in preparation. Further, he had already—before the Lynchburg debate—debated Morris or Gish as often as anyone else in the world. He had debated them four times—equaled only by Vincent Sarich and Kenneth Miller[1]. It wasn't as if Doolittle were inexperienced in this matter.

Why Doolittle, who had so much experience debating creationists, would make such a foolish error as not timing his presentation properly is hard to understand. The true depth of his humiliation is seen by his statement after the debate: "How am I going to face my wife after making such a fool of myself?"

I wonder what she said.

---

[1]   Fred Edword, Administrator of the American Humanist Association, has also debated Morris and/or Gish four times. However, two of these debates came after the Liberty Baptist College debate.

Chapter 39

Looking Both Ways

This past decade has been an astounding period of history, both in the creation-evolution controversy and in the reorganization of evolutionary thought. Virtually every tenet of evolution is being challenged—except, of course, the "fact" of evolution itself. Because the concept of evolution is an ideal naturalistic explanation for the origin of the universe and of life, it will continue to flourish as it has for thousands of years.

The turmoil within the evolutionist community stands out in bold relief in these 136 Morris/Gish debates. Some evolutionists claim that there are thousands of transitional forms. Others confess that there are none. Some state that evolution is observable today. Others admit that it is not. Some evolutionists recognize that evolution is a random process. Others have insisted that it isn't. Some have seen the second law of thermodynamics as a genuine problem for evolution. Others feel that it presents no difficulties at all. The origin of life is considered by some to be outside of evolutionary theory. Others see it as an integral part of evolution. Some recognize that the only legitimate evidence for evolution must come from the fossil record. Others seek to utilize a wide spectrum of evidences for the theory. Some declare that evolution's pace is slow and steady. Others prefer to think that it is fast and jerky. Mutations and natural selection have long been held to be the major mechanisms of evolution. Both are now being challenged. And on it goes.

While we all recognize that challenge and conflict are a part

of the scientific method, it is obvious that something far
deeper is brewing. Changes will continue to be made
in the way evolution is presented in the schools and to the
public. It is significant that this most severe challenge to
evolution theory is contemporaneous with an intense and
increasing interest in creationism. Some of us believe that
there is a cause-and-effect relationship. A reviewer writing in
the November-December 1982 issue of *American Scientist*
confesses: "Evolutionary biology is in a state of ferment and
restructuring, partly because of fundamentalist pressure on the
public schools . . . . "

Because the term "fundamentalist" has a negative connota-
tion in many circles, evolutionists continually present the
creationist movement as just an attempt by fundamentalists to
impose their "narrow religion" on the public schools.
Thankfully, informed people are beginning to see the issues as
much more profound. These creation-evolution debates
directed primarily to the student world are having a telling
effect.

The geographical distribution of these debates is revealing.
Twenty-seven have been held in California and ten in Illinois.
Five each have been held in Florida, Kansas, and Missouri,
four each in Iowa, Louisiana, Texas, and Wisconsin, and
three each in Michigan, Ohio, Virginia, and Washington. In
all, 36 states have hosted at least one creation-evolution
debate. Glaring omissions are New York state and
Washington, D.C., where none have been held.

Fifteen debates have been held in Canada, seven of these
being in the Province of Ontario. Six of Canada's provinces
have hosted at least one creation-evolution debate. Since it is
obvious that these Morris/Gish debates would have to be
confined to English-speaking areas, it is not surprising that
the other countries having debates are England, Australia,
New Zealand, the West Indies, and The Netherlands—where
English is common.

Of interest also is the question of how many people have
seen, heard, or read a Morris/Gish debate. There are four
categories involved in determining this figure. By far the
easiest figure at which to arrive—and the most accurate—is
the total attendance of these debates. This total attendance
figure, obtained from attendance estimates of the individual

debates, is 129,550. Although not all of the debates were held
before a live audience, the average attendance of those that
were is 1,028.

Incidental to some of the public debates was a radio or
television audience. Some of the debates were broadcast live.
Others were recorded or videotaped for later airing. Only a
portion of these situations are known, and estimates of even
these are difficult. Station estimates in this category give a
listener/viewer audience of 36,000.

A third category involves those that were primarily radio or
television debates. In some cases there was also a small studio
audience which has been included in the attendance figures in
category one. In consultation with the stations involved, what
I believe to be a conservative listener/viewer estimate has been
determined to be 5,230,000. The individual estimates are as
follows.

Date	Debate	Audience
Feb. 1975	Winnipeg debate broadcast over CBC	100,000
April 20, 1976	KTRH Houston Radio Talk-Show debate	160,000
April 14, 1977	KFH Wichita Radio Talk-Show debate	250,000
Oct. 21, 1980	WHO Des Moines Radio Talk-Show debate	1,500,000
Sept. 21, 1982	KMOX St. Charles, MO., Radio debate	10,000
March 2, 1974	WTVT Tampa debate	50,000
Nov. 1974	Toronto TV Talk-Show debate	50,000
March 31, 1977	WGN Chicago TV panel	280,000
Oct. 1977	Utrecht, The Netherlands, debate televised nationwide	500,000
March 1980	Kansas City TV debate PTL Club	300,000
Feb. 10, 1982	Salt Lake City public television debate	20,000
1981-1982	Liberty Baptist College TV debate	2,000,000
Sept. 28, 1982	Kitchener, Ontario TV debate	10,000
		5,230,000

The fourth category involves debates that have been printed
in periodicals. I have determined the circulation of these
periodicals and then arbitrarily used the figure of one-fourth
that amount to estimate the number who actually read the
debate. Obviously, this estimate is the most difficult one to
determine with accuracy. This estimate comes to 228,000

readers. The individual debates and the circulation figures for the periodicals are as follows:

Date	Periodical	Readers
Sept. 19, 1975	*San Diego Union* newspaper debate	182,000
Nov.-Dec. 1977	*The Humanist* magazine debate	100,000
Oct. 1981	*Science Digest* debate	542,000
		824,000
Estimated one-fourth readership		206,000

In the following situations, I have estimated a three-fourths readership of the total circulation.

Date	Periodical	Readers
1975	*Acts and Facts* reprint of *San Diego Union* debate	20,000
1981-82	Printed text of Liberty Baptist College debate	10,000
		30,000
Estimated three-fourths readership		22,500

I have thus estimated that a total of 5,624,000 people have seen, heard, or read a creation-evolution debate involving Henry Morris and/or Duane Gish. I believe that these figures are conservative. However, even if they should be over-estimated in some areas, it is obvious that the impact of these two men has been amazing. Remember, this figure involves only their *debates*—cases where one or more evolutionists have been on the podium or program with them. It does not include their lectures and seminars—as well as their many books—which have reached far more people than have the debates.

As for the present, the debates continue. Six have already been held in the first semester of the 1982-83 school year. Morris has debated at Bemidji State University, Bemidji, Minnesota, and at the University of West Virginia, Morgantown. Gish has debated at the University of Western Ontario, London, and at the University of Toronto. He has also had a television debate at Kitchener, Ontario, and a radio debate at

St. Charles, Missouri. Since the average number of debates per school year has been thirteen, and two-thirds of the debates have been in the Spring Semester, the 1982-83 school year has started well.

The future of the debates promises to be even more exciting than the past has been. The reason is that evolutionists are getting organized in order to more effectively respond to the creationist challenge. Writing in the November issue of *Science 82,* a publication of the American Association for the Advancement of Science, science journalist Robert Schadewald (who debated Gish on Station WHO, Des Moines, in 1980) believes that because of better preparation and an organized network, evolutionists are beginning to win some of the Morris/Gish debates. This is a rather subjective statement on his part since no attempt is made to determine an official "winner."

Admitting that creationists "won" virtually all of them in the past, Schadewald feels that the turning point was the Morris/Miller debate at Brown University in the Spring of 1981. He states that a small group of evolutionists have formed an informal communications network to exchange information. Miller, whom Schadewald calls "the most successful anti-creationist debater," estimated that about half of his arguments came from that network.

Schadewald implies that creationists will now lose their taste for debating. Not so! Morris has continually stated his dislike for debating and has tried to avoid as many as possible in the past. Why does he do it? He has declared that creationists are not as interested in winning debates as they are in winning a hearing. Creationists have continually challenged evolutionists to answer their arguments. A study of recent debates involving Miller and others reveals that while evolutionists are becoming better debaters, they are still not squarely facing the evidences against evolution. In the recent University of West Virginia debate, no debater from that campus could be found to face Morris. Emmanuel Sillman from Duquesne University, Pittsburgh, was brought in. He is the Pennsylvania coordinator for the new information network established by evolutionists. Yet, he reportedly did poorly.

An interesting detail of this information network was not reported by Schadewald. He stated that the coordinator of this information network for evolutionists is a man named Fred Edwords. Edwords has debated Morris and Gish four times. What Schadewald neglected to mention is that Edwords, who is not a scientist but a philosopher, is the Administrator of the American Humanist Association. It is understandable why Schadewald would not advertise that fact, although he obviously was aware of it. It is very significant that the national head of the humanist movement should feel that there is so much at stake in the creation-evolution issue as to personally head up this communications network for evolutionist debaters. It tends to confirm what Morris and Gish have emphasized all along—the creation-evolution issue is far deeper than just a scientific controversy. It is a battle of two world-views affecting every area of life.

Of all the things that took place in the 136 debates over a period of ten years, two contrasting incidents stand out sharply in my mind. They dramatically illustrate the two possible responses in this battle of world-views.

The first incident came out of the Des Moines Area Community College debate in 1980. During the question period, a student asked debater John Patterson, an evolutionist and an atheist, what kind of evidence it would take for him to consider a supernatural cause in the origin of things. Patterson began by referring to the remarkable fact that in living proteins and DNA all of the amino acids are left-handed, while all of the sugars have a right-handed configuration. This fact alone is so totally removed from what happens naturally that it is a powerful testimony to the God of Creation.

Patterson then suggested that people, apparently Christians, gather around an empty enclosed chamber and call upon God to create in the chamber a life form having molecules of the opposite orientation. If God would create a life form having D-amino acids and L-sugars, Patterson said that he would be impressed! He did not say that even then he would become a Christian or a creationist.

This "experiment" Patterson likened to the demonstration which the Old Testament character, Gideon, asked of God regarding the fleece. However, Patterson's absurd request was just a clever way of saying that there is simply no evidence that he would accept as being sufficient to prove a Creator.

However, his detailed knowledge of the account of Gideon suggests that he had an evangelical Christian background. He seems to be a classic illustration of the spiritual wreckage which evolution leaves in its wake.

The contrasting incident which has stuck in my memory was an illustration Gish gave in the Pennsylvania State University debate in 1973. The story impressed me so much that I have wondered why Gish has not used it before or since. He suggested that you imagine yourself in a flask in which a biochemist was synthesizing the highly complex organic substance, insulin. Being inside the flask, you would not know that there was an intelligent being outside the flask that had planned the experiment and was directing it. All you would see would be the natural laws operating. You would see chemical bonds being formed and broken, charged particles interacting, and chemical groups attracting one another. The only way you would know that there was someone outside the flask planning and directing everything would be by the nature of the finished product. You would see a highly complex structure form that could not come about by natural, random processes. You would see something come into being in contrast to the way chemistry and physics normally operate. Because of the finished product, you would know that there was an intelligence behind it all who had planned and directed it.

In the same way, we are in a very complex universe. A universe, Gish emphasized, that could not have come about by natural, random processes. It is by the nature of the finished product, our complex universe, that we know that there is a Creator who planned and directed it all. With those words he concluded his presentation at the Penn State debate. His words were in complete accord with the words of St. Paul:

> For since the creation of the world, God's invisible
> qualities—His eternal power and divine nature—have
> been clearly seen, being understood from what has been
> made, so that men are without excuse.
>
> Romans 1:20 (N.I.V.)

Appendix I

Alphabetical List of Debates By Cities

Academic positions mentioned are positions held by the debaters at the time of their participation in the creation-evolution debates listed.

Ames, Iowa. Debate on the origin of life held on the campus of Iowa State University on October 22, 1980, with 1,500 in attendance. Duane Gish vs. Russell F. Doolittle (Professor of Biochemistry, University of California, San Diego). Sponsored by Students for Origins Research, a local campus organization.

Amherst, Massachusetts. Debate held on the campus of the University of Massachusetts on April 28, 1976, with 900 in attendance. Henry Morris vs. David J. Klingener (Associate Professor of Zoology and Vertebrate Paleontology) and Bruce R. Levin (Associate Professor of Zoology and Population Genetics). Sponsored by several Christian student organizations.

Ankeny, Iowa. Debate held on the campus of the Des Moines Area Community College on January 16, 1980, with 200 in attendance. Duane Gish vs. John W. Patterson (Professor of Materials Science and Engineering, Iowa State University). Sponsored by the Office of Student Affairs and the Student Government Association of Des Moines Area Community College.

Ann Arbor, Michigan. Debate held on the campus of the University of Michigan on March 17, 1982, with 2,000 in attendance. Duane Gish vs. C. Loring Brace (Professor of Physical Anthropology). Sponsored by the local Campus Crusade for Christ organization. The debate was broadcast locally on WUOM.

Auckland, New Zealand. Debate held on the campus of Auckland University in July 1973, with 1,500 in attendance. Henry Morris vs. C. Loring Brace (Professor of Physical Anthropology, University of Michigan).

Austin, Texas. Debate held on the campus of the University of Texas on March 24, 1977, with 2,200 in attendance. Henry Morris and Duane Gish vs. Larry Gilbert and Alan Templeton (both of the Department of Zoology). Sponsored by the University of Texas.

Baraboo, Wisconsin. Debate held in the Civic Center on October 24, 1980, with 250 in attendance. Duane Gish vs. Newtol Press (Professor of Zoology, University of Wisconsin, Milwaukee). Sponsored by the First Baptist Church, Baraboo.

Bellingham, Washington. Debate held on the campus of Western Washington University on October 9, 1980. Attendance was 800. Duane Gish vs. Donald C. Williams (Professor of Biochemistry). Sponsored by the Associated Students of Western Washington University.

Bemidji, Minnesota. Debate held on the campus of Bemidji State University on September 20, 1982, with 650 in attendance. Henry Morris vs. Evan Hazzard (Professor of Biology).

Berkeley, California. Debate on the origin of life held on the campus of the University of California, Berkeley, on May 19, 1977, with 400 in attendance. Duane Gish vs. Harold J. Morowitz (Professor of Molecular Biophysics, Yale University). Sponsored by the University of California, Berkeley.

Blacksburg, Virginia. Debate held on the campus of the Virginia Polytechnic Institute and State University on November 8, 1975, with 1,100 in attendance. Henry Morris vs. Richard K. Bambach (Associate Professor of Paleontology). Sponsored by Genesis, a student organization.

Bridgewater, Massachusetts. Debate held on the campus of Bridgewater State College on April 29, 1976, with 300 in attendance. Henry Morris vs. Richard Enright (Department of Geology) and John C. Jahoda (Associate Professor of Biology).

Brighton, England. Debate held at Sussex University on February 12, 1979, with 550 in attendance. Duane Gish vs. John Maynard Smith (Professor of Biology and Chairman of the Department). Sponsored by Campus Crusade for Christ of Great Britain.

Burnaby, British Columbia, Canada. Debate held on the campus of Simon Fraser University in November 1974, with 250 in attendance. Duane Gish vs. R.M.F.S. Sadleir (Professor of Biology).

Calgary, Alberta, Canada. Panel held on the campus of the University of Calgary on February 21, 1974. Attendance figures unavailable. Duane Gish vs. three faculty members from the University of Calgary.

Calgary, Alberta, Canada. Debate held on the campus of the University of Calgary in February 1981. Attendance was 200. Duane Gish vs. Val Geist (Department of Geology) and William Costerton (Department of Biochemistry).

Carbondale, Illinois. Debate held on the campus of Southern Illinois University on October 19, 1978, with 2,000 in attendance. Duane Gish vs. Howard Stains (Professor of Zoology). Sponsored by Word of Life Fellowship, a local organization.

Cave Hill, Barbados, British West Indies. Debate held on the Cave Hill campus of the University of the West Indies in November 1981, with 350 in attendance. Duane Gish vs. Wayne Hunt (Department of Biology) and Dr. Madison (Professor of Biology and Chairman of the Department.).

Chapel Hill, North Carolina. Debate held on the campus of the University of North Carolina on January 21, 1974, with 500 in attendance. Henry Morris vs. William Pollitser (Professor of Anatomy and Anthropology). Sponsored by the local Campus Crusade for Christ organization.

Charleston, South Carolina. Debate held in the Municipal Auditorium on February 10, 1980, with over 1,000 in attendance. Duane Gish vs. E. Roy Epperson (Professor of Chemistry, High Point College, North Carolina).

Charlottesville, Virginia. Debate held on the campus of the University of Virginia on March 22, 1982, with 500 in attendance. Duane Gish vs. James Murray (Professor of Biology) and Jerry Wolff (Assistant Professor of Biology). Sponsored jointly by the Faculty Forum for Science Research and the local chapter of Sigma Xi national honorary scientific research society.

Chicago, Illinois. Debate held in the auditorium of Lake Park High School on March 30, 1976. No attendance figures. Henry Morris vs. James Bond (biologist).

Chicago, Illinois. Debate held in the auditorium of Glenbrook High School, Glenview, on April 5, 1976, with 200 in attendance. Duane Gish vs. Robert Demar (Department of Geology, University of Illinois, Chicago Circle Campus).

Chicago, Illinois. Debate held on the Chicago Circle Campus of the University of Illinois on April 5, 1976, with 250 in attendance.

Duane Gish vs. Robert Demar (Department of Geology) and Steven Weller (Department of Biology).

Chicago, Illinois. Station WGN television panel on "Cromie's Circle" moderated by Dr. Robert Cromie, recorded on March 31, 1977. Henry Morris vs. Peter J. Wyllie (Professor of Geology, University of Chicago).

Chico, California. Debate held on the campus of California State University, Chico, on November 19, 1976, with 1,400 in attendance. Duane Gish vs. Michael Erpino (Department of Biological Science).

Cincinnati, Ohio. Debate held on the campus of the University of Cincinnati on October 24, 1974, with 1,500 in attendance. Duane Gish vs. Alex Fraser (Professor of Biology and Genetics). Sponsored by The Overcomers, a local student organization.

College Park, Maryland. Debate held on the campus of the University of Maryland on October 14, 1976, with 1,300 in attendance. Duane Gish vs. Geerat J. Vermeij (Associate Professor of Zoology) and Isidora Adler (Professor of Chemistry and Chairman of the Geochemistry Division).

Columbia, Missouri. Debate held on the campus of the University of Missouri, Columbia, on October 20, 1975, with 1,500 in attendance. Duane Gish vs. James Gavan (Professor of Anthropology and Chairman of the Department). Sponsored jointly by the university Department of Anthropology and the Missouri Association for Creation.

Columbia, Missouri. Panel discussion held on the campus of the University of Missouri, Columbia, on September 22, 1976, with 500 in attendance. Duane Gish with David Shear (Associate Professor of Biochemistry), Thomas Freeman (Professor of Geology), Olan Brown (microbiologist and Assistant Director of the Dalton Research Center), and Robert Marshall (Professor of Food Science and Nutrition). Sponsored jointly by the Missouri Students Association and the Missouri Association for Creation.

Columbus, Georgia. Debate held on the campus of Columbus College on May 6, 1981, with 1,000 in attendance. Henry Morris and Harold Slusher vs. David Schwimmer and William Frazier (both of the Department of Geology).

Costa Mesa, California. Debate held at Calvary Chapel on November 17, 1975, with 2,800 in attendance, as well as a radio audience. Henry Morris and Duane Gish vs. Bayard Brattstrom (Professor of Zoology, California State University, Fullerton) and William

Presch (Assistant Professor of Zoology, California State University, Fullerton). Sponsored by Calvary Chapel.

Costa Mesa, California. Debate held at Calvary Chapel on October 1, 1976, with 3,100 in attendance. Duane Gish and Harold Slusher vs. Gary Lynch (Professor of Neurobiology, University of California, Irvine) and George Miller (Professor of Chemistry, University of California, Irvine). Sponsored by Calvary Chapel.

Cupertino, California. Debate held on the campus of DeAnza College on August 29, 1974, with 2,300 in attendance. Duane Gish vs. Sheldon Matlow (Instructor in Mathematics, West Valley College, Saratoga, California, and owner of a mining and manufacturing company). Sponsored by Citizens for Scientific Creation, a local organization.

Cupertino, California. Debate held on the campus of DeAnza College on May 31, 1979, with 1,600 in attendance. Duane Gish vs. Vincent Sarich (Professor of Anthropology, University of California, Berkeley). Sponsored by Citizens for Scientific Creation, a local organization.

Cypress, California. Debate held on the campus of Cypress College on October 20, 1977, with 700 in attendance. Duane Gish vs. R. Erving Taylor (Professor of Anthropology, University of California, Riverside). Sponsored by student government organizations.

Davis, California. An informal debate on the campus of the University of California, Davis, in the Spring of 1972 with 1,000 in attendance. After a lecture on campus by Duane Gish, G. Ledyard Stebbins (Professor of Genetics and Chairman of the Department) challenged Gish in a 2½ hour confrontation. This was the first "debate" involving men of the Institute for Creation Research.

Dayton, Ohio. Debate held on the campus of Wright State University in February 1980, with 600 in attendance. Duane Gish vs. Bryan Gregor (Department of Geology). Sponsored by the University Senate, the Newman Club, and the Anthropology Club of Wright State University.

Dearborn, Michigan. Debate held on the Dearborn Campus of the University of Michigan on April 18, 1977, with 200 in attendance. Duane Gish vs. David J. Krause (Department of Geology, Henry Ford Community College, Dearborn). Sponsored by the Detroit Creation-Science Association.

Des Moines, Iowa. Radio debate over station WHO on October 21, 1980. Duane Gish vs. Robert Schadewald (science writer).

Durango, Colorado. Panel discussion held on the campus of Fort Lewis

College on March 30, 1977, with 400 in attendance. Duane Gish with Daniel Gibbons (Professor of Physics), Donald Barrs (Professor of Geology), and Donald Gordon (Professor of Anthropology). Sponsored by Fort Lewis College.

Edmonton, Alberta, Canada. Debate held in the Jubilee Auditorium on February 26, 1981, with 2,800 in attendance. Duane Gish vs. Richard Fox (Professor of Geology and Zoology, University of Alberta). Sponsored by the Creation Science Association of Alberta.

El Paso, Texas. Forum held on the campus of the University of Texas, El Paso, on February 17, 1977, with 700 in attendance. Duane Gish and Harold Slusher with Peter Chrapluvy (Professor of Biology), Walter Whitford (Professor of Biology, New Mexico State University, Las Cruces), and Robert Dinegar (chemist at the University of California Los Alamos Laboratory and an ordained Episcopal priest). Sponsored by the University United Ministries.

Emporia, Kansas. Panel held on the campus of Emporia State University on February 14, 1977, with 500 in attendance. Duane Gish with John E. Peterson (biologist and Dean of the School of Liberal Arts and Science). Sponsored by the University Forum Committee.

Emporia, Kansas. Panel held on the campus of Emporia State University on February 15, 1977, with 300 in attendance. Duane Gish with Thomas Bridge (Department of Geology), Samuel Dicks (Department of History), David Dumas (Department of Philosophy), H. Michael LeFever (Department of Biology), and Dallas Roark (Department of Religion). Sponsored by the University Forum Committee.

Eugene, Oregon. Debate held on the campus of the University of Oregon on January 20, 1977, with 600 in attendance. Duane Gish vs. Arthur J. Boucot (Professor of Geology, Oregon State University, Corvallis).

Eugene, Oregon. Debate on the origin of man held on the campus of the University of Oregon on January 21, 1977, with 600 in attendance. Duane Gish vs. Paul Simonds (Professor of Anthropology).

Eureka, California. Debate held in the Eureka High School Auditorium on April 15, 1980, with 700 in attendance. Duane Gish and Harold Slusher vs. Timothy Lawer (Professor of Biology) and Richard Stepp (Professor of Physics), both of Humboldt State University, Eureka.

Evanston, Illinois. Debate held on the campus of Northwestern University on April 4, 1977, with 1,600 in attendance. Henry Morris and Duane Gish vs. Michael E. Ruse (Professor of Philosophy of Science, University of Guelph, Ontario) and Donald Weinshank (Associate Professor of Natural Science, Michigan State University, East Lansing). Sponsored by the local Campus Crusade for Christ organization.

Fargo, North Dakota. Debate held on the campus of North Dakota State University on April 28, 1979, with 1,500 in attendance. Duane Gish vs. Vincent Sarich (Professor of Anthropology, University of California, Berkeley). Sponsored by North Dakota State University Campus Attractions.

Fort Collins, Colorado. Debate held on the campus of Colorado State University on October 7, 1977, with 2,000 in attendance. Duane Gish and Harold Slusher vs. Michael Charney (Professor Emeritus of Anthropology) and Charles G. Wilber (Professor of Zoology). Sponsored by the University Honors Program and the local organizations of Campus Crusade for Christ, The Navigators, and Inter-Varsity Christian Fellowship.

Fort Lauderdale, Florida. Debate held at the Coral Ridge Presbyterian Church on March 14, 1974, with 1,500 in attendance. Duane Gish vs. Joel Warren (Professor of Microbiology, Nova University, Fort Lauderdale). Sponsored by Coral Ridge Presbyterian Church.

Fort Lauderdale, Florida. Debate held at the Coral Ridge Presbyterian Church on March 2, 1982, with 1,500 in attendance. Henry Morris vs. David Fisher (Professor of Marine Geology, University of Miami). Sponsored by Coral Ridge Presbyterian Church.

Fort Wayne, Indiana. Debate held at the First Missionary Church on July 17, 1979, with 600 in attendance. Duane Gish vs. Vincent D'Orazio (organic chemist, Johnson Wax Company, Racine, Wisconsin). Sponsored by the Institute for Creation Research Midwest Center and the Fort Wayne Bible College.

Guelph, Ontario, Canada. Debate held on the campus of the University of Guelph on February 2, 1982, with 800 in attendance. Duane Gish vs. Fred Edwords (Administrator, American Humanist Association).

Halifax, Nova Scotia, Canada. Debate held on the campus of Dalhousie University in November 1974, with 300 in attendance. Duane Gish vs. Mark Ragan (doctoral candidate in biochemistry, Dalhousie University).

Hobart, Tasmania, Australia. Debate held in the Hobart Town Hall in the Summer of 1975, with 400 in attendance. Duane Gish vs. Richard W. Haines (Professor of Anatomy, retired, Tasmania University). Sponsored by the Evolution Protest Movement.

Houston, Texas. Radio debate held on April 20, 1976, in the studios of station KTRH, 50,000 watts. Duane Gish vs. Mrs. Madalyn Murray O'Hair, nationally known spokeswoman for atheism.

Kalamazoo, Michigan. Debate held on the campus of Western Michigan University on October 29, 1975, with 1,500 in attendance. Duane Gish vs. Elizabeth Baldwin (Professor of Anthropology). Sponsored by the local Campus Crusade for Christ organization.

Kansas City, Kansas. Television debate held on March 7, 1980, with 400 in attendance at the television studio. Duane Gish vs. Vincent Sarich (Professor of Anthropology, University of California, Berkeley). Sponsored by the PTL Club. The debate was videotaped for rebroadcast over the Christian Broadcasting Network.

Kansas City, Missouri. Debate held on the campus of the University of Missouri, Kansas City, on October 11, 1972, with 400 in attendance. Henry Morris vs. Richard J. Gentile (Professor of Geology). Sponsored by the local Campus Crusade for Christ organization. This was the first formal debate involving the men of the Institute for Creation Research.

Kansas City, Missouri. Panel held on the campus of the University of Missouri, Kansas City, on September 20, 1976, with 400 in attendance. Duane Gish with Frank Millich (Professor of Chemistry), Paul Hilpman (Professor of Geology), and Richard Wilson (Professor of Biology, Rockhurst College, Kansas City, Missouri). Sponsored jointly by the Missouri Students Association and the Missouri Association for Creation.

Kitchener, Ontario, Canada. Television debate on Station CTKW on September 28, 1982. Duane Gish vs. Michael Ruse (Professor of Philosophy of Science, University of Guelph, Ontario).

Knoxville, Tennessee. Debate held on the campus of the University of Tennessee on January 14, 1975, with 2,400 in attendance. Henry Morris and Duane Gish vs. George K. Schweitzer (Professor of Chemistry) and Arthur Jones (Professor of Biology). Sponsored jointly by the University Issues Program, the New Life fellowship of Knoxville, and the local Campus Crusade for Christ organization.

Lamoni, Iowa. Debate held on the campus of Graceland College on January 17, 1980, with 200 in attendance. Duane Gish vs. John

W. Patterson (Professor of Materials Science and Engineering, Iowa State University). Sponsored by Graceland College.

Laramie, Wyoming. Panel held on the campus of the University of Wyoming on February 8, 1974, with 450 in attendance. Henry Morris and Duane Gish with Donald Boyd (Professor of Geology and Invertebrate Paleontology), George Gill (Professor of Physical Anthropology), and Robert George (Professor of Biology). Sponsored by the University of Wyoming.

Lawrence, Kansas. Debate held on the campus of the University of Kansas on September 17, 1976, with 3,500 in attendance. Henry Morris and Duane Gish vs. E. O. Wiley (vertebrate paleontologist and Assistant Curator of the Kansas Museum of Natural History, Lawrence) and Marion Bickford (Professor of Geology). Sponsored by the Creationist Club of the University of Kansas.

Leeds, England. Debate held on the campus of the University of Leeds on February 1, 1979, with 400 in attendance. Duane Gish vs. J. Alexander (Professor of Zoology and Chairman of the Department). Sponsored by Campus Crusade for Christ of Great Britain.

Lethbridge, Alberta, Canada. Debate held on the campus of the University of Lethbridge on February 21, 1974, with 300 in attendance. Duane Gish vs. Job Kuijt (Professor of Botany). Sponsored by the Alberta Committee for True Education.

Lima, Ohio. Debate held in the Memorial Auditorium on September 14, 1976, with 1,200 in attendance. Duane Gish vs. Charles Good (Assistant Professor of Biology, Ohio State University, Lima). Sponsored by the Lima Baptist Temple. The debate was also broadcast on local radio.

Lincoln, Nebraska. Debate held on the campus of the University of Nebraska on March 2, 1979, with 1,000 in attendance. Duane Gish vs. Michael R. Voorhies (Associate Professor of Geology and Associate Curator of Vertebrate Paleontology of the Nebraska Natural History Museum). Sponsored by the Creation Coalition, a student organization.

London, Ontario, Canada. Panel held on the campus of the University of Western Ontario on November 1, 1974, with 1,000 in attendance. Duane Gish with David Ankney (Professor of Zoology), Allan Richardson (Professor of the History of Science), and C.P.S. Taylor (Professor of Biochemistry). Sponsored jointly by the London District Association Youth and the London Chapter of the Bible-Science Association of Canada.

London, Ontario, Canada. Debate held on the campus of the University of Western Ontario on September 29, 1982, with 500 in attendance. Duane Gish vs. Fred Edwords (Administrator, The American Humanist Association). Sponsored by a student Christian association and The Philosophy Club.

Los Angeles, California. Debate held on the campus of the University of California at Los Angeles on May 10, 1977, with 1,200 in attendance. Duane Gish vs. Henry Hespenheide (Assistant Professor of Biology). The distinguished scholar, Everett C. Olson (Professor of Paleontology and Biology at UCLA), served as moderator. Sponsored by the Evolution Inquiry Association, a student organization.

Louisville, Kentucky. Debate held in the Memorial Auditorium on March 18, 1982, with 1,000 in attendance. Duane Gish vs. Craig Nelson (Associate Professor of Biology, University of Indiana).

Lubbock, Texas. Debate held on the campus of the Texas Tech University on February 9, 1975, with 2,700 in attendance. Henry Morris and Duane Gish vs. Rae Harris (Professor of Earth Sciences) and Robert Baker (Professor of Biology). Sponsored by the Baptist Student Union and by the First Baptist Church of Lubbock. The debate was also broadcast locally.

Lynchburg, Virginia. Debate held on the campus of Liberty Baptist College on October 13, 1981, with 5,000 in attendance. This debate and the debate at the University of Minnesota, Minneapolis, are the two with the largest attendance. Duane Gish vs. Russell F. Doolittle (Professor of Biochemistry, University of California, San Diego). The debate was sponsored by the Old Time Gospel Hour and was scheduled for national television coverage in 1982.

Madison, Wisconsin. Debate held on the campus of the University of Wisconsin on February 10, 1978, with 3,300 in attendance. Duane Gish vs. John T. Robinson (Professor of Zoology and Paleoanthropology). Sponsored by the Lutheran Collegians and the Creation-Science Association of Madison.

Minneapolis, Minnesota. Debate held on the campus of the University Minnesota on April 29, 1977, with 5,000 in attendance. Duane Gish vs. Samuel Kirkwood (Professor of Biochemistry). Sponsored by the Twin Cities Creation-Science Association and the local Campus Crusade for Christ organization. This debate and the debate at Liberty Baptist College, Lynchburg, Virginia, are the two with the largest attendance.

Morgan Hill (San Jose), California. Debate held in the Live Oak High School Auditorium on November 9, 1978, with 400 in attendance.

Duane Gish vs. Vincent Sarich (Professor of Anthropology, University of California, Berkeley). Sponsored by private citizens.

Morgantown, West Virginia. Debate held on the campus of the University of West Virginia on November 5, 1982, with 800 in attendance. Henry Morris vs. Emmanuel Sillman (Professor of Biology, Duquesne University, Pittsburgh, Pennsylvania). Sponsored by the local Campus Crusade for Christ organization.

Naperville, Illinois. Debate on thermodynamics held on the campus of North Central College on July 14, 1979, with an attendance of 100 limited to those with a background in thermodynamics. Duane Gish vs. Vincent D'Orazio (organic chemist, Johnson Wax Company, Racine, Wisconsin). Sponsored by the Institute for Creation Research Midwest Center.

New Britain, Connecticut. Debate held on the campus of Central Connecticut State College on April 1, 1982, with 1,000 in attendance. Duane Gish vs. Michael Alan Park (Associate Professor of Anthropology). Sponsored by the Student Center Program Council of the college.

New Orleans, Louisiana. Debate held on the campus of the University of New Orleans on February 3, 1975, with 400 in attendance. Henry Morris vs. William Craig (Professor of Geology and Acting Chairman of the Department). Sponsored by Iktheus, a student organization.

New Orleans, Louisiana. Debate on thermodynamics held on the campus of University of New Orleans on February 4, 1975, with 300 in attendance. Henry Morris vs. Max Herzberger (Professor of Physics and a protege and colleague of Albert Einstein). Sponsored by Iktheus, a student organization.

New Orleans, Louisiana. Panel discussion held on the campus of Tulane University on February 4, 1982, with 400 in attendance. Duane Gish with Michael Kane (Department of Biology), Elizabeth Watts (Department of Anthropology), John Glenn (Department of Philosophy), and Timothy O'Neil (Department of Political Science).

New Orleans, Louisiana. Debate held at the Fountain Bay Hotel on February 6, 1982, with 500 in attendance. Duane Gish vs. Melton Fingerman (Professor of Biology and Chairman of the Department, Tulane University). Sponsored by private citizens.

Norman, Oklahoma. Debate held on the campus of the University of Oklahoma on January 15, 1973, with 1,000 in attendance. Henry

Morris and Duane Gish vs. David Kitts (Professor of Geology) and Hubert Frings (Professor of Zoology). Sponsored by the local Campus Crusade for Christ organization.

Northridge, California. Debate held on the campus of California State University, Northridge, on November 17, 1981, with 450 in attendance. Duane Gish vs. Michael Leneman (Department of Geology) and Clay Singer (Department of Anthropology).

Olympia, Washington. Debate held on the campus of Evergreen State College on April 11, 1979, with 400 in attendance. Duane Gish vs. David Milne (Department of Biology). Robert Utter, Chief Justice of the Supreme Court of the State of Washington, served as moderator. Sponsored by students of Evergreen State College.

Pasadena, California. Debate on creation vs. theistic evolution held at the First Congregational Church on May 17, 1977, with 400 in attendance. Duane Gish vs. Jerry Albert (research biochemist, Mercy Hospital, San Diego, California). Sponsored by student organizations at Fuller Theological Seminary, Pasadena.

Peoria, Illinois. Panel discussion on the origin of life held on the campus of Bradley University on June 15, 1974, with 400 in attendance. Duane Gish with Merrill Foster (Professor of Geology) and Richard L. Hoffmann (Professor of Chemistry, Illinois Central College, East Peoria). Sponsored by the Creation-Science Association of Central Illinois and the local organizations of Campus Crusade for Christ and Inter-Varsity Christian Fellowship

Philadelphia, Pennsylvania. Debate held at the Arch Street Presbyterian Church on April 19, 1977, with 1,000 in attendance. Henry Morris vs. Herman W. Pfefferkorn (Assistant Professor of Geology, University of Pennsylvania). Sponsored by the Philadelphia College of Bible.

Port of Spain, Trinidad, British West Indies. Panel discussion held on the Port of Spain campus of the University of the West Indies in November 1981, with 1,000 in attendance. Duane Gish with Dipak Basu (Department of Physics), Maura Imbert (Department of Biochemistry), and Robin Bruce (Department of Zoology).

Princeton, New Jersey. Debate held on the campus of Princeton University on April 12, 1980, with 2,000 in attendance. Duane Gish vs. Ashley Montagu (Professor of Anthropology). Sponsored by the Princeton Evangelical Fellowship.

Providence, Rhode Island. Debate held on the campus of Brown University on April 10, 1981, with 1,800 in attendance. Henry Morris vs. Kenneth Miller (Assistant Professor of Biology). Sponsored by the Dean of the College, the Dean of Student Life, and several campus organizations.

Racine, Wisconsin. Debate held in Memorial Hall on May 1, 1978, with 1,000 in attendance. Duane Gish vs. Vincent D'Orazio (organic chemist, Johnson Wax Company, Racine). Sponsored by the Institute for Creation Research Midwest Center.

Racine, Wisconsin. Debate held in the J. I. Case High School Fieldhouse on June 18, 1982, with 1,500 in attendance. Duane Gish vs. David Bantz (Assistant Professor of Philosophy, University of Illinois). Sponsored by Racine Christian Academy.

Reading, England. Debate held on the campus of Reading University on February 9, 1979, with 650 in attendance. Duane Gish vs. E. G. Halstead (Professor of Zoology). Sponsored by Campus Crusade for Christ of Great Britain.

Reno, Nevada. Debate held on the Reno campus of the University of Nevada on October 4, 1977, with 800 in attendance. Henry Morris vs. Michael Kendall (Professor of Anatomy). Sponsored jointly by the University of Nevada, Reno, and the local Inter-Varsity Christian Fellowship. The debate was also broadcast on local radio.

Sacramento, California. Debate held on the campus of Sacramento State University on March 1, 1973, with 1,500 in attendance. Duane Gish and James Boswell vs. G. Ledyard Stebbins (Professor of Genetics and Chairman of the Department, University of California, Davis) and Richard M. Lemmon (Associate Director, Biodynamics Laboratory, University of California, Berkeley). Sponsored by Sacramento State University.

Sacramento, California. Debate held on the campus of Sacramento State University on April 12, 1982, with 150 in attendance. Duane Gish vs. Richard Hughes (Department of History).

Salt Lake City, Utah. Debate held on Public Broadcasting Service TV on February 10, 1982. Duane Gish vs. Duane Jeffries (Department of Biology, Brigham Young University, Provo, Utah).

Salt Lake City, Utah. Debate held on the campus of the University of Utah on February 10, 1982, with 600 in attendance. Duane Gish vs. Cedric Davern (biologist and Vice-President for Academic Affairs, University of Utah).

San Diego, California. Debate held on the campus of the University of California, San Diego, in the Fall of 1972, with 1,000 in attendance. Duane Gish vs. Russell F. Doolittle (Professor of Biochemistry, University of California, San Diego).

San Diego, California. Debate held in the *San Diego Union* newspaper University, Spring or Fall of 1973. No attendance figures. Duane Gish vs. Russell F. Doolittle (Professor of Biochemistry, University of California, San Diego).

San Diego, California. Debate held in the San Diego Union newspaper on September 19, 1975. Henry Morris vs. Russell F. Doolittle (Professor of Biochemistry, University of California, San Diego).

San Diego, California. Debate held on April 7, 1976. No attendance figures. Henry Morris and Duane Gish vs. Fred Edwords (philosopher and President of the San Diego Humanist Society) and Mr. Nolo.

San Diego, California. Debate held on the campus of San Diego State University on April 7, 1976, with 1,400 in attendance. Henry Morris and Duane Gish vs. Benjamin Banta (Professor of Zoology) and Hale Wedberg (Professor of Botany). Sponsored jointly by the university Zoology Club and the Aztec Christian Fellowship. During the question and answer period, Dr. Banta asked Dr. Stanley Miller (Professor of Biochemistry, University of California, San Diego, and famed for his origin of life experiments) to come to the platform from the audience and respond to a question on the origin of life. A brief exchange between Miller and Gish then took place regarding Miller's experiments.

San Diego, California. Debate held on the campus of San Diego State University on April 26, 1977, with 1,500 in attendance. Henry Morris and Duane Gish vs. Frank Awbrey and William Thwaites (both Professors of Genetics).

San Diego, California. Debate held in a public school auditorium on April 12, 1978, with 700 in attendance. Henry Morris and Duane Gish vs. Fred Edwords (philosopher and President of the San Diego Humanist Society) and Phillip Osmond (physicist and Vice President of the San Diego Humanist Society). Sponsored by the San Diego Humanist Society.

San Diego, California. Debate held on the campus of San Diego State University on September 28, 1981, with 250 in attendance. Duane Gish vs. Jerry Albert (research biochemist, Mercy Hospital, San Diego). Sponsored by Students for Jesus, a campus organization.

San Marcos, California. Debate held on the campus of Palomar College on November 7, 1979, with 1,000 in attendance. Duane Gish and Gary Parker vs. Frank Awbrey and William Thwaites (both Professors of Genetics, San Diego State University).

Santa Barbara, California. Debate held on the campus of the University of California, Santa Barbara, on May 24, 1976, with 1,100 in attendance. Henry Morris and Duane Gish vs. Preston Cloud (Professor of Biogeology) and Aharon Gibhor (Professor of Plant Physiology). Sponsored jointly by the University of California, Santa Barbara, and the Creation Society of Santa Barbara, a student organization.

Saskatoon, Saskatchewan, Canada. Panel discussion held on the campus of the University of Saskatchewan on February 20, 1981, with 600 in attendance. Duane Gish with Taylor Steves (Department of Biology), Willie Braun (Department of Geology), and Peter Shargool (Department of Biochemistry). Sponsored by the Creation Science Association of Saskatchewan.

Seattle, Washington. Debate on the origin of man held on the campus of the University of Washington on November 19, 1980, with 1,000 in attendance. Duane Gish vs. Eugene Hunn (Associate Professor of Social Anthropology). Sponsored by students of the University of Washington.

St. Charles, Missouri. Radio debate on Station KMOX on September 21, 1982. Duane Gish vs. John Dwyer (Professor of Biology, St. Louis University).

Tampa, Florida. Television debate on station WTVT on March 2, 1974, with 800 in attendance in the television studio. Henry Morris and Duane Gish vs. Evelyn Kessler (Professor of Anthropology) and John Betz (Assistant Professor of Biology), both from the University of South Florida, Tampa. Sponsored by WTVT Productions and Pat Colmenares, TV talk show hostess.

Tampa, Florida. Debate held in the Thomas Jefferson High School Auditorium on September 19, 1981, with 1,200 in attendance, as well as a radio audience. Henry Morris vs. Kenneth Miller (Assistant Professor of Biology, Brown University, Providence, Rhode Island). Sponsored by a citizen's group.

Tampa, Florida. Debate held in the Thomas Jefferson High School Auditorium on March 20, 1982, with 300 in attendance, as well as a radio audience. Duane Gish vs. Kenneth Miller (Assistant Professor of Biology, Brown University, Providence, Rhode Island). Sponsored by a citizen's group.

Tempe, Arizona. Debate held on the campus of Arizona State University on May 2, 1977, with 450 in attendance. Duane Gish vs. Fred Plog (Professor of Cultural Anthropology). Sponsored by several Arizona State University students.

Toronto, Ontario, Canada. Debate held on the campus of York University on November 2, 1974, with 150 in attendance. Duane Gish vs. Thomas H. Leith (Professor of Philosophy of Science).

Toronto, Ontario, Canada. Television debate on the Norm Perry TV show in November 1974. Duane Gish vs. Christopher Nichols (Professor of Biology, York University, Toronto).

Toronto, Ontario, Canada. Panel held on the campus of the University of Toronto in September 1982 with 800 in attendance. Duane Gish vs. Christopher McGowan (Curator, The Royal Ontario Museum, Toronto).

Tucson, Arizona. Debate held on the campus of the University of Arizona on February 12, 1982, with 2,100 in attendance. Henry Morris and Duane Gish vs. Kenneth Miller (Assistant Professor of Biology, Brown University, Providence, Rhode Island) and David Milne (Professor of Biology, Evergreen State College, Olympia, Washington).

University Park, Pennsylvania. Debate held on the campus of Pennsylvania State University on October 10, 1973, with 1,600 in attendance. Duane Gish vs. Roger Cuffey (Department of Geosciences). Sponsored by the Penn State Overcomers, a student organization.

Utrecht, The Netherlands. Debate held in Congress Hall on October 1, 1977, with 1,100 in attendance. Duane Gish, Harold Slusher, and Donald Chittick (Professor of Chemistry, George Fox College, Newberg, Oregon) vs. Cees Laban (geologist with the Geological Service of Holland), Carl Koppeschaar (astronomer and science journalist), and Mels Sluijser (biologist with the Dutch Cancer Institute). Sponsored by Evangelische Omroep (Evangelical Broadcasting) of Utrecht. The debate was videotaped for broadcast throughout The Netherlands.

Van Nuys, California. Debate held at the First Baptist Church in September 1973, with 1,500 in attendance. Henry Morris and Duane Gish vs. David M. Morafka (Assistant Professor of Biology, California State College, Dominguez Hills) and William T. O'Day (Postdoctoral fellow in biology, University of Southern California). Sponsored jointly by the Van Nuys Christian College and the First Baptist Church of Van Nuys.

Ventura, California. Debate held on the campus of Ventura College on October 5, 1976, with 1,100 in attendance. Henry Morris and Duane Gish vs. Thomas O'Neill (Department of Biology) and Paul Aiello (Department of Anthropology). Sponsored by the Religion-in-Life Committee of Ventura College.

West Lafayette, Indiana. Debate held on the campus of Purdue University on October 29, 1981, with 2,100 in attendance. Henry Morris vs. Craig Nelson (Associate Professor of Biology, Indiana University, Bloomington).

Wheaton, Illinois. Panel on flood geology held on the campus of Wheaton College on November 19, 1974, with 300 in attendance. Henry Morris vs. Dr. Frank Roberts (Instructor in Earth Science, Delaware County Christian High School, Newtown Square, Pennsylvania). Sponsored by the Wheaton College Science Division.

Wheaton, Illinois. Panel on the age of the earth held on the campus of Wheaton College on May 2, 1978, with 500 in attendance. Duane Gish and Marvin L. Lubenow (Senior Pastor, First Baptist Church, Fort Collins, Colorado) vs. David L. Willis (Professor of Biology and Chairman of the Department of General Science, Oregon State University, Corvallis) and Walter C. Kaiser, Jr. (Professor of Semetics and Old Testament, Trinity Evangelical Divinity School, Deerfield, Illinois). Sponsored jointly by the Science Division and the Biblical Studies Division of Wheaton College.

Wichita, Kansas. Radio debate on Station KFH "Night Line" held on April 14, 1977. Duane Gish and Harold Slusher vs. Louis Bussjaeger (Professor of Biology, Kansas Newman College, Wichita) and George Potts (Professor of Biology, Friends University, Wichita). Sponsored by the Mid-Kansas Branch of the Bible-Science Association.

Winnipeg, Manitoba, Canada. Debate held on the campus of the University of Manitoba on February 6, 1975, with 400 in attendance. Duane Gish vs. Martin Samoiloff (Professor of Cell Biology and Genetics) and Kenneth Stuart (Professor of Zoology). Sponsored by the University of Manitoba. The debate was taped and broadcast over CBC Radio Canada.

Science Digest debate, October 1981. Duane Gish vs. Isaac Asimov (biochemist and America's most prolific science writer).

The Humanist magazine debate, November-December, 1977. Duane Gish vs. William V. Mayer (Director, Biological Sciences Curriculum Study, Boulder, Colorado) and Preston Cloud (Professor of Biogeology, University of California, Santa Barbara).

Appendix II

Alphabetical List of Debate Participants

Academic positions mentioned are positions held by the debaters at the time of their participation in the creation-evolution debates listed.

Adler, Isidora. Professor of Chemistry and Chairman of the Geochemistry Division, University of Maryland, College Park. University of Maryland debate, October 14, 1976.

Aiello, Paul. Department of Anthropology, Ventura College, Ventura, California. Ventura College debate, October 5, 1976.

Albert, Jerry. Research biochemist, Mercy Hospital, San Diego, California. Pasadena, California, debate on theistic evolution, May 17, 1977, and San Diego State University debate, September 28, 1981.

Alexander, J. Professor of Zoology and Chairman of the Department, Leeds University, Leeds, England. Leeds University debate, February 1, 1979.

Ankney, David. Professor of Zoology, University of Western Ontario, London, Ontario, Canada. University of Western Ontario panel, November 1, 1974.

Asimov, Isaac. Biochemist and America's most prolific science writer. Debate in the October 1981 issue of *Science Digest*.

Awbrey, Frank. Professor of Genetics, San Diego State University, San Diego, California. San Diego State debate, April 26, 1977, and Palomar College, San Marcos, California, debate, November 7, 1979.

Baker, Robert. Professor of Biology, Texas Tech University, Lubbock. Texas Tech debate, February 9, 1975.

Baldwin, Elizabeth. Professor of Anthropology, Western Michigan University, Kalamazoo. Western Michigan University debate, October 29, 1975.

Bambach, Richard. Associate Professor of Paleontology, Virginia Polytechnic Institute and State University, Blacksburg. Virginia Polytech debate, November 8, 1975.

Banta, Benjamin. Professor of Zoology, San Diego State University, San Diego, California. San Diego State debate, April 7, 1976.

Bantz, David. Assistant Professor of Philosophy, University of Illinois. Racine, Wisconsin, debate, June 18, 1982.

Barrs, Donald. Professor of Geology, Fort Lewis College, Durango, Colorado. Fort Lewis College panel, March 30, 1977.

Basu, Dipak. Department of Physics, University of the West Indies, Port of Spain, Trinidad. University of the West Indies, Port of Spain, panel, November 1981.

Betz, John. Assistant Professor of Biology, University of South Florida, Tampa. Tampa TV debate, March 2, 1974.

Bickford, Marion. Professor of Geology, University of Kansas, Lawrence. University of Kansas debate, September 17, 1976.

Bond, James. Biologist. Lake Park High School, Chicago, Illinois, debate, March 30, 1976.

Boswell, James C. Pastor, Christian Disciples Church, Carmichael, California. Creationist debater in the Sacramento State University debate, March 1, 1973.

Boucot, Arthur J. Professor of Geology, Oregon State University, Corvallis, and Adjunct Professor, Museum of Natural History, University of Oregon, Eugene. University of Oregon debate, January 20, 1977.

Boyd, Donald. Professor of Geology and Invertebrate Paleontology, University of Wyoming, Laramie. University of Wyoming panel, February 8, 1974.

Brace, C. Loring. Professor of Physical Anthropology, University of Michigan, Ann Arbor. University of Auckland, New Zealand, debate, July 1973, and University of Michigan debate, March 17, 1982.

Brattstrom, Bayard. Professor of Zoology, California State University, Fullerton. Costa Mesa, California, debate, November 17, 1975.

Braun, Willie. Department of Geology, University of Saskatchewan, Saskatoon. University of Saskatchewan panel, February 20, 1981.

Bridge, Thomas. Department of Geology, Emporia State University, Emporia, Kansas. Emporia State University panel, February 15, 1977.

Brown, Olan. Microbiologist and Assistant Director, Dalton Research Center, University of Missouri, Columbia. Creationist on the University of Missouri, Columbia, panel, September 22, 1976.

Bruce, Robin. Department of Zoology, University of the West Indies, Port of Spain, Trinidad. University of the West Indies, Port of Spain, panel, November 1981.

Bussjaeger, Louis. Professor of Biology, Kansas Newman College, Wichita, Kansas. Wichita radio debate, April 14, 1977.

Charney, Michael. Professor Emeritus of Anthropology, Colorado State University, Fort Collins. Colorado State University debate, October 7, 1977.

Chittick, Donald. Professor of Chemistry, George Fox College, Newberg, Oregon. Creationist debater in the Utrecht, The Netherlands, debate, October 1, 1977.

Chrapluvy, Peter. Professor of Biology, University of Texas, El Paso. University of Texas, El Paso, panel, February 17, 1977.

Cloud, Preston. Professor of Biogeology, University of California, Santa Barbara. University of California, Santa Barbara, debate, May 24, 1976, and *The Humanist* magazine debate, November-December, 1977.

Costerton, William. Department of Biochemistry, University of Calgary, Calgary, Alberta, Canada. University of Calgary debate, February 1981.

Craig, William. Professor of Geology and Chairman of the Department, University of New Orleans, New Orleans, Louisiana. University of New Orleans debate, February 3, 1975.

Cuffey, Roger. Department of Geosciences, Pennsylvania State University, University Park. Pennsylvania State University debate, October 10, 1973.

Davern, Cedric. Biologist and Vice President for Academic Affairs, University of Utah, Salt Lake City. University of Utah debate, February 10, 1982.

Demar, Robert. Department of Geology, University of Illinois, Chicago Circle Campus, Chicago. University of Illinois, Chicago Circle, debate, April 5, 1976, and Glenbrook High School, Chicago, debate, April 5, 1976.

Dicks, Samuel. Department of History, Emporia State University, Emporia, Kansas. Emporia State University panel, February 15, 1977.

Dinegar, Robert. Chemist, University of California Los Alamos Laboratory, Los Alamos, New Mexico, and an ordained Episcopal priest. University of Texas, El Paso, panel, February 17, 1977.

Doolittle, Russell F. Professor of Biochemistry, University of California, San Diego. University of California, San Diego, debate, Fall 1972; San Diego State University debate, Spring or Fall 1973; *San Diego Union* (newspaper) debate, September 19, 1975; Iowa State University, Ames, debate on the origin of life, October 22, 1980; and Liberty Baptist College, Lynchburg, Virginia, TV debate, October 13, 1981.

D'Orazio, Vincent T. Organic chemist, Johnson Wax Company, Racine, Wisconsin. Racine debate, May 1, 1978; North Central College, Naperville, Illinois, debate on thermodynamics, July 14, 1979; and Fort Wayne, Indiana, debate, July 17, 1979.

Dumas, David. Department of Philosophy, Emporia State University, Emporia, Kansas. Emporia State University panel, February 15, 1977.

Dwyer, John. Professor of Biology, St. Louis University. St. Charles, Missouri, radio debate, September 21, 1982.

Edwords, Fredrick. Philosopher, President, San Diego Humanist Society, San Diego, California, and later Administrator of the American Humanist Association. San Diego debate, April 7, 1976; San Diego debate, April 12, 1978; University of Guelph, Ontario, Canada, debate, February 2, 1982, and University of Western Ontario debate, September 29, 1982.

Enright, Richard. Department of Geology, Bridgewater State College, Bridgewater, Massachusetts. Bridgewater State College debate, April 29, 1976.

Epperson, E. Roy. Professor of Chemistry, High Point College, High Point, North Carolina. Charleston, South Carolina, debate, February 10, 1980.

Erpino, Michael. Department of Biological Science, California State University, Chico. California State University, Chico, debate, November 19, 1976.

Fingerman, Melton. Professor of Biology and Chairman of the Department, Tulane University, New Orleans, Louisiana. New Orleans debate, February 6, 1982.

Fisher, David. Professor of Marine Geology, University of Miami, Miami, Florida. Fort Lauderdale debate, March 2, 1982.

Foster, Merrill. Professor of Geology, Bradley University, Peoria, Illinois. Bradley University panel on the origin of life, June 15, 1974.

Fox, Richard. Professor of Geology and Zoology, University of Alberta, Edmonton, Alberta, Canada. Edmonton debate, February 26, 1981.

Fraser, Alex. Professor of Biology and Genetics, University of Cincinnati, Cincinnati, Ohio. University of Cincinnati debate, October 24, 1974.

Frazier, William. Department of Geology, Columbus College, Columbus, Georgia. Columbus College debate, May 6, 1981.

Freeman, Thomas. Professor of Geology, University of Missouri, Columbia. University of Missouri, Columbia, panel, September 22, 1976.

Frings, Hubert. Professor of Zoology, University of Oklahoma, Norman. University of Oklahoma debate, January 15, 1973.

Gavan, James. Professor of Anthropology and Chairman of the Department, University of Missouri, Columbia. University of Missouri, Columbia, debate, October 20, 1975.

Geist, Val. Department of Geology, University of Calgary, Calgary, Alberta, Canada. University of Calgary debate, February 1981.

Gentile, Richard. Professor of Geology, University of Missouri, Kansas City. University of Missouri, Kansas City, debate, October 11, 1972.

George, Robert. Professor of Biology, University of Wyoming, Laramie. University of Wyoming panel, February 8, 1974.

Gibbons, Daniel. Professor of Physics, Fort Lewis College, Durango, Colorado. Fort Lewis College panel, March 30, 1977.

Gibhor, Aharon. Professor of Plant Physiology, University of California, Santa Barbara. University of California, Santa Barbara, debate, May 24, 1976.

Gilbert, Larry. Field Biologist, Department of Zoology, University of Texas, Austin. University of Texas debate, March 24, 1977.

Gill, George. Professor of Physical Anthropology, University of Wyoming, Laramie. University of Wyoming panel, February 8, 1974.

Gish, Duane T. Associate Director of the Institute for Creation Research. After receiving his doctorate in biochemistry from the University of California, Berkeley, he served on postdoctoral research appointments at Berkeley and Cornell University. He was for many years a research biochemist at the Upjohn Company, Kalamazoo, Michigan. He was one of the founding members of the Creation Research Society. In 1971, he joined Dr. Henry Morris as Associate Director of the ICR. Since then, he has participated in 115 creation-evolution debates and panels.

Glenn, John. Department of Philosophy, Tulane University, New Orleans, Louisiana. Tulane University panel, February 4, 1982.

Good, Charles. Assistant Professor of Biology, Ohio State University, Lima. Lima debate, September 14, 1976.

Gordon, Donald. Professor of Anthropology, Fort Lewis College, Durango, Colorado. Fort Lewis College panel, March 30, 1977.

Gregor, Bryan. Professor of Geology, Wright State University, Dayton, Ohio. Wright State University debate, February 1980.

Haines, Richard W. Professor of Anatomy, retired, Tasmania University, Hobart, Tasmania, Australia. Hobart debate, Summer 1975.

Halstead, E. G. Professor of Zoology, Reading University, Reading, England. Reading University debate, February 9, 1979.

Harris, Rae. Professor of Earth Science, Texas Tech University, Lubbock. Texas Tech debate, February 9, 1975.

Hazzard, Evan. Professor of Biology, Bemidji State University, Bemidji, Minnesota. Bemidji State University debate, September 20, 1982.

Herzberger, Max. Professor of Physics, University of New Orleans, New Orleans, Louisiana. University of New Orleans debate on thermodynamics, February 4, 1975.

Hespenheide, Henry. Assistant Professor of Biology, University of California at Los Angeles. UCLA debate, May 10, 1977.

Hilpman, Paul. Professor of Geology, University of Missouri, Kansas City. University of Missouri, Kansas City, panel, September 20, 1976.

Hoffmann, Richard L. Professor of Chemistry, Illinois Central College East Peoria. Bradley University panel on the origin of life, June 15, 1974.

Hughes, Richard. Department of History, Sacramento State University, Sacramento, California. Sacramento State debate, April 12, 1982.

Hunn, Eugene. Associate Professor of Social Anthropology, University of Washington, Seattle. University of Washington debate on the origin of man, November 19, 1980.

Hunt, Wayne. Department of Biology, University of the West Indies, Cave Hill, Barbados. University of the West Indies, Cave Hill, debate, November 1981.

Imbert, Maura. Department of Biochemistry, University of the West Indies, Port of Spain, Trinidad. University of the West Indies, Port of Spain, debate, November 1981.

Jahoda, John C. Associate Professor of Biology, Bridgewater State College, Bridgewater, Massachusetts. Bridgewater State College debate, April 29, 1976.

Jeffries, Duane. Department of Biology, Brigham Young University, Provo, Utah. Salt Lake City, Utah, Public Broadcasting Service TV debate, February 10, 1982.

Jones, Arthur. Professor of Zoology, University of Tennessee, Knoxville. University of Tennessee debate, January 14, 1975.

Kaiser, Walter C., Jr. Professor of Semetics and Old Testament, Trinity Evangelical Divinity School, Deerfield, Illinois. Wheaton College, Wheaton, Illinois, panel on the age of the earth, May 2, 1978.

Kane, Michael. Department of Biology, Tulane University, New Orleans, Louisiana. Tulane University panel, February 4, 1982.

Kendall, Michael. Professor of Anatomy, University of Nevada, Reno. University of Nevada, Reno, debate, October 4, 1977.

Kessler, Evelyn. Professor of Anthropology, University of South Florida, Tampa. Tampa TV debate, March 2, 1974.

Kirkwood, Samuel. Professor of Biochemistry, University of Minnesota, Minneapolis. University of Minnesota debate, April 29, 1977.

Kitts, David B. Professor of Geology, University of Oklahoma, Norman. University of Oklahoma debate, January 15, 1973.

Klingener, David J. Associate Professor of Zoology and Vertebrate Paleontology, University of Massachusetts, Amherst. University of Massachusetts debate, April 28, 1976.

Koppeschaar, Carl. Astronomer and Dutch science journalist. Utrecht, The Netherlands, debate, October 1, 1977.

Krause, David J. Department of Geology, Henry Ford Community College, Dearborn, Michigan. University of Michigan, Dearborn, debate, April 18, 1977.

Kuijt, Job. Professor of Botany, University of Lethbridge, Lethbridge, Alberta, Canada. University of Lethbridge debate, February 21, 1974.

Laban, Cees. Geologist, Geological Service of Holland, The Netherlands. Utrecht, The Netherlands, debate, October 1, 1977.

Lawer, Timothy. Professor of Biology, Humboldt State University, Eureka, California. Eureka debate, April 15, 1980.

LeFever, H. Michael. Department of Biology, Emporia State University, Emporia, Kansas. Emporia State University panel, February 15, 1977.

Leith, Thomas H. Professor of Philosophy, York University, Toronto, Ontario, Canada. York University debate, November 2, 1974.

Lemmon, Richard M. Associate Director, Chemical Biodynamics Laboratory, University of California, Berkeley. Sacramento State University debate, March 1, 1973.

Leneman, Michael. Department of Geology, California State University, Northridge. California State University, Northridge, debate, November 17, 1981.

Levin, Bruce R. Associate Professor of Zoology and Population Genetics, University of Massachusetts, Amherst. University of Massachusetts debate, April 28, 1976.

Lubenow, Marvin L. Senior Pastor, The First Baptist Church, Fort Collins, Colorado. Wheaton College, Wheaton, Illinois, panel on the age of the earth, May 2, 1978.

Lynch, Gary. Professor of Neurobiology, University of California, Irvine. Costa Mesa, California, debate, October 1, 1976.

Madison,   . Professor of Biology and Chairman of the Department, University of the West Indies, Cave Hill, Barbados. University of the West Indies, Cave Hill, debate, November 1981.

Marshall, Robert. Professor of Food Science and Nutrition, University of Missouri, Columbia. University of Missouri, Columbia, panel, September 22, 1976.

Matlow, Sheldon T. Instructor in Mathematics, West Valley College, Saratoga, California, and owner of a mining and manufacturing company. DeAnza College, Cupertino, California, debate, August 29, 1974.

Mayer, William V. Director, Biological Sciences Curriculum Study, Boulder, Colorado. *The Humanist* magazine debate, November-

December, 1977.

McGowan, Christopher. Paleontologist and Curator of the Royal Ontario Museum, Toronto, Canada. University of Toronto panel, September 1982.

Miller, George. Professor of Chemistry, University of California, Irvine. Costa Mesa, California, debate, October 1, 1976.

Miller, Kenneth. Assistant Professor of Biology, Brown University, Providence, Rhode Island. Brown University debate, April 10, 1981; Tampa, Florida, debate, September 19, 1981; University of Arizona, Tucson, debate, February 12, 1982; and Tampa, Florida, debate, March 20, 1982.

Miller, Stanley. Professor of Biochemistry, University of California, San Diego. Famous for his origin of life experiments, he took part in the discussion period following the debate at San Diego State University, April 7, 1976.

Millich, Frank. Professor of Chemistry, University of Missouri, Kansas City. University of Missouri, Kansas City, panel, September 20, 1976.

Milne, David. Professor of Biology, Evergreen State College, Olympia, Washington. Evergreen State College debate, April 11, 1979, and University of Arizona, Tucson, debate, February 12, 1982.

Montagu, Ashley. Professor of Anthropology, Princeton University, Princeton, New Jersey. Princeton University debate, April 12, 1980.

Montgomery, John Warwick. Dean of the Simon Greenleaf School of Law. Moderator of the Fort Lauderdale, Florida, debate, March 2, 1982.

Morafka, David. Assistant Professor of Biology, California State College, Dominguez Hills. Van Nuys, California, debate, September 1973.

Morowitz, Harold. Professor of Molecular Biophysics, Yale University, New Haven, Connecticut. University of California, Berkeley, debate on the origin of life, May 19, 1977.

Morris, Henry M. Founder and Director of the Institute for Creation Research, San Diego, California. He received his doctorate from the University of Minnesota, majoring in engineering hydraulics and hydrology. From 1957 to 1970 he was Chairman of the Department of Civil Engineering at the Virginia Polytechnic Institute and State University. He is the author of a definitive textbook on hydrology. He was one of the founders of the Creation

Research Society and served five years as its president. In 1970 he founded what is now the Institute for Creation Research. He has taken part in 38 creation-evolution debates and panels.

Murray, James. Professor of Biology, University of Virginia, Charlottesville. University of Virginia debate, March 22, 1982.

Nelson, Craig. Associate Professor of Biology, University of Indiana, Bloomington. Purdue University, West Lafayette, Indiana, debate, October 29, 1981, and Louisville, Kentucky, debate, March 18, 1982.

Nichols, Christopher. Professor of Biology, York University, Toronto, Ontario, Canada. Toronto TV debate, November 1974.

Nolo,   . No information available. San Diego Humanist debate, April 7, 1976.

O'Day, William T. Postdoctoral fellow, University of Southern California, Los Angeles. Van Nuys, California, debate, September 1973.

O'Hair, Madalyn Murray. Leader of the American atheist movement. Houston, Texas, radio debate, April 20, 1976.

Olson, Everett C. Professor of Paleontology and Biology, University of California at Los Angeles. Moderator of the UCLA debate, May 10, 1977.

O'Neil, Timothy. Department of Political Science, Tulane University, New Orleans, Louisiana. Tulane University panel, February 4, 1982.

O'Neill, Thomas. Department of Biology, Ventura College, Ventura, California. Ventura College debate, October 5, 1976.

Osmond, Phillip. Physicist, Vice President, San Diego Humanist Society, San Diego, California. San Diego debate, April 12, 1978.

Park, Michael Alan. Associate Professor of Anthropology, Central Connecticut State College, New Britain. Central Connecticut State College debate, April 1, 1982.

Parker, Gary. Research Associate in Bioscience, Institute for Creation Research, and Professor of Biology, Christian Heritage College, San Diego, California. Participated in the Palomar College, San Marcos, California, debate, November 7, 1979. Dr. Parker, as well as other ICR staff members, has been involved in a number of creation-evolution debates which are not considered by this study.

Patterson, John W. Professor of Materials Science and Engineering, Iowa State University, Ames. Des Moines Area Community College, Ankeny, Iowa, debate, January 16, 1980, and Graceland College, Lamoni, Iowa, debate, January 17, 1980.

Peterson, John E. Biologist, Dean of the School of Liberal Arts and Science, Emporia State University, Emporia, Kansas. Emporia State University forum, February 14, 1977.

Pfefferkorn, Hermon W. Assistant Professor of Geology, University of Pennsylvania, Philadelphia. Philadelphia debate, April 19, 1977.

Plog, Fred. Professor of Cultural Anthropology, Arizona State University, Tempe. Arizona State University debate, May 2, 1977.

Pollitser, William. Professor of Anatomy and Anthropology, University of North Carolina, Chapel Hill. University of North Carolina debate, January 21, 1974.

Potts, George. Professor of Biology, Friends University, Wichita, Kansas. Wichita radio debate, April 14, 1977.

Presch, William. Assistant Professor of Zoology, California State University, Fullerton. Costa Mesa, California, debate, November 17, 1975.

Press, Newtol. Professor of Zoology, University of Wisconsin, Milwaukee. Baraboo, Wisconsin, debate, October 24, 1980.

Ragan, Mark. Doctoral candidate in biochemistry, Dalhousie University, Halifax, Nova Scotia, Canada. Dalhousie University debate, November 1974.

Richardson, Allan. Professor of the History of Science, University of Western Ontario, London, Ontario, Canada. University of Western Ontario panel, November 1, 1974.

Roark, Dallas. Department of Religion, Emporia State University, Emporia, Kansas. Emporia State University panel, February 15, 1977.

Roberts, Frank. Instructor in Earth Science, Delaware County Christian High School, Newtown Square, Pennsylvania. Wheaton College, Wheaton, Illinois, panel on flood geology, November 19, 1974.

Robinson, John T. Professor of Zoology and Paleoanthropology, University of Wisconsin, Madison. University of Wisconsin debate, February 10, 1978.

Ruse, Michael. Professor of the Philosophy of Science, University of Guelph, Guelph, Ontario, Canada. Northwestern University, Evanston, Illinois, debate, April 4, 1977, and Kitchener, Ontario, television debate, September 28, 1982.

Sadleir, R.M.F.S. Professor of Biology, Simon Fraser University, Burnaby, British Columbia, Canada. Simon Fraser University debate, November 1974.

Samoiloff, Martin. Professor of Cell Biology and Genetics, University of Manitoba, Winnipeg, Manitoba, Canada. University of Manitoba debate, February 6, 1975.

Sarich, Vincent. Professor of Anthropology, University of California, Berkeley. Morgan Hill, California, debate, November 9, 1978; North Dakota State University, Fargo, debate, April 28, 1979; DeAnza College, Cupertino, California, debate, May 31, 1979; and Kansas City, Kansas, TV debate, March 7, 1980.

Schadewald, Robert. Science writer. Radio debate over Station WHO, Des Moines, Iowa, October 21, 1980.

Schweitzer, George. Distinguished Professor of Chemistry, University of Tennessee, Knoxville. University of Tennessee debate, January 14, 1975.

Schwimmer, David. Associate Professor of Geology, Columbus College, Columbus, Georgia. Columbus College debate, May 6, 1981.

Shargool, Peter. Department of Biochemistry, University of Saskatchewan, Saskatoon, Saskatchewan, Canada. University of Saskatchewan panel, February 20, 1981.

Shear, David. Associate Professor of Biochemistry, University of Missouri, Columbia. University of Missouri, Columbia, panel, September 22, 1976.

Sillman, Emmanuel. Professor of Biology, Duquesne University, Pittsburgh, Pennsylvania. University of West Virginia debate, November 5, 1982.

Simonds, Paul. Professor of Anthropology, University of Oregon, Eugene. University of Oregon debate on the origin of man, January 21, 1977.

Singer, Clay. Department of Cultural Anthropology, California State University, Northridge. California State University, Northridge, debate, November 17, 1981.

Sluijser, Mels. Biologist, Dutch Cancer Institute. Utrecht, The Netherlands, debate, October 1, 1977.

Slusher, Harold. Research Associate in Geophysics and Astronomy, Institute for Creation Research, and Chairman of the Physical Sciences Department, Christian Heritage College, San Diego, California. He is also a member of the Department of Physics, University of Texas, El Paso, and has served as the Director of the University of Texas Kidd Memorial Seismic Observatory in El Paso. Besides participating in many creation-evolution debates on his own, he has participated in the following debates covered by this study: Costa Mesa, California, debate, October 1, 1976; University of Texas, El Paso, panel, February 17, 1977; Wichita, Kansas, radio debate, April 14, 1977; Utrecht, The Netherlands, debate, October 1, 1977; Colorado State University, Fort Collins, debate, October 7, 1977; Eureka, California, debate, April 15, 1980; and Columbus College, Columbus, Georgia, debate, May 6, 1981.

Smith, John Maynard. Professor of Biology and Chairman of the Department, Sussex University, Brighton, England. Sussex University debate, February 12, 1979.

Stains, Howard. Professor of Zoology, Southern Illinois University, Carbondale. Southern Illinois University debate, October 19, 1978.

Stanley, Steven M. Professor of Paleobiology, Johns Hopkins University, Baltimore, Maryland. Professor Stanley was a visiting lecturer on the University of Wyoming campus at the time of the evolution-creation panel there, February 8, 1974, and took part in the discussion period following the panel.

Stebbins, G. Ledyard. Professor of Genetics and Chairman of the Department, University of California, Davis. University of California, Davis, "informal debate," Spring 1972, and Sacramento State University debate, March 1, 1973.

Stepp, Richard. Professor of Physics, Humboldt State University, Eureka, California. Eureka debate, April 15, 1980.

Steves, Taylor. Department of Biology, University of Saskatchewan, Saskatoon, Saskatchewan, Canada. University of Saskatchewan panel, February 20, 1981.

Stuart, Kenneth. Professor of Zoology, University of Manitoba, Winnipeg, Manitoba, Canada. University of Manitoba debate, February 6, 1975.

Taylor, C.P.S. Professor of Biochemistry, University of Western Ontario, London, Ontario, Canada. University of Western Ontario panel, November 1, 1974.

Taylor, R. Erving. Professor of Anthropology, University of California, Riverside. Cypress College, Cypress, California, debate, October 20, 1977.

Templeton, Alan. Department of Zoology, University of Texas, Austin. University of Texas debate, March 24, 1977.

Thwaites, William. Professor of Genetics, San Diego State University, San Diego, California. San Diego State debate, April 26, 1977, and Palomar College, San Marcos, California, debate, November 7, 1979.

Utter, Robert. Chief Justice of the Supreme Court of the State of Washington. Moderator, Evergreen State College, Olympia, Washington, debate, April 11, 1979.

Vermeij, Geerat J. Associate Professor of Zoology, University of Maryland, College Park. University of Maryland debate, October 14, 1976.

Voorhies, Michael R. Associate Professor of Geology, University of Nebraska, Lincoln, and Associate Curator of Vertebrate Paleontology, Nebraska Natural History Museum. University of Nebraska debate, March 2, 1979.

Warren, Joel. Professor of Microbiology, Nova University, Fort Lauderdale, Florida. Fort Lauderdale debate, March 14, 1974.

Watts, Elizabeth. Department of Anthropology, Tulane University, New Orleans, Louisiana. Tulane University panel, February 4, 1982.

Wedberg, Hale. Professor of Botany, San Diego State University, San Diego, California. San Diego State debate, April 7, 1976.

Weinshank, Donald. Associate Professor of Natural Science, Michigan State University, East Lansing. Northwestern University, Evanston, Illinois, debate, April 4, 1977.

Weller, Steven. Department of Biology, University of Illinois, Chicago Circle Campus, Chicago. University of Illinois, Chicago Circle, debate, April 5, 1976.

Whitford, Walter. Professor of Biology, New Mexico State University, Las Cruces. University of Texas, El Paso, panel, February 17, 1977.

Wilber, Charles. Professor of Zoology, Colorado State University, Fort Collins. Colorado State University debate, October 7, 1977.

Wiley, E. O. Vertebrate paleontologist and Assistant Curator of the Kansas Museum of Natural History, Lawrence. University of Kansas, Lawrence, debate, September 17, 1976.

Williams, Donald C. Professor of Biochemistry, Western Washington University, Bellingham. Western Washington University debate, October 9, 1980.

Willis, David L. Professor of Biology and Chairman of the Department of General Science, Oregon State University, Corvallis. Wheaton

College, Wheaton, Illinois, panel on the age of the earth, May 2, 1978.

Wilson, Richard. Professor of Biology, Rockhurst College, Kansas City, Missouri. University of Missouri, Kansas City, panel, September 20, 1976.

Wolff, Jerry. Assistant Professor of Biology, University of Virginia, Charlottesville. University of Virginia debate, March 22, 1982.

Wyllie, Peter J. Professor of Geophysical Sciences, University of Chicago. Chicago TV Station WGN Roundtable panel, recorded March 31, 1977.

In addition to the above, there were three unknown faculty members from the University of Calgary, Calgary, Alberta, Canada, panel, February 21, 1974.

Total Participants	185
Creationist Debaters	10
Evolutionist Debaters	172
Moderators	3
Women Debaters	5
Men Debaters	177

Other Books of Interest From
CLP PUBLISHERS
P. O. Box 15908
San Diego, California 92115

What is Creation Science? *Henry Morris & Gary Parker*
Answers to the question being asked around the world today.
Over 50 illustrations. Written in understandable language by
outstanding scientists. **No. 187**

Evolution? The Fossils Say No! *Duane T. Gish*
The only *solid* evidence in the discussion of origins is the fossil
record—anything else is circumstantial evidence and conjecture.
Powerful testimony. Over 100,000 in print. **No. 055**

Dinosaurs: Those Terrible Lizards *Duane T. Gish*
Did dinosaurs and humans live at the same time? Are dragons
just imaginary? This beautifully color-illustrated book for
children tells about dinosaurs and why they no longer exist.
8½" x 11". **No. 046**

Scientific Creationism *Henry M. Morris*
Comprehensive, documented exposition of the scientific
evidence of origins. **General Edition No. 140**
Nonreligious Edition No. 141

Evolution in Turmoil *Henry M. Morris*
Captivating report detailing the battle that is currently raging in
the evolutionary camp—"slow-and-gradual" evolution . . . or
"hopeful monsters"? Dr. Morris shows that *neither* is scientifically acceptable. Sequel to *The Troubled Waters of Evolution*. **No. 271**

Creation and Its Critics *Henry M. Morris*
A booklet prepared by Dr. Morris answering the many questions, accusations, and aspersions raised against creationist
scientists, parents, and educators who desire to have creation
science taught in the public schools in addition to evolution.
No. 273

Scientific Case for Creation *Henry M. Morris*
A brief introduction to the broad field of scientific creationism.
Science only, no theology. Some scientific background helpful.
No. 139